Copts and the Security State

Stanford Studies in Middle Eastern and Islamic Societies and Cultures

Copts and the Security State

VIOLENCE, COERCION, AND SECTARIANISM IN CONTEMPORARY EGYPT

Laure Guirguis

Stanford University Press
Stanford, California

Stanford University Press
Stanford, California

A version of this work was originally published in French in 2012 under the title *Les Coptes d'Egypte: Violences communautaires et transformations politiques (2005–2012)* [Egyptian Copts: Sectarian Violence and Political Transformations (2005–2012)] ©2012, Editions Karthala—Paris.

Printed in the United States of America on acid-free, archival-quality paper

Library of Congress Cataloging-in-Publication Data

Names: Guirguis, Laure, author.
Title: Copts and the security state : violence, coercion, and sectarianism in contemporary Egypt / Laure Guirguis.
Other titles: Coptes d'Egypte. English
Description: Stanford, California : Stanford University Press, 2016. | Series: Stanford studies in Middle Eastern and Islamic societies and cultures | "Originally published in French in 2012 under the title Les coptes d'Egypte." | Includes bibliographical references and index. | Description based on print version record and CIP data provided by publisher; resource not viewed.
Identifiers: LCCN 2016021295 (print) | LCCN 2016020170 (ebook) | ISBN 9781503600805 (e-book) | ISBN 9780804798907 (cloth : alk. paper) | ISBN 9781503600782 (pbk. : alk. paper) | ISBN 9781503600805 (ebook)
Subjects: LCSH: Copts—Political activity. | Copts—Government relations. | Coptic Church—Political activity. | Egypt—Politics and government—1981-
Classification: LCC DT72.C7 (print) | LCC DT72.C7 G8413 2016 (ebook) | DDC 323.1193/2—dc23
LC record available at https://lccn.loc.gov/2016021295

Typeset by Bruce Lundquist in 10/14 Minion Pro

To Samer Soliman

CONTENTS

ACKNOWLEDGMENTS

It took me years of running away to be drawn back to Egypt and the Middle Eastern turmoil at the turn of the twenty-first century. After writing a master's thesis on art, ideology, and resistance in the philosophy of Theodor W. Adorno, and carrying out studies in Chinese language and civilization, focused mainly on philosophic and aesthetic literature, I traveled to Cairo—a short trip but, as I had not been to Egypt since 1992, a decisive step forward that had important consequences for me. A new culture of protest seemed to be surfacing in Egypt at that time. I ultimately decided to pursue my reflection on coercion, power, and resistance in a Middle Eastern context. But when Professor Alain Roussillon suggested that I devote my research to the "Coptic issue," which was arising anew in the limelight, I reacted negatively: "No, anything but the Copts." He convinced me that my own concerns with power and resistance, state coercion, and political change could open a path to rethink the sectarian problem in Egypt, which, at that time, remained entangled in debates on minorities and Islam. I first wish to thank him here, as well as my supervisor, Professor Hamit Bozarslan, who has paid sustained attention to my research and advised and encouraged me with extraordinary patience and great generosity.

In conducting this research, I benefited from the double advantage of a familiarity with the Egyptian and Coptic landscapes, thanks to which I could guess the unspoken, and understand implicit rules, while my externality permitted me to maintain the indispensable distance of the observer. Being in contact with people from a wide variety of social and geographic backgrounds, from the villages of Upper Egypt to the intellectual and political circles of the capital, I took into account a diversity of experiences and points of view; observations and informal discussions often remain the most reliable way to collect materials on this sensitive issue in an authoritarian situation. I nevertheless also undertook interviews on a regular basis with certain people. In several cases, out of respect for the anonymity of the individuals I was interviewing, I have not cited their names (for example, concerning religious conversions). I am grateful to all those I met during my research and who accorded me their time and attention for discussions or interviews.

This research refers to a good deal of excellent academic research written in Arabic by Egyptian scholars, such as the studies of Nabil ʿAbd al-Fattah on the relations between religious institutions and the state or the texts of Sherif Younes on the Nasserist regime and the paradoxes of modernity. The various exchanges with Egyptian researchers, activists, lawyers, and journalists, among other public personalities, have not only provided me with an array of testimonies, information, and documents but have allowed me to always further my reflections, to constantly challenge, question, and untangle what is commonly regarded as truth. I am especially grateful to Samer Soliman, Mounir Megahed, Nabil ʿAbd al-Fattah, Tewfik Aclimandos, Sherif Younes, Kamal Zakher, Samir Morcos, Mohamed El-Baz, Adel Guindy, William Wissa, Muhammad Afifi, Emad Thomas, Basma Moussa, Anwar Moghith, Peter and Ramses Naggar, Yara Sallam, Husam Tammam, Atef Gendy, Rafiq Habib, Bahey eldin Hassan, Magdi Khalil, Hani Labib, Khaled Ali, Husam Bahgat, Nader Choukri, Samih Fawzi, Butros Butros Ghali, Nabil Ghubrial, Naguib Ghubrial.

This research also relies on the testimonies of prominent figures in the Egyptian press (Musa Sabry, Muhammad Hasanayn Haykal, Samih Fawzi, Usama Salama), on a great number of post-2005 texts published by journalists, Muslim Brotherhood authors (or those close to the Brotherhood), independent or activist Coptic authors, a variety of public figures, and the reports of NGOs and associations (a literature that remained largely unexplored). It draws heavily on "gray" literature: tracts, publications of associations and activists, national and communitarian written and audiovisual press—certain papers that are only distributed within the confines of the church (like *al-Tariqa* and *al-Katiba al-Tibiyya*), videos and films broadcast in Coptic circles. I systematically reviewed the leading Egyptian newspapers between 2006 and 2011.

This book would not have seen the light of day without the lively exchanges with several colleagues, through informal café discussions, as well as through seminars and conferences: Mona Abaza, Febe Armanios, Dominique Avon, Joel Beinin, Sarah Ben-Néfissa, Nathalie Bernard-Maugiron, Laurent Bonnefoy, Bernard Botiveau, Patrice Brodeur, Virginie Collombier, Fanny Colonna, Grégoire Delhaye, Blandine Destremeau, Marie Duboc, Baudouin Dupret, Gaétan Du Roy, Souad Ferrié, Séverine Gabry, Aurélien Girard, Patrick Haenni, Chaymaa Hassabo, Bernard Heyberger, François Ireton, Lina Khatib, Mustapha

Khayati, Elisabeth Longuenesse, Dina Makram-Ebeid, Jacques Masson, Marlene Nasr, Didier Monciaud, Jean-Jacques Pérennès, Olivier Roy, Giedre Sabaseviciute, Jihane Sfeir, Jana Tamer, Thomas Scheffler, and Nelly Van Doorn-Harder, among others.

My thanks also go to the institutions that financially or logistically supported realizing the translated version of this book: the Centre d'Études et de recherches internationales (CÉRIUM); the Canada Research Chair in Religious Pluralism and Ethnicity; and the Canada Research Chair in Islam, Pluralism, and Globalization at the University of Montreal; as well as to the associations L'Oeuvre d'Orient and Solidarity-Orient.

Last but not least, I thank Kate Wahl, the editor-in-chief at Stanford University Press, who followed the entire process of publishing the research's English version with exemplar attention and great generosity. I cannot praise highly enough Allison McManus, who has successfully met the challenge to translate this book into English, and I am grateful to Russell Craig Richardson who provided the finishing touches to the English text.

Copts and the Security State

INTRODUCTION

"Wa entī mā lik, ya masīḥiyya!?" (Hey Christian, what's your problem!?) spat Egyptian Member of Parliament 'Abd al-Rahim al-Ghul at his fellow parliamentarian Ibtisam Habib during a People's Assembly meeting on the subject of *'urfī* (common law) marriage. "I am the Muslim president of an Islamic State," declaimed Egyptian president Anwar al-Sadat (1970–81) in his memorable speech on May 14, 1980. But Sadat's 1980 speech does not mark a starting point; rather, several centuries of history are entangled within it. Yet from one formulation to the next everything has changed. Most curious, perhaps, is the almost imperceptible character of the successive mutations. Everything seems to be repeating *ad nauseam*: "I am the Muslim president of an Islamic state"; "Wa entī mā lik, ya masīḥiyya!?" The two statements are embedded into two different *dispositifs* of domination.

In his speech, given during a celebration of the "Corrective Revolution,"[1] Sadat refers confusedly to what this "Islamic state" would be:

> If Article 2 is the cause of all of this,[2] I now ask my sons, the Copts, to listen to me. I tell you, and I tell my people, that from the day I governed in Egypt, I ruled as a Muslim president. Let's just call it what it is: Egypt is an Islamic state. Not an ordinary Islamic state, no: it holds a position of leadership in the Islamic world, a position as a guide, for al-Azhar has preserved the Islamic heritage for a thousand years, to which all Muslims testify. And the demons of sedition (*fitna*) should understand that Islam is the true guarantor of Christianity in Egypt. When I say "Muslim president of an Islamic state," this in no case signifies that the rights of Muslims come before those of Christians. But, this state has been

> an Islamic state since the Patriarch Benjamin entered into an alliance with the Arab armies of Amr ibn al-'As . . . in order to put an end to the religious oppression endured under the Byzantine yoke. I am the Muslim president of an Islamic state who knows his responsibilities. According to the Qur'anic text, I am responsible for the Jews and Christians of Egypt, the same as I am for the Muslims.[3]

In his speech Sadat alludes to the pact of *dhimma* (protection, safeguard). This pact was meant to guarantee protection for the *ahl al-dhimma* (protected peoples),[4] insofar as they submit to the sovereign authority of the Muslim ruler and pay a tax, the *jizya*. Hence, Sadat refers to a status perceived as all the more ignominious from the Christian point of view, in hindsight, now that notions of equal rights and citizenship have replaced the distinct and hierarchical positions of subjects. By evoking this bygone practice of subjugating Christians, Sadat ignores their current status, as well as the specificities of the contemporary processes of minoritization. Originating in the rules and practices of the prerepublican era, discrimination against Christians harks back to a redefinition of the religious/political nexus: with the shock of confrontation with the Great Powers in the nineteenth century and the emergence of nationalisms that followed, religion became a marker of identity. As a fledgling nation-state Egypt began to define itself against its occupier following an identitarian logic—that is to say, by excluding the other. And Islam allowed the newly born Egyptian state to demarcate itself from the occupying powers, which were viewed as Christian. Then, at the apogee of Arab and Egyptian nationalism, the Nasserite security-state crystallized the identitarian dynamics, thus furthering and transforming the minoritization processes. In the wake of the 1967 Arab defeat Sadat's rise to power (1970) represented the triumph of the religious right wing of the Free Officers, which has fostered sectarian authoritarianism.

The parliamentarian al-Ghul's exclamation brutally reveals a notable aspect of contemporary discrimination endorsed by the modern Egyptian state and by most citizens. Without explicit reference to Islam the interjection "Wa entī mā lik, ya masīḥiyya!?" signals that the term *Christian* does not simply constitute a category for classifying an individual; it is literally an insult. A sedimentation of multifaceted, century-old practices, language enforces discrimination—sometimes falling short of the intentions of the speaker, without referencing any transcendent principle that would underlie its classifying power.

• • •

In 2005, a time of both crisis and hope, antagonisms that tormented, forged, and undermined Egyptian society appeared, glaring in the harsh light of the media. In February Hosni Mubarak had amended Article 76 of Egypt's Constitution to allow for multicandidate presidential elections, sparking a brief moment of enthusiasm and the resurgence of political activism in several parts of society. Tongues loosened. Activists renewed demands to promote citizenship and, thus, the respect of political, civil, and personal rights. Thanks to these changes, the taboo that had weighed on the "Coptic issue" was momentarily lifted. This emblematic issue was situated at the heart of demands for political reform.

A few years later, the first revolutionary situation, the eighteen days from January 25 to February 11, 2011, revealed to an international audience the aspirations for political change shared by so many Egyptians. This moment was marked by the rejection of the authoritarian hierarchies that characterized both the Egyptian state and political organizations, heightening the generational tensions at work in most of these formations. At that time not only did revolutionary discourses comply with the requirements to respect a political ethic and subjective rights, but several practices of civility expressed these values, turning the ephemeral Tahrir Square of that eighteen days into a here-and-now "Ideal City" in revolutionary memory. But the revolution also featured heavy street fighting. It was born from the visceral rejection of police brutality, which momentarily united different sectoral demands: the young Khalid Saʿid, beaten to death by police in Alexandria in June 2010, initially embodied the people's anger. During these eighteen days the people seemed to be assisting at their own birth and worked it into slogans, videos, and chants. Young and old, workers and bosses, women and men, Christians and Muslims, all joyously chanted, "Ṣūt al-ḥurriyya beynādī fī kull shawāriʿ bilādī!" (The voice of freedom sings in all the streets of my country!), the lyrics from a music video disseminated on YouTube. Egyptians brandished both the cross and the crescent in the streets. Some Copts publicly demonstrated against Mubarak's government, and, in so doing, they were also protesting against the Coptic Orthodox pope, Shenuda III (1971–2012), as he had reaffirmed his support for the president and directed his community not to participate in the revolutionary movement. Tensions between Christians and Muslims would have been nothing but a bad dream, the result of machinations plotted by the reviled regime. Thus, rumors increased about an alleged plot between the minister of interior and the Salafis, who were accused of having schemed together to carry out the

2010 bombing at the Church of the Two Saints in Alexandria at the dawn of the New Year.

Nonetheless, Copts did not descend in huge numbers into Tahrir Square. In the several years up until that time they had often adopted a sectarian pattern of expressing discontent. As early as autumn 2005, the late Samer Soliman and Alain Roussillon were wondering whether Coptic activism could constitute a "path to democracy,"[5] a spearhead in the struggle for the "necessary secularity of institutions and society,"[6] or if it would reinforce sectarianism in political life. Was it one of its symptoms? After February 2011 a new wave of attacks against Copts occurred, resulting in clashes among Copts, Salafis, and the military. Indeed, the revolutionary event had reactivated structural tendencies and, in particular, the sectarianization of Egyptian society and political life. Sectarianization even became visible in a redrawn geography of downtown Cairo. As Tahrir Square was embodying the vibrant heart of the revolution, a rediscovered national pride, and the unity of the "two elements of the nation," another center of dissent formed farther away, toward Maspero. Certainly, secular activists, like members of the group MARED (Miṣriyūn Against Religious Discriminations / Miṣriyūn ḍidd al-tamyīz al-dīnī), organized demonstrations there. More often, however, marches were led by Coptic associations, whose demands focused exclusively on the attacks against Christians and churches that had been launched after Mubarak's resignation. Meanwhile, all Islamist currents played the religion card during the March 2011 referendum on amending electoral procedures, thereby worsening tensions and negating the hope of living together that had been raised by the revolutionary momentum. Later on, during the presidency of Muhammad Mursi (June 2012–July 2013), the Muslim Brotherhood relied heavily on sectarian policies and discourses. But they did not target only Copts; they defiantly stigmatized all non-Brotherhood individuals and groups. Then, although resolutely hostile to the Muslim Brothers and apparently promoting a renewed religious discourse, President ʿAbd al-Fattah al-Sisi (2014–present) nevertheless pursued a counterrevolutionary politics. From the beginning he plugged the slight breach that the revolutionary event had opened in the vicious circle of sectarianism:

> The forces of change in Egypt will not move forward until they are capable of including the individuals and organizations of the Christian minority. This is neither strange nor new. We should turn our attention to the revolution

of 1919, and observe how it shaped the national understanding around the claim to national independence: at this epoch, Egypt was divided into numerous categories and social communities, between wealthy landowners and poor peasants, between men and women, between landed aristocracy and city dwellers, between capitalists and workers, between the literate and the illiterate. The 1919 revolution did not build a national understanding through the union of the previously mentioned groups, but forged it solely on the religious division between Muslims and Christians. Hence, the slogans "Union of the Crescent and the Cross" or "Religion for God, and the Nation for All" became the most significant watchwords of the time. This fact is worth thinking about for the future. Christians in Egypt only account for around ten percent of the population. Why did their participation in the national consensus hold such importance? Because the 1919 revolution was based on a sectarian society, such is the most logical response."[7]

A sectarian society that is unique in several ways. The union of the two elements of the nation always presupposes an initial division. Yet it became a core value of the nationalist narratives. But sectarian discrimination rarely requires a legal basis; confessional geographic groupings do not appear significant; power-sharing according to religious cleavages seems impossible; and political sectarianism is not institutionalized as is the case in Lebanon. In contrast, in Lebanon, in Iraq, and in Syria the national space emerges out of the superimposition of clan-based, tribal, and confessional territories. In these three cases no group accounts for a proportion of the population as large as the Egyptian Sunnis (around 93 percent), and religious affiliation most often determines political allegiance. Although they once formed a numerical majority, Lebanese Christians now account for only around 35 percent of the population. Conversely, in Egypt, despite the existence of multiple forms of insidious and pervasive discrimination, we are currently witnessing the exacerbation of two tendencies that have long characterized the Coptic relationship to the nation in a more or less determinant manner: first, the desire for integration in the national framework or the centripetal tendency toward alleged universal values; second, a withdrawal into community institutions, symbols, values, and demands.

• • •

Given that Egypt is a "sectarian society," the objective of this book is twofold. First, it paints a dynamic picture of this sectarian society. The construction of the modern Egyptian state has reproduced sectarianism, while at the same time transforming it. Decentering the debate from Islam and religion as such,[8] I examine the affinity—the "family resemblance"—between authoritarian and identitarian logics, both of which put an emotional dynamic of fear to work. They reinforce each other and constitute a matrix of meaning that establishes security as a normative concept. In other words I argue that sectarianism should not be analyzed through the lens of secularism or authoritarianism, nor should it be considered as a typically Middle Eastern product. It should rather be understood as a by-product of a global security-turn, which puts to work identitarian practices of legitimization and veridiction, as Foucault would put it. New kinds of multiform violence unfold from the security-identity nexus. This book aims at understanding the specificities of Egyptian structural violence, while taking into account this global change, which interacts with local dynamics. Vivienne Jabri argues that this security-turn can be traced back to 9/11 and the subsequent "war against terrorism [that] is constructed as a global war, transcending space and seemingly defiant of international conventions."[9] This new world order, namely the security-identity order, was shaped, I would venture, during the Cold War. But that is another story, to be further explored at a later date; for now, I will maintain my focus on the Egyptian situation.

Second, I raise the question of transformation: which forces and which individuals have attempted to break the vicious cycle of identitarian dynamics, and how have they done this? And is it possible to evaluate the results of these actions at this point in time?

In this respect the contemporary literature in the field of Coptic studies has fashioned an extremely stimulating renewal of approaches, objects, and methods of investigation. The Copts had long been kept prisoners of inquiry by authors who were sometimes lax in their application of scientific criteria and who addressed this issue in terms of Christian minorities in the lands of Islam.[10] The most common fault of this literature has been to describe the current status of Christians in the light of the concept of *dhimma*. In so doing, it neglects the variety of situations that took shape even within the unique Egyptian arena beginning in the seventh century, and it supposes a historical continuity that prohibits identifying the contemporary specificities of the minoritization processes. Often sympathetic to Christians, this literature makes the mistake of reducing them to victims and denying them any form of agency, as Paul Sedra has duly noted.[11] These traits still characterize a notable portion of activist literature.[12]

In contrast to these approaches, and with greater concern for scientific criteria, the research produced on the subject in the years from 1980 to 1990 in France, in Egypt, and in the English-speaking world has sought to paint a more complex and better-documented picture of Coptic participation in Egyptian political life and intracommunity dynamics.[13] It was not until the 2000s, however, that the literature saw a diversification of objects, questions, and methods, in great part thanks to earlier work carried out in Arabic and French, notably that of Tariq al-Bishri and of Dina El-Khawaga, not to mention the many testimonies of Egyptian journalists.[14] Contemporary scholarship emphasizes the diversity of Coptic protagonists, narratives, and behaviors. In the words of Paul Sedra, "The victim has become an actor."[15] The studies of Alastair Hamilton in 2006, Paul Sedra in 2004 and 2011, and Heather Sharkey in 2008 show the ambivalent relationship between the Coptic Church and Western missions, underscoring the impact of the latter on transformations in the Egyptian church and in the religious field in Egypt from the nineteenth century to the mid-twentieth.[16] Other researchers have examined the current influence of charismatic Protestant currents on the religious practices of Christians in Egypt.[17] And historians have explored the Ayyubid and Ottoman worlds to give a more precise image of the everyday relationships between Christians and Muslims, as well as those between Christians and their rulers.[18] Researchers have adopted varied and often complementary approaches to understanding the transformations in representations of identity and community, from the study of Coptic music to media.[19] The Coptic issue has also interested legal experts,[20] and political scientists have studied the judicial domain as a new space of dissent. More recent works analyze the renewal of Coptic dissent in the 2000s in the context of a national revival of political activism.[21] This new scholarship was necessary to shatter the image of the Copts as a monolithic bloc, the subject of decades of critiques by Egyptian analysts, for political reasons. Nevertheless, a complete and dynamic picture of the structural tendencies of Egyptian society still remains to be painted in order to accurately assess the impact of critical and dissenting Coptic actions, as well as determining to what extent key personalities on the communitarian and national scenes actually are representative of the majority view.

Thus, I propose a synthetic analysis, combining micro, meso, and macro scales, articulating different regimes of historicity, and drawing on methods from several different disciplines—social history, political sociology, and ethnography. Following the advice of Claude Lefort, I analyze actions and representations. For

> [it is] impossible to establish a barrier between the order of action and the order of representation. Certainly, the distinction is well-established at a certain level, but political analysis is only worth its name; it only ceases to be confused with what is commonly referred to as political facts when it does not stop at the obvious and particular traits of actions and representations, when it combines the study of behavior and institutions with that of the narratives and ideas they convey, the research of the system in which they are arranged, or the logic that animates them, which we cannot say is either the logic of action or representation, for it is exercised in both registers.[22]

Indeed, the complexity of the issue requires a multiperspective approach: how does sectarianism take shape, and how is it exercised in both registers, the logic of action and the logic of representation? Identitarian logic governs sectarianization: religion as an identity marker determines the possibility, the modalities, and the limits of professional, social, and political relationship, as well as the relationships between individuals and state institutions. It sets out the criteria for exclusion and modes of categorization. More than just causing the minoritization processes that structure Egyptian society, the reference to religion has become "a principle of internalization lending support to a particular mode of differentiation, and of linking classes, groups, and conditions, and, simultaneously, of a particular mode of discrimination markers to organize the experience of coexistence—economic, juridical, aesthetic, and religious."[23] It represents the intelligibility principle of a signifying order, which is formed and transformed through multiple practices—be they political, discursive, or symbolic—governed by specific rules, and embedded in various historical narratives. This initial definition leads to a number of questions that determine the plan of this work, the fields of study it engages, and its methodology.

Although sectarianism depends on a legal and political order partly inherited from the Ottoman Empire, this legacy does not explain its contemporary specificities. Sectarianism has endured to the extent that the modern state has consolidated it, while profoundly modifying it. In other words the state is the principal agent enforcing sectarianism, in part owing to the historical circumstances of its construction and the nationalist discourse of legitimacy that followed. And the state apparatus has all too often favored violence and discriminatory practices. In Foucauldian terms the specific governmentality of the Egyptian state has encouraged certain conducts and forbidden others.[24] Therefore, in the first chapter I analyze the state as the implementation site for multiform minoritization processes. Yet, here as elsewhere, the Leviathan does not loom over society: "The state's history should come from the practices of men themselves, from what they have done and the manner in which they think. The state as a way of doing, the state as a way of thinking."[25] To disentangle the effective modalities of the minoritization processes such an analysis "should not concern itself with the regulated and legitimate forms of power in their central locations. It should rather [be] concerned with power at its extremities, at the points where it becomes capillary, in its regional and local forms and institutions; the point where power surmounts the rules of right which organize and delimit it and extends itself beyond them, oversteps those rules and is invested in institutions, is embodied in techniques and acquires the material means to intervene, sometimes in violent ways."[26] The sphere of governmentality refers to the "technologies of power," or "micro-powers," that forge the political order and ensure its longevity but also its modification, be it slow or sudden. Hence, governmentality also implies the formation of meaning-making processes and of regimes of veridiction. It puts a specific rationality to work. Whereas Adorno interprets the process of modernization as the historical advent of instrumental rationality, Foucault purposefully distances himself from this approach by identifying several types of rationalities and, therefore, several regimes of veridiction and truth. Hence, the crucial element in understanding the specific rationality and governmentality of the sectarian order is the notion of practice. Institutional, social, and discursive practices become structured institutions' routines, as well as lived experience, and they constitute structuring continuities. A multiplicity of daily practices reproduces sectarianism. And they are the products as well as the vectors that perpetuate and transform the sectarian order. To understand the "conditions governing the continuity or transformation of structures and, therefore, the reproduction of systems,"[27] one must take into account the historical specificity of each of these processes. Indeed, the legal *dispositif*, the electoral scene, activist literature (from NGO reports to pamphlets), media discourse, common representations, government policies, religious practices, the Coptic Church—each of these domains involves a different set of rules and narratives. Hence, for each scale of analysis and for each domain that I explore, I consider several time frames: the long time frame of the twentieth century, the short but dense period coming at the beginning of the 2000s (which includes the intensification of violence against the Copts, the renewal of political activism, runaway neoliberal measures, and the ascension of the president's son, Gamal Mubarak, along with his cohorts in the ruling National Democratic Party [NDP]), and the following period through al-Sisi's rise to the presidency.

In the first chapter I focus on three areas to reveal the subtle workings of power and violence. I start with the most visible and spectacular phenomenon, namely "interconfessional" violence, and examine how security agencies have dealt with and exerted violence. I then turn to governmental narratives on this issue. In this regard I show how government initiatives to promote a pacifist discourse not only failed to stem the spread of hate speech but are also governed by identitarian logics. I then turn toward the practices of institutional agents of the state in charge of religious conversions: the Ministry of the Interior, religious institutions, and the judiciary. Analyzing these interconnected practices helps us to decipher the sectarian order's specific rationality and regimes of veridiction. These case studies bring to light a salient trait of this rationality. The rules of the electoral game do not allow for differentiation between authoritarian and democratic logics. Yet analyzing the technologies of power in different sectors and scales of the state apparatus enables us to further distinguish between these two logics: "Hybrid regimes include situations characterized by a 'plurality of normative fields' that confront participants with the inadequacies of old regimes of justification and with the heterogeneity of possible new references. . . . In this regard, the question of the game participants' 'security' seems definitive. Authoritarian and democratic situations distinguish themselves from one another based on this criteria of security and, correspondingly, in the margin of the exercise of competences."[28]

In other words authoritarian situations are characterized by a *margin of informality* between laws and practices—a margin that deepens at whim. Thus, authoritarian and democratic situations distinguish themselves according to a criterion that Michel Camau indicates without naming it: an emotion, fear. Authoritarian and sectarian logics reinforce one another: in the name of identity or of national union, defining friends and foes appears as the criterion of the political, and security becomes a normative concept.[29]

In this regard the new centrality of purity in social, discursive, and symbolic practices signals the radicalization of speech and the increasing mistrust between the followers of the two religions, fueled by several government initiatives. Hence, in the second chapter I analyze the concurrent formation of national and Coptic symbolic configurations at the end of the nineteenth century and then radicalized discourses throughout the twentieth century prominent in the ethnicization of the definition of community.[30] To uncover significant traits in contemporary practices, I show how they are embedded in multiple discursive and symbolic frames, by drawing on images of the "other," as well as by reinvesting, or referring to, older images and narratives. In so doing, I shed light on the unprecedented link between security and purity: security as a norm currently pervades and defines the ideal of purity prevalent in sectarian discourses.

In the third and fourth chapters I take on the communal scale. The politicization of the patriarchal function that started during the reign of Cyril VI (1959–71), the formation of Shenuda III's theological-political project, and social sectarianization were all dependent on the constitution of the security state under Nasser's presidency (1954–70), as well as on intracommunitarian dynamics.[31] As a state institution, the church both submits to the arbitrariness of the state regime and provides a place of refuge within it, thereby fostering the elaboration of a counterdiscourse. But the state-imposed identitarian logic governs this sectarian counterdiscourse, which, thus, fails to form a real alternative. By doubling up on the state-enforced subjugation, the church further requires Copts to submit to patriarchal authority (Chapter 3).[32]

Yet the Coptic pope has partly failed in imposing religious, political, and social hegemony. Not only have intracommunitarian rivalries and divergences multiplied, but critics have raised their voices to call into question the patriarch's theological orientation, the patriarchal management of communitarian affairs, and the clergy's allegiance to power. Critique of the church's patriarch and critique of the regime often went hand in hand until the fall of Mubarak in 2011.[33] Despite the diversification of dissenting actions from the 2000s until the years just after the first revolutionary situation of January 25, 2011, admirably described by Mariz Tadros,[34] the community's attachment to the church and its support for the regime characterize the attitude of the overwhelming majority of Copts. The election of al-Sisi in May 2014 reinforced this tendency when he presented himself as the champion of a reformed religious discourse and sought to reassure Copts after the brief rule of Muslim Brotherhood president Mursi from June 2012 to July 2013. Simultaneously, the significant increase in conducts that combine attachment to the community and the church with resistance to the religious, social, and political rules dictated by the patriarch indicates the contemporary reconfigurations of the relations between religious practices, community belonging, and national commitment (Chapter 4).

In Chapter 5 I continue an analysis of the interconnected sectarian and authoritarian logics, while observing how the controlled pluralization of the Egyptian political scene has strengthened sectarianism, though not without several changes. I analyze transformations of the Egyptian political scene throughout the course of the twentieth century, with a focus on the last thirty years. Like the agents of state institutions, political figures are confronted with "a plurality of normative fields and the heterogeneity of new possible references."[35] In the context of controlled pluralization under more or less lax international pressure, Islamist political formations were summoned to prove that their doctrinal orientation hindered neither the recognition of equality for all citizens nor the fundamental principles of the modern state. The position of the Society of Muslim Brothers with respect to Copts therefore constituted a litmus test in measuring its capacity to adopt a conception of the state and citizenship according to which Christians would have the same rights as their Muslim counterparts. While affirming their adherence to these principles, however, the majority of political protagonists fulfilled a requirement to respect so-called Islamic norms and values. This was especially the case as the National Democratic Party (NDP) endeavored to build a democratic facade in the 2000s with the intent of ensuring hereditary transmission of power at the ballot box. The ruling party therefore had to compete with Islamists on the electoral scene. From the 1980s to the present, political actors have used two tactics, susceptible to infinite variations: the exhibition of Copts as an empty signifier and the stigmatization of Christians.

Nonetheless, the analysis of the current Egyptian situation demands that we clarify a few assumptions. Several researchers suppose, guess, or hope that Egypt is in a phase of democratic transition—failed or postponed. In her gripping work on the Copts, Mariz Tadros asks from the outset about the construction of an inclusive democracy.[36] But is the distinction between authoritarian and democratic regimes, as well as the idea of a transition from one to the other, still relevant?[37] Limited pluralism, which "appears as the principal distinctive criterion of authoritarianism versus democracy,"[38] does not permit the differentiation between one regime and another: "Swathes of limited pluralism are currently emerging in democracies. . . . Governance appears in this respect as a form of elitist selection of actors integrated into networks of action closed unto themselves and separated from 'electoral politics' (Hermet 2004). For their part, elitist authoritarianisms are presumed to demonstrate the forms of pluralistic openness to supposed 'civil society' participants, most often under the guidance of international funding."[39]

Consequently, if democracy remains a normative principle or an ideal, this notion does not constitute a pertinent heuristic and methodological tool to analyze political mutations, either in the Middle East or elsewhere. Consensual connotations poorly mask the elitist character and the confiscation of power by experts that shape the very notion of governance. Rather, the Foucauldian notion of governmentality allows us to better shed light on the exercise of social, political, and symbolic power in contemporary societies, as well as on the interconnections between micro and macro scales of analysis. And the notion of practices enables us to push further the reflection on the reproduction, as well as on the transformation, of the sectarian order. The repetition of discriminatory practices ensures the reiteration of dominant norms.[40]

Nevertheless, repetition does not occur automatically. The state has, up to the present day, encouraged discriminatory practices and thus the reproduction of the sectarian order. But subversive practices also occur regularly, and sectarian society does not remain unchanged. In the sixth chapter I analyze Coptic strategies of resistance to the minoritization processes. I also examine how the regime and the Coptic Church have integrated or neutralized critics. Finally, I interrogate advocacy activism's impact on social changes, while slightly shifting the terms of debate on the role of "civil society." If we were to suppose that the world is now in a phase of "de-democratization,"[41] how should we reassess the impact of advocacy activisms, and of the January 25 revolution, on social and political change? Discriminatory practices create structuring effects in the long term. Yet transformative practices, were they reiterated, also create structuring effects.

1 INSTITUTIONALIZED VIOLENCE AND THE IDENTITY STATE

HASSAN AND MARCUS

Egyptian cinema showed the representation of civil war for the first time in 2007. This unnamed, troubling thing, this projected phobia that haunted people's spirits and sometimes appeared under the mask of a proper noun ("Lebanon," "Iraq," . . .), became an image. The last scene in *Hassan and Marcus* shows two massive armies, face-to-face. Weapons fire; heavy, spinning, batons hit skulls; the wounded collapse, stunned; and flames invade the screen. Yet tenuous hope remains, perhaps, for the nation-state to be saved. In the heart of the battlefield, their faces charred by fire, six characters advance hand in hand: two fathers in the center, then their wives, then the son of Marcus and the daughter of Hassan, who have fallen in love. Having both been threatened by their radical co-religionists, Hassan and Marcus had unwittingly used the same subterfuge by temporarily adopting the religious identity of the other. Not realizing the sectarian front that separated them, the two families became friends. Finally, they preserved these bonds to meet the challenge posed by the love between their children.

The debates in the Egyptian press were both animated and bitter. Some praised the intention of denouncing sectarianism and pointing out its dangers; others pointed to a lack of realism in the exact parallels drawn between the two parties, implying the presence of two forces of equal strength and with an equitable distribution of wrongdoing. But the dynamics of denial shaped all discussion about the film: although recognizing the existence of the trauma, or of the problem, discussions about its representation still denied the very dynamic that nourished it. Such is the nature of denial.

Indeed, the allusion to the 1954 film *Hassan, Marcus, and Cohen*, adapted from the stage, escaped no one, and no one—or almost no one—failed to underscore the fact that Cohen, the Jew, was missing.[1] What would become of Marcus, the Christian? Do we Egyptians wish that Marcus, too, would take the path of exodus? The reference to this imagined past offered the audience a chance to once again embroider a work that never ceases to unravel and that, just like Penelope, keeps hope alive to one day attain the "nation." *Hassan, Marcus, and Cohen* conjured nostalgia for a golden era; the film's creators described the cheerful ties and friendship that united members of diverse religions under the Egyptian sun. Lamenting the "sectarian" incident—real or onscreen—they idealized the past period and then concluded that the current unfortunate state of affairs was only a passing phase. Yet denial transcends the personal sphere and pervades most narratives related to the "Coptic issue" in general and "sectarian violence" in particular. Salah Jahin presented a humorous riff on this denial in a cartoon published in *al-Ahram* on June 22, 1981,[2] at the end of a decade punctuated by violence: "They [unity, harmony, secularity] are my children and I know they are kind, but you, whose child are you?" asks Mother Egypt, astonished, to an unlikely offspring, a hirsute and enraged monster named *fitna ṭā'ifiyya* (sectarian strife).

That Salah Jahin dared to count secularity (*'ilmāniyya*) among the three children of Mother Egypt was the motivation for the criticism and insults that the artist suffered at the time of the cartoon's publication—the height of irony given the collective dynamic of denial. Denial determines the modalities of apprehension and interrogation; it bedevils the most sophisticated analyses of what is deemed *fitna ṭā'ifiyya*; it accompanies an acute awareness of all the "givens" of the problem. Denial, by definition, only exists in full knowledge of the facts.

• • •

In this chapter I analyze the security, discursive, and legal *dispositifs* of minoritization, relying on three case studies: the treatment of violence, the production of a consensual discourse on the relations between Muslims and Christians, and religious conversions. Taking "power in its forms and its most regional and local institutions, especially where this power, overstepping the rules of law that organize and delimit it, extends beyond these rules,"[3] I highlight the principal feature of Egypt's authoritarian situation: the margin of informality that allows for the arbitrary and establishes a reign of fear.

PRODUCING FITNA ṬĀ'IFIYYA

From the 1970s, attacks on Christians became a recurrent feature of Egyptian society. Physical violence represents only one particular form of violence, merely determined by political power relations and government policies. Generally, three periods of violence can be distinguished, throughout which the motives—or pretexts—for outbreaks of hostility have been generically similar. Regime policies and the police agencies have played a crucial role in determining the forms, the duration, the extent, and the intensity, as well as the agents of violence, from the 1972 attacks in Khanka in the Nile Delta region to the military repression that bloodied the Maspero Bridge in the center of Cairo in October 2011.

A Christian association, Friends of the Holy Book (*Aṣdiqa' al-Kitāb al-Muqaddas*), had legally carried out activities in the village of Khanka since 1946. In 1970 it had constructed new buildings on recently acquired plots of land (one from a Copt and the other from a Muslim) and used one as a place of worship without having first obtained the necessary church-building license. This roused the anger of the Muslim neighborhood. The building was burned down on November 6, 1972. Pope Shenuda III appealed to martyrdom and sacrifice; the church ran bus and taxi services to send its clergy. The morning of November 12, hundreds of Cairene priests descended on the site to celebrate Sunday Mass. Having been ordered to warn the clergy that they would not be able to get all the way to Khanka, State Security cordoned off the road to prevent them from reaching their destination. No incidents occurred during Mass, but several Muslim neighbors retaliated that same evening after gathering in the mosque. They formed a procession that police only partially dispersed, headed toward the Arab Socialist Union (*al-ittiḥād al-ishtarākī al-'arabī*) building,[4] burning, destroying, and looting Copts' houses and stores along the way. A government committee headed by Gamal al-'Utayfi was charged with conducting an inquiry into the causes of the incident.[5] The committee determined that the principal motivations for the outbreak of violence and, afterward, the Copts' anger and mobilization were disputes over sacred places: religious symbols, women's bodies, land, and, particularly, places of worship.

Since the Assiut conference in 1911, suggested by the British and organized by Christian lay elites,[6] Copts have discussed the idea of unifying legislation on Christian and Muslim places of worship. The actual regulations are one of the rare cases where religious discrimination has a legal basis. The regulations are partially derived from the *Hatti Humayuni*, enacted in 1856 during the

Tanzimat reforms,[7] which conditions the building and restoration of Christian places of worship upon the issuance of a sovereign authority. Only Egyptian presidents have the power to grant building permits to Christian denominations. Certainly, subordination to the goodwill of a ruler represents a violation of the principle of equality. De facto, Gamal Abdel Nasser (1954–70) authorized Cyril VI (1959–70) to erect twenty-five churches, and together the president and pope laid the cornerstone of Saint Mark's Cathedral in ʿAbasiyya, the current seat of the Patriarchate in Cairo; Sadat (1970–81) allowed Shenuda III the right to construct fifty more. But the 1934 *Izabi* ministerial decree had enumerated ten conditions (notably the respect of a minimum one hundred–yard distance between any church and the closest mosque, as well as the prior procurement of the assent of neighboring Muslim populations)[8] that, on a local scale, have seriously interfered with the construction of churches even after authorization has been granted. Shenuda III did not fail to mention these obstacles each time that Sadat boasted of having doubled the number of authorizations of his predecessor.[9]

Mubarak (1981–2011) issued two decrees (in 1998 and 1999) with the objective of simplifying procedures for church restoration. In 2005 he put forward one more (291/2005). The text of the law delegated the power to authorize the expansion and renovation of churches to the twenty-six provincial governors, stipulating that the governors must review all requests no later than thirty days after their date of submission and that any rejections should be explained. It also mentioned that maintenance work may be undertaken with a simple written notification to the local authorities. Several years after the enactment of the decree, Egyptian church representatives noted that local authorities continued to pose obstacles to construction, whether by demanding the presentation of documents impossible to procure (for example, a presidential decree authorizing the existence of a church built during the monarchy), by classifying simple maintenance work under the rubric of "expansion/reconstruction" and so arguing that a written notice would not suffice, or by State Security's obstruction of church-building despite the presence of all prior necessary documents.[10] Finally, if a mosque were to be erected between the date of authorization and the start of work, the neighborhood would no longer consider the authorization valid. Church construction, renovation, and expansion, therefore, have been highly dependent on personal relationships between the clergy and the local authorities. Weary of the toil required to overcome these obstacles, Christians sometimes use private locations or those of associations to worship and carry out necessary activities without permits. These unauthorized initiatives regularly provoke Muslim neighbors' anger and represent one of the primary pretexts for attacks against Copts and churches. To date, the People's Assembly (*majlis al-sha'b*) has not examined any of the proposals for a unified law applicable to all houses of worship. In one of these proposals Muhammad al-Juwayli, then president of the Suggestions and Complaints Committee in the People's Assembly, suggested a single regulation: to be governed by law 176 of 1976 pursuant to civil construction. The unified regulation would apply to construction work, maintenance, and repair of all Muslim, Jewish, and Christian houses of worship. The law's author aimed to free the construction of houses of worship from "the political and security influence to which it is currently subjected" and to put an end to the power "that governors and State Security officers exercise in this domain, their irresponsible actions in refusing, without explanation, to grant the permits required to undertake work, and their hindrance of [permits'] proper implementation."[11] Al-Juwayli presented the draft to the People's Assembly in May 2005, hoping that it would be reviewed before the end of the parliamentary session.[12] In a second draft, commissioned by the National Council for Human Rights (NCHR)—an organization formed by the regime—the editors placed the issuance of permits back under the control of local authorities and the State Security services. Yusif Sidhum was critical of this second draft, which would "preserve political and police dominance." He asked: "Has the role of the NCHR been hijacked, so that instead of protecting human rights it protects those of the authorities?"[13]

Christian and Muslim associations' renewed activity constituted a defining feature of the era after the shock of the Arab defeat in 1967. And the authors of the 'Utayfi report noted the impact of *da'wa* (call, or preaching, typically reserved for Islam) and of *tabshīr* (proselytizing, typically reserved for Christianity) on the exacerbation of tensions between the two religious groups. They also counted the conversion (two years earlier) of two young boys in Alexandria among the incidents that had heightened emotions before the eruption of hostility in Khanka.

Throughout the first period of violence (1972–97), which was marked by the growth in power of Islamist organizations (*al-jamā'āt al-islāmiyya*)[14] and the critical peak in 1981, the Egyptian state showed a general complacency with regard to radical groups, followed by increasingly repressive measures undertaken to combat them. Just after the 1967 defeat to Israel, leftist and Islamist activism in Egypt reorganized. Having reached the presidency in 1970, Sadat removed 'Ali Sabri's (his adversary in government) pro-Soviet faction, triggering the "corrective revolution" (*al-thawra al-taṣlīḥiyya*, May 1971). He then encouraged the rise of Islamist movements on university campuses as a countercurrent to the influence of Nasserist and left-wing organizing; from 1970 to 1972 the latter had been more and more urgently demanding the warrior's revenge Sadat had promised. The strategy of rapprochement with the religious right and the concomitant adoption of Islamic rhetoric ensured the success of Sadat's primary objectives: to make peace with Israel and, correspondingly, to promote economic policies of openness (*infitāḥ*), breaking down the Nasserist outlook and the figure of Nasser. The Islamization of political rhetoric, beginning with the implementation of Nasser's socialist politics and renewed with the activity of Islamist movements at Sadat's instigation, had repercussions at all levels of society.[15] Although violence was frequently grafted onto local quarrels over land or interfaith romances, the *jama'at* exacerbated these existing tensions and launched attacks against churches, Copts, and their property. This was particularly the case in Upper Egypt, Alexandria, and in numerous informal areas in the outskirts of Cairo. The tensions weighed on the daily activities of students, both Muslim and Christian, particularly at universities in Assiut, Minya, and Alexandria. Islamist militants kept a watchful eye, sometimes using force, so that everybody would respect the laws they deemed mandatory according to shari'a; they pressured women to cover their heads, forbade celebrating Christian holidays, and imposed the payment of *jizya* on a Coptic youth rooted in the church and the evocation of martyrdom for Christ.[16]

In June 1981 the Zawaya al-Hamra episode marked the climax of this first phase of violence. A dispute between a Christian and a Muslim over land in the peripheral Cairo neighborhood of Zawaya al-Hamra, where a church was supposed to be built, gave way to a battle that was carried out over the course of three long days. At Zawaya al-Hamra, and to a lesser degree at Khanka, the security forces' behavior favored the spread, prolongation, and intensification of violence. Coptic activists, among others, denounced State Security's sluggishness in curbing the violence and the agency's complicity with the assailants. The accusation was justified in the case of the Zawaya al-Hamra events. Although they surrounded the combat zones, security forces did not intervene during the first days, allowing a good number of members from the more radical *Jama'a al-Islamiyya* and *al-Jihad* to come from other districts and lend arms and other assistance to the Zawaya residents.[17] After the battle of Zawaya al-Hamra and Sadat's assassination by Khalid al-Islambuli (who rose in the wake of the Egyptian Islamic Jihad, where his brother was a member), Mubarak's policies integrated those Islamists judged to be "moderate" into public life, though the initiative was controlled and punctuated by phases of repression. The regime also started promoting an official version of Islam, all the while extirpating radical groups.[18] In the 1980s and early 1990s the police carried out extrajudicial repression and killing, whose intensity varied depending on the different orientations of the various governors and ministers of the interior. Faced with the ever more rapid reconstitution of radical cells and attacks on tourists, State Security hardened its tone and brought militants before military courts (*al-maḥākim al-'askariyya*).[19] The repression transformed into a veritable war, epitomized by the siege of Imbaba in 1992 and the battles in Assiut against the *Jama'a* in the early 1990s.[20] The war seemed to have been won in 1997 when the *Jama'a* declared its renunciation of violence, with the exception of a last deadly jolt, in Luxor, carried out by a dissident faction.

The 2004 attacks on a tourist complex in Taba (South Sinai) marked the end of a fleeting period of calm. Throughout the course of this period (1997–2004), the proliferation of rival Islamist narratives, coupled with the formation of a Coptic *imaginaire* that centered on communitarian values, ultimately broke the remaining ties between the followers of the two religions. In this climate of congestion and social segregation latent tensions and old grudges imbued even the slightest incident, and disputes between Christians and Muslims often resulted in attacks and reprisals. The murders perpetrated in al-Kushih in 1999 and 2000 indicated the changeover to a third phase (2004–11) marked initially by the resurgence of violence, then by its organized character.[21] The authors of a 2010 report based on systematic surveys, published by the Egyptian Initiative for Personal Rights (EIPR), found that violence between 2008 and 2010 erupted in areas where it had not happened before (like Marsa Matruh in 2009), seemed less related to local conflicts, and was often more prolonged, destructive, and deadly than throughout the previous years, particularly in Middle and Upper Egypt. Additionally, their surveys revealed that actions that appeared spontaneous were in fact often organized and that weekly prayers played a mobilizing role.[22] After 2004 new radicalized factions and individuals committed attacks against Christians and tourists.

The government authorities' actions and rhetoric after any deadly episode followed a similar pattern. The government's position was typically to give a disclaimer, alleging the externality of causes: the foreign nationality or insanity of the criminal or the isolated and "nonsectarian" nature of the incident. For example, on January 1, 2011, after the attack at the Two Saints Church in Alexandria, Mubarak spoke on state television: "This attack is a terrorist operation and bears the mark of foreign hands wishing to transform Egypt, and even the entire region, into another terrorist landscape." A variation on the theme of externality, *fitna* was often presented as the isolated work of a madman. The causes and agents of *fitna* were only recognized as national elements when, pushing the envelope of unreason, their actions relegated them to the periphery of normality. And the representatives of religious institutions depicted presumed national unity by showcasing the solidarity between the Imam of al-Azhar and the Coptic Orthodox pope. With only one exception, no penal sentence was ever handed to the perpetrators of crimes and abuses against Christians before the fall of Mubarak. So-called sectarian incidents were generally subject to customary reconciliation sessions (*jalasāt al-ṣulḥ*). The parties in conflict would be called to publicly reconcile in the presence of religious representatives and local notables. In most cases these sessions proved ineffective, even counterproductive. Most often organized under the pressure of State Security officers worried about avoiding any legal action, they were rarely initiated by the locals concerned. In 2008, for example, during a dispute between the monastery of Abu Fana, a Muslim family, and the state in the district of Mallawi (Minya Province), State Security services forced the monks and bishop of Mallawi to waive their property rights to the plot of land, which was the object of the conflict, and to submit to this parody of reconciliation. According to rigorous analyses carried out in 2010 and based on a large selection of case studies, the negative aspects of this type of conflict mediation were predominant. The absence of legal punishment for guilty parties fed antagonism and sowed the seeds of the violence to come, as evidenced by the fact that conflict was often repeated in the same locations where reconciliation sessions occurred.[23]

Nevertheless, it is untrue that the government does not "sanction." It represses. From 1980 to 1990 the cases of several militant Islamists were referred to military court, often when crimes included attacks against Copts. Because of repression and secret processes, however, there was no official recognition of the damages that Christians suffered. The actions taken after the attack on the Two Saints Church were paradigmatic of the Egyptian government's modus operandi. The government launched several operations in tandem with calming rhetoric and symbolic gestures. Obediently following the security service's narrative of a "foreign hand," the daily newspapers announced that police were trying to identify foreigners who had recently entered the country, harassing Afghanis and Pakistanis. State Security agents carried out heavy-handed raids on Alexandria hotels, interrogating any foreigners. They conducted an investigation and published the results: the body of a young unemployed man, presumed guilty postmortem, had been found. Neither Afghan nor Pakistani, he was Egyptian. At the same time, a police officer summoned a young man named Sayyid Bilal to the precinct, advising him to bring a blanket. Whether he was a "practicing Muslim" or a "Salafi" differs according to opinion. Already married and the father of a family, Sayyid was an unlikely culprit for the attack on the Two Saints Church. Twenty-four hours after his summons, the police delivered his corpse to his family, covered in his blanket; they forced his wife to retract her complaint demanding an investigation into her young husband's death.

The explosion at the Two Saints Church influenced the verdict on Hammam al-Kamuni, the individual who had opened fire on Christians on January 6, 2010, in a church in Nag' Hammadi (Suhag Province). Indeed, the date set for the trial after repeated delays—January 16, 2011—came not only after the drama in Alexandria but also after a set of serial bombings in Iraq targeting Christians. The perpetrators of those bombings accused the Egyptian church of having detained young women who wished to convert to Islam. The crime in Alexandria mobilized the attention of the international media and, for the first time in Egypt, a penal sentence was handed down to a Muslim who had committed a crime against Christians. Sentenced to death, al-Kamuni took advantage of a lapse in prison defenses to regain his liberty during the revolutionary heyday in January 2011, although he was caught and executed several months later.[24]

CHRISTIANITY, ISLAM, AND NATIONAL UNITY: CONSENSUAL DISCOURSES

From the 1990s onward Mubarak's government undertook several initiatives intended to improve relations between Christians and Muslims, aside from symbolic measures to satisfy long-standing Christian demands, such as the 2002 declaration of Coptic Christmas as a national holiday (despite the fact that for Copts, Easter, which is not a public holiday, is more important than Christmas).

The government encouraged national interfaith dialogues under the auspices of the minister of Awqaf (Muhammad 'Ali Mahjub, and then his successor Mahmud Zaqzuq).[25] It broadcast speeches from representatives of official Islamic institutions on government television, showcasing their fraternal attitude toward their Christian compatriots. Throughout the second half of the 1990s the shaykh Muhammad Sayyid al-Tantawi hosted a weekly program to counter the hostile diatribes that more and more preachers were delivering against Christianity in mosques and on television broadcasts. Shaykh al-Sha'rawi's similar program, for example, had gained popularity in the 1980s.[26] This initiative did not achieve its objective. To make state Islamic religious institutions the promoters of a "moderate" Islam, it would have been necessary for their positions to be clear and unequivocal. If the Ministry of Awqaf was an integral part of government and followed government policies unwaveringly, the two principal official Islamic institutions, al-Azhar and Dar al-Ifta', maintained a more complex relationship with the ruler. Like the Imam of al-Azhar, the Grand Mufti, who presides over Dar al-Ifta', is appointed by the president of the republic. Founded in 1895, Dar al-Ifta' is affiliated with the Ministry of Justice and, as such, is the state institution charged with issuing *fatwas*. But both al-Azhar and an internal committee in the Ministry of Awqaf are also authorized to do so, creating tensions not only between these institutions but also within them. When Mubarak tasked al-Azhar with his campaign to counter radical Islamists, several clergymen refused to endorse the operations, and others expressed opinions contrary to those of al-Azhar. Since the 1980s, al-Azhar has seen diverse political tendencies.[27] Certain clerics have been members of Islamic associations specializing in *da'wa* and have fed conceptions in line with those of the Muslim Brotherhood. Finally, a boom in satellite television programming led to the proliferation of different and simultaneous discourses, drowning the official vision in the stream of a thousand others. To win support, the majority of these rival visions had other means than simply the sheer force of their word: the Brothers and a variety of other Islamic associations inscribed their discourse in the fabric of daily practices, the exchange of services, and solidarity on the local, city, village, and neighborhood scale.

The government also endeavored to promote inspiring and educational discourses, financing and supervising publications on Egyptian history, Islamic-Christian relations, Christianity, and Islam. In 1991 the Ministry of Awqaf edited a series of booklets entitled "This Is Islam" in an "Islamic Culture" collection. "Tolerance in Islam and the Rights of the Non-Muslim" (*samāḥāt al-islām wa ḥuqūq ghayr al-muslimīn*, 1991) gave advice on how to develop trusting and friendly relationships with non-Muslims and counted peace and national harmony among the happy consequences of overcoming barriers of fear.[28] They underlined the principle of noncoercion in matters of faith, as well as equality in rights and responsibility between followers of the two religions, "even if this religion is the religion of the state."[29] In another collection, "Reading for

All," prompted by Suzanne Mubarak, First Lady of Egypt until February 2011, the administration published several historical and sociological texts. Their authors highlight Coptic nationalism and the fraternity that unites Christians and Muslims in Egypt. In one of these, focused without great originality on 1914–21, the author invokes Coptic contributions to national construction, describing at length the Egyptian rally at Saint Mark's Cathedral as a sign of opposition to the Milner Commission in 1920. In another booklet in the series Edwar Ghali al-Dahabi (a Christian, appointed by Hosni Mubarak to the People's Assembly in 2010) insists on piety as a unifying national cement—a piety that "comes from a just understanding of the essence of religion."[30]

In *Christianity and Islam in Egypt* Husayn Kafafi paints a picture of Egyptian history centered on Muslim-Christian relations beginning in the first centuries of the Common Era and reaching the 1919 revolution. The author brings supposedly unanimous elements to the forefront, like the figure of the Virgin Mary in the account of Christianity's introductory period; the Coptic Church during resistance to Roman and then Byzantine occupation; and, finally, Salah al-Din, under whom Christians and Muslims once again united against invaders. He describes the transition from the Coptic to Arabic language as one that took place without pressure or strife and highlights the common source of both languages. In an original take he refers to Akhenaton as the "first unifier,"[31] the father of monotheism. This being neither a thesis nor even a hypothesis, but simply a literary allusion, Kafafi does not seek to support his claim. Akhenaton allows Kafafi to represent the so-called religious character of the Egyptian people and thereby embodies the values of "faith and unity." Allegedly defining the "essence" of Egyptianness, the theme of religiosity surfaces from time to time, although it does not constitute the main leitmotif of nationalist discourse. In one variation this religiosity confers on Egyptians their unity regardless of separate religions. In another this attachment to faith explains the inevitable character of friction between members of different religions. With the figure of Akhenaton the author confusingly evokes the heritage of a native Egyptian monotheism, from which the three monotheisms emerged, and which embodies the common values of Egyptians at the same time as those shared by Christians and Muslims. This idea, in a more sophisticated and less Egyptcentric form, does have a history, which Kafafi may have been aware of.[32]

But the official discourse rarely evoked the rights and the role of the state to overcome the "sickness" of sectarianism. It proposed faith and fraternal sentiments or national solidarity, defined by the unity of Christians and Muslims and considered to be the antidote to sectarianism. Yet such unity does not imply than equality between the two elements that compose it, as evidenced in the governmental *Weltanschauung* delivered in Egyptian schoolbooks.

In a speech presented at the second conference organized by MARED, the Egyptian historian Sherif Younes demonstrated how, in history manuals for middle and high school students, a "dual containment" structure determined the arrangement of Coptic, Egyptian, and Islamic identities: the Islamic identity encompasses the Egyptian one, which in turn contains the Coptic identity.[33] Eschewing "the study of Christianity's emergence and the progress of evangelization, with its problems and its struggles," the authors of these manuals confined the history of Christianity to that of Egyptian Christianity and then assigned Coptic history to a circumscribed place in the course of Egyptian history: the Roman epoch. It follows, therefore, that Christianity holds a unique value: to manifest an "already-existing Egyptian-ness, both politically and culturally." "A formidable weapon in the hands of the Egyptian resistance to Roman power," Christianity became "an *instrument* to express the desire for liberation from the Byzantine yoke."[34] Egyptian identity itself appears embedded in Islamic identity, which is conceived as encompassing the totality of truth:

> The manuals did not present Islam as one of the manifestations of Egyptian nationalism. On the contrary, it was the Egyptians that played a role in defending Islam. Islam is, in and of itself, foundational. It has no Egyptian attribute and nothing indicated the existence of an Egyptian command of Islam. It is not an instrument of Egyptian nationalism. It is, simply, the true religion: "The new religion rests on divine law, the Qur'an, untouched by error."[35] In summary, Egyptian nationalism completely absorbs the Christian period, to the point that its value is reduced almost solely to its status as the manifestation of an instrument of Egyptian-ness that precedes it. Whereas, Egyptian identity itself is absorbed by Islam and expressed in such a way that it lacks all specificity (contrary to what actually happened in reality).[36]

Disconnected from personal concerns and individualized religious practices, the supposedly edifying publications were no more successful in rivaling the Salafist and Brotherhood discourses than was the promotion of an official Islam. Furthermore, they failed because they presented a conception of the nation and relations between Christians and Muslims that rested on the same principles as those of their supposed adversaries. In effect, far from being the invention of school textbooks, the "dual containment" structure that Younes highlighted draws on conceptions of a "civilizational Islam" presented by several so-called liberal Islamist thinkers still anxious to integrate Christians into the *umma*. The founders of the al-Wasat Party put forward a recent variation on this theme.

• • •

The idea of creating a political party had long nagged at the Muslim Brothers, or at least the idea of creating a party from among their ranks. Activists from the so-called intermediary generation, Abu al-'Ila Madi, 'Isam al-'Iryan, and 'Abd al-Mon'im Abu al-Futuh, to name the better-known, wanted to be granted decision-making positions and greater responsibility within the Society of Muslim Brothers. Their successful efforts in the struggle for control in professional unions in the 1980s justified these pretentions, in their eyes. But they were not heard.[37] Aside from this dissension within the Brotherhood, the repression of radical Islamists in the 1990s reinforced the idea to al-Wasat's founders that it was urgent to explicitly distance themselves from these groups and to establish an "open, moderate [Islam], that did not hold a monopoly on truth and that defended a pluralist political system."[38] Followed by a faction from the Brotherhood, Madi founded the al-Wasat Party. This was done at the instigation of the former Supreme Guide, Mahdi 'Akif,[39] whom the Christian Rafiq Habib[40] met at this time. When the Committee of Parties refused to grant them legal status, they formed an organization headed by Salim al-'Awwa, and their activities were therefore governed by the 1999 law on associations, which restricted funding sources to members' fees and donations only.

Although they claimed to set a precedent and model for Islamic movements in the Arab world, their endeavor was not entirely new, even in Egypt. The cadres of al-Wasat valorized the notion of a civilizational Islam that had reappeared in Egyptian political debates after an alliance forged in 1987 between the Socialist Labor Party (*ḥizb al-'amal al-ishtirākī*), the Liberal Party (*ḥizb al-aḥrār*), and the Muslim Brothers. As with the leaders of the Socialist Labor Party, they drew theoretical inspiration from the texts of Yusif al-Qaradawi, Muhammad 'Imara, the columnist Fahmi Huwaydi, and, especially, Salim al-'Awwa and Tariq al-Bishri. Al-'Awwa posited that the pacts of *dhimma* (safeguard, protection) and *jizya* were in fact abolished the moment "that the Islamic state fell into the hands of occupying powers and that its sons, Muslims and Christians, having struggled side by side to rid their lands of occupation, acquired the right to citizenship in full equality."[41] This argument, advanced by numerous figures on the political scene, implied that equality for Christians had to be won, their loyalty proven and paid for in blood. Nothing indicated that the process was irreversible. Concerning the functions of authority (*wilāya al-'āmma*), al-'Awwa testified that any pretense to restrict access to governmental functions (*ḥukm*) for members of any particular religion in a multifaith state had no foundation in shari'a.[42] Al-Bishri set forth a more elaborate reflection on the institutions and state functions in a modern state. In the 1980s al-Bishri was firmly committed to finding a formula relying on Islamic jurisprudence, while permitting a guarantee for the equality of Muslims and non-Muslims in a modern nation-state, which, in this perspective, would also be an Islamic state. According to him, political Islamic doctrine did not prescribe a specific format for institutions and government, as it simply defined Muslims as a political community to govern themselves with the recommended application of shari'a. He legitimated access to the highest functions of state for non-Muslims, arguing that, in the modern state, officials hold impersonal roles that are dictated by law. Those occupying the highest positions, up to that of the president of the republic, have only the power and authority of delegates. Hence, in democratic regimes they are simply functionaries that represent the will of the democratically elected majority, not that of their personal identity.

Along with these two thinkers, al-Wasat Party members pledged to respect the Constitution and the sovereignty of the people and to submit to the will of the majority even when it expressed an opinion contrary to Islamic teachings. Deeming *jizya* inappropriate for the administration of a modern society, they considered Christians to be citizens endowed with the same rights as Muslims, including ascension to the presidency. They viewed shari'a as the principal, indeed only, source of legislation, according to flexible and adaptable modalities.[43] To this day the authors of the charter for al-Wasat refer to so-called Islamic values that hinder the recognition of several clauses in international treaties. In particular, these include the Universal Declaration of Human Rights articles concerning rationality requirements, religious freedom,[44] and freedom of conscience. Therefore, they also face problems in dealing with conversion and proselytism. At a MARED conference in Cairo in December 2009, in response to the question "Do we need a law on religious conversion?" Madi said, "In this country where both Muslims and Christians live, the authorization for [Christian] proselytism could only encourage tensions between the followers of the two religions. Conversion is fine if it is carried out discreetly and if converts do not disturb public order." In a March 2010 conversation with me, Rafiq Habib held the same opinion.[45]

APOSTASY AND CONVERSION: THE STATE OF EXCEPTION

Muhammad the Christian

The image appears in the Egyptian press on August 4, 2007: Muhammad Higazi, his wife Zaynab, Christ, and the Gospel. Muhammad had changed his name to Bishuy Armia upon conversion, and Zaynab changed hers to Christiane. Two versions of the same image: side by side, a representation of Christ hanging on the wall behind them, Muhammad and Zaynab watch us or, on the contrary, ignore us, broken, in front of the camera, contemplating a text from the Gospel. He became Christian in secret, Higazi explains, at the age of sixteen. He is now twenty-five. He is going to have a child. "If it is a boy, we will name him Ramy; if it is a girl, we will name her Sarah." They want their child to be officially recognized as a Christian. They introduce a case to the Court of Administrative Justice in the State Council in order to make their conversion to Christianity official and to change the religion as officially registered on their identification papers.

The first press coverage mainly relays legal information about this "unprecedented" request. The lawyer Mamduh Nakhla, specializing in Coptic media affairs, director of the al-Kalima center for human rights, refers to Articles 40 and 46 of the 1971 Constitution and a *fatwa* from 'Ali Jum'a, then Grand Mufti, which advocates no worldly punishment for apostasy by citing the Qur'anic verse: "no coercion in religion" (*lā ikrāh fī al-dīn*).[46] The clergymen appeal to the state for clemency. They flatter the wisdom and equanimity of the judges even though, in a bad omen, judge Muhammad al-Husayni will be presiding over the chamber tasked with hearing the case. Al-Husayni has already rejected the appeals of Christians who, after converting to Islam, wished to return to their original Christian identity.

Everything spins very quickly into another register. We watch as if Higazi were being butchered and his parts exhibited in public space. With the exception of *al-Ahali*, *al-Wafd*, and *al-Badil* every paper—*al-Masri al-Yawm*, *al-Jumhuriyya*, *al-Dustur*, *Nahda Masr*, *al-Fajr*—delights in a display of stories and fabrications around Higazi, who disappears in this overexposure: "*al-Jumhuriyya* in the Port Said Apostate's House";[47] "Failed Poet Higazi Shamelessly Tries Out Every Religion, Including Christianity";[48] "Higazi's Father: My Son Was Harassed by Proselytizers to Convert";[49] "Higazi Demonstrates for the Victory of the Prophet, Defends the Muslim Brotherhood . . . Then Becomes Christian";[50] "Higazi Is Psychologically Unstable and a Member of Kifaya";[51] "The Higazi Show";[52] "Higazi's Family Demands Their Son's Arrest for the Irresponsibility of His Actions."[53]

Suddenly attributed all the flaws of creation in the eyes of his family, colleagues, friends, and acquaintances, the young man also draws the ire of Islamists. With Yusif al-Badri in the lead, they enter into the fray in the early days of the case. Al-Badri, and he prides himself on this, will not be silent.[54] He accuses the lawyer of defaming Islam (*isā'at al-islām*) and with others calls for the application of the Islamic penalties for apostasy. The Coptic Orthodox Church, through the words of its pope, denounces the media pandemonium and then distances itself from the affair, anxious not to appear vulnerable to accusations of proselytism, while many priests take a hostile position toward foreign evangelizers. Several voices are raised simultaneously, criticizing the opinions of the *'ulama'* or *fuqaha'*, denouncing the venality of the lawyers, or accusing the regime, the Ministry of the Interior, the ruling party, the opposition party, the press, society, and so on.

On August 7 Higazi's lawyer, Nakhla, abandons the case, privately citing death threats he received from Islamists. In interviews given to journalists, he explains his withdrawal with other reasons. Higazi, Nakhla says, has not provided the necessary documents, nor has he communicated valid contact information. He has generously distributed his phone number to the press despite his lawyer's advice not to discuss the details of an ongoing case. Nakhla cites advice from the church, which denies having ruled on the case but also specifies not having submitted to "any pressure" from State Security. Finally, he calls Jihad 'Awda (a Muslim and a member of the al-Kalima center and the political committee *lajna al-siyāsiyyāt*) into question: Higazi had hesitated, argued Nakhla. He never would have brought the case if 'Awda had not offered to cover all the costs of the trial. Earlier, Nakhla had underscored Higazi's determination and his own goodwill in taking the case pro bono aside from the procurement of necessary documents. 'Awda denies any involvement with a case that, he argues, falls under the purview of Nakhla as a lawyer and not al-Kalima. Sticking with his version, Nakhla confesses that 'Awda's opinion had influenced his own personal decision to take the case. After the August 10 arrest of two members of the Middle East Christian Association (MECA), Peter 'Izzat and 'Adil Fawzi, Higazi's case takes on international dimensions. The true perpetrator is denounced, with quasi unanimity: Christian proselytism—that is to say the "foreign hands"—that tries to undermine the unity of the "two elements of the nation." *Al-Dustur*, for example, reports on August 12, 2007: "Deputies of the People's Assembly, Muslim Brotherhood or independent, have warned against sedition (*fitna*) that is the work of a hidden hand moving to incite the two elements of the nation, Coptic and Muslim." The government press makes a thunderous entry: "Proselytizing Organizations Inflame Port Said."[55] "National and international agents conspire in the alleged oppression of Egypt's Copts. One international organization convenes crooked Coptic organizations."[56] "The Truth About Proselytism in the Middle East."[57] "Al-Azhar: Foreign Organizations Are Behind Cases of Conversion."[58] The magazines *Ruz al-Yusuf*, *Akhir Sa'a*, and *al-Musawwar* devote multipage spreads to proselytism in the span of several days. The driving idea behind the majority of these exposés is simple: proselytism is colonization by other means and with obviously different ends.

The little-documented connection between MECA and Higazi is decried in a rhyming slogan: "Higazi . . . Fawzi . . . agents of sedition in Egypt" (*Higazi . . . Fawzi . . . lī ishghāl al-fitna fī miṣr*). MECA had been in the crosshairs of State Security since it demanded compensation for the victims of violence in al-Kushih in 1999 and 2000. Just after these events, and in a similar fashion to that of the debates around the Higazi affair, the problem of foreign funding and diaspora organizations' intervention burrowed into the heart of the press's preoccupations. This happened to such a degree that the numerous victims were not even part of the discussion. Similarly, when Egyptian American Sa'ad al-Din Ibrahim planned to organize a conference on minorities in the Arab world, the press and most public personalities followed the lead of Muhammad Hasanayn Haykal. They diverted the debate on the sectarian issue and denounced the foreign funding granted to civil society organizations, in this case the Ibn Khaldun Center.[59]

In 2006 two Islamist lawyers brought a case against the members of MECA in Egypt, accusing them of practicing proselytism and contempt of Islam (*izdirā' al-islām*). No law forbade proselytism; the charges brought after the activists' nighttime arrest and the search of their apartment in August 2007 were possession of a weapon without a permit, possession of unauthorized copies of the Qur'an, and spreading slogans intended to disrupt the social order. A text entitled *al-Muḍṭahadūn* (The Oppressed) was seized as evidence.[60] Several witnesses and lawyer Ramsis al-Naggar questioned the motivations of the prosecution in considering this case at the same time as the outbreak of the Higazi affair. Canadian organizations supported MECA's request to strip Egypt of its standing as a member of the World Assembly of Human Rights. Italy intervened to offer asylum to Higazi, while Copts in Italy, supported by parties from the Italian right, protested in front of the Egyptian embassy in Rome to oppose *fatwas* that had condemned Higazi to death. Higazi refused to leave and expressed his disagreement with the Canadian demand. Peter ʻIzzat and ʻAdel Fawzi's pretrial detention period was extended, by court decision, until the end of September. They were released at the end of November, but another member of the organization was detained.

On November 24, 2007, the independent daily *al-Masri al-Yawm* ran the front-page headline "The Preacher of a Mosque Discovers Two Counterfeit Volumes of the Qur'an in Matruh." Redundantly, an image of two pages of the Qur'an sat under the title, while a subtitle announced, "The MECA Stops Its Activity in Egypt and Declares: Some Christians Sold Their Souls to the Devil." At the bottom of the page a third article proclaimed, "Coptic leadership in diaspora refuses the invitation of the National Council for Human Rights (NCHR) to participate in today's conference on citizenship."

The Court of Administrative Justice, presided over by al-Husayni, considered Higazi's case and rejected his request on January 29, 2008. His child, a daughter, was born: Muhammad Higazi and his wife name her Miryam.

• • •

Despite the antagonistic opinions, contradictory decrees, and secret circulars promulgated under the guise of national security, one conclusion is obvious: Egypt's constitutional and legal framework permits conversion to Christianity. The rejection of conversion happens in daily practices and is merely legitimized by reference to Islamic teachings, whether as social actors conceive of them or as they believe others conceive of them. The obstacles presented to conversion in the administrative and judicial systems rest on the "informal institutionalization," ex post facto, of the arbitrariness of the Egyptian regime and state institutions' agents. Jurists and social science researchers, as well as activists in advocacy groups, have thoroughly analyzed the judicial, legal, and constitutional aspects of these affairs. Although it provides a brief overview of this legal and judicial imbroglio, the following section is principally intended to show how government decisions, often in the margins of legality, orient the actions taken by institutional agents. It also shows how those involved skillfully pass from one normative field to another in order to achieve their given objectives.

National Identity, Religious Affiliation, and Civil Status

Religion does not simply refer to national and community *imaginaires*. Printed on official documents, it is a physical mark of the state machine and compels individuals to define themselves through reference to religious categories at every stage of their lives. Acquiring a national identity card, mandatory at the age of sixteen,[61] requires affiliation with one of the three heavenly religions recognized by the Egyptian state: Judaism, Christianity, or Islam; this excludes Bahai and other religions.[62] Written on official documents, the designation determines the rules of law applied in issues of personal status, and a minor's religion, which also dictates the religious discipline studied in school.

Muslim, Christian, and Jewish communities used to be governed by their own courts and their own laws. In the course of the twentieth century, Egyptian substantive law was codified, borrowing from European legal systems and uncodified rules of Islamic jurisprudence, particularly in the area of family law. In family law, ratified with *Hatti Humayuni* (1856) and then partly renewed by the Egyptian state (laws 8/1915, 462/1955, and 1/2000), several laws partially regulate different domains, owing to the lack of a comprehensive and structured code. Established on the basis of Islamic legal cases, these laws apply to the whole of the Egyptian population and cover inheritance rights, guardianship of property and people, and certain situations touching on personal status, like payment of alimony. However, personal status (*al-aḥwāl al-shakhsiyya*), related to matters of marriage and divorce, remains governed by sectarian laws.[63] Yet, since the 1955 judicial reform carried out under Nasser,[64] the separate confessional courts were abolished; therefore, state courts decide personal status issues following sectarian laws.

Officially changing one's religion implies the consequent change of religious affiliation recorded on official documents. And law 143/1994 on civil status (*qānūn al-aḥwāl al-madaniyya*) stipulates that it is incumbent on those wishing to change any information on their identity card to present themselves to the Civil Registry (Article 53) and to the Civil Status Department with a "demonstration of proof from appropriate authorities" (Article 47) in order to modify the religion written on their identity card, national registration form, and birth certificate. Only two Muslim-born individuals had attempted to officially convert to Christianity (one in the 1950s, the other in 1979) before the Higazi scandal, and several cases afterward inspired heated public discussion in Egypt. In a slightly different context, since the year 2000, several hundred Copts who have been registered incorrectly as Muslims (for one reason or another) have legally tried to recuperate their Christian identity. In 2004 a judge ruled in favor of these "reconverts" (*al-'ā'idīn li-l-masīḥiyya*, literally: those who return to Christianity).

The legal procedure for conversion to Islam is governed by internal regulations in the Ministry of Justice, which houses the Real Estate and Documentation Authority (*maṣlaḥat al-ishār al-ʿaqqārī wa-l-tawthīq*). This body is charged with validating all Egyptian citizens' official documents, according to law 48/1967 on notary acts. The chapter entitled "Certification of Declaration (of Conversion) to Islam" (*tawthīq ishār al-islām*) requires that candidates for conversion, being at least sixteen years of age, go to the police station to initiate the process by expressing their desire to embrace Islam. They must renew this declaration at the Bureau of Conversion at al-Azhar. Officers are required to organize counseling and guidance sessions (*jalasāt al-nuṣḥ wa-l-irshād*) throughout the course of which a Christian representative interviews the potential convert to ensure that the decision is made with full autonomy, under no pressure or coercion, and that faith alone dictates the choice to convert. If the individual remains resolute throughout these sessions, the Real Estate and Documentation Authority will deliver a statement of proof—the only official document that is exempt from any fees—to present to the Civil Status Department in order to proceed with changing religious affiliation on any identification documents. Set forth in Ordinance 5 of July 1970, the obligation to hold these sessions was not initially part of the regulations. It followed the December 6, 1969, dissemination of a secret circular from the Ministry of Interior, number 40, undoubtedly at the demand of the church. The church had in all likelihood first initiated this practice—the existence of which is evidenced in the 1930s, although it remains unclear if these sessions were regularly and systematically organized[65]—and might have wished to confer legal status on it during a period marked by an increase in conversions to Islam. The authorities concerned do not, however, always strictly follow this regulation. It is often sufficient to simply make the necessary stops at al-Azhar, the documents department, and the Civil Status Department. Institutional functionaries rarely impede the completion of the process. Al-Azhar has declined several applications for conversion to Islam, especially those made by the wives of Coptic Orthodox priests, angering some religious men and Muslim jurists who point out that a circular (no. 40 of 1969) and an ordinance (no. 5 of 1970), not presented to the People's Assembly, lack any legal weight. For their part advocacy groups, including the EIPR, opposed the initiative, arguing that, far from protecting individual rights, the sessions only put pressure on the individual to abandon the decision to convert. Indeed, the candidate for conversion faced an embarrassing quandary, being compelled to reveal the motivations for the decision in the presence of clerics, police officers, and sometimes family members. In 2008 a rumor circulated, according to which the minister of the interior had reportedly issued a decree to remove the counseling sessions and guidance. But on March 4, 2008, the State Council's Court of Administrative Justice rejected a lawyer's demand to remove the sessions, because there was no such decree.[66]

But no law provides for conversion to Christianity. The Real Estate and Documentation Authority never established a framework to allow for registration of Christian conversion. A single circular issued by the minister of the interior in June 1971 recommended that requests to convert to Christianity be written on the same form as requests for conversion to Islam, and he justified this by declaring that "Islamic shari'a does not allow apostasy."[67] Although Egyptian substantive law does not forbid apostasy (*ridda*), the Court of Cassation and the Supreme Administrative Court have been brought to rule on apostasy and so have contributed in this way to its legal definition. In accordance with the four schools of Islamic jurisprudence, court decisions have usually agreed on prohibiting apostasy, as well as on its legal repercussions. Indeed, apostasy, or leaving Islam, has legal repercussions that directly extend to matters of personal status. Hence, leaving Islam negates any contracts entered into by the apostate, including marriage, inheritance rights, and guardianship of children. Yet opinions differ on whether apostasy should be punished and what penalties (*ḥadd*, pl. *ḥudūd*) should be applied if the apostate does not repent and return to Islam. Those who advocate for worldly punishment often support the death penalty, when apostasy is accompanied by acts of provocation that are likely to disturb public morals and order, making it akin to crimes of high treason. Judges are presented with two scenarios. In one, the more frequent, the accusation of apostasy is used as a legal tactic in an attempt to invalidate a contract, with accused and accuser both implicated in the issue being reviewed.[68] In the other the applicants use the *ḥisba* procedure to introduce legal action without motivation other than the obligation that enjoins a Muslim to do good deeds and reject evil (*al-amr bi-l-ma'rūf wa-l-nahī 'an al-munkar*),[69] an obligation reiterated in many *ahadīth*.

Muslim Theologians and Apostasy

By relaunching the debate over whether shari'a prescribes worldly punishment for apostasy, the conversion affairs that polarized Egyptian opinion are embedded in a lineage of polemic debates that regularly surface in the Egyptian political media. They testify to reconfigurations of the religious and political in an idiomatic framework governed by reference to Islam. They provide the occasion for public personalities to expound their views on modes of reference to Islamic norms and, thus, to take a stance against each other in a political game where the rise of political Islam's competing currents merely governs alliances and rivalries. To mention only the theologians' positions, there exists a full range of intermediary stances between two standards: those who support the restoration of "pure" Islam, purged of any foreign intrusion, and those who advocate for a conciliation, or even an original accord, between the foundational Islamic texts and the requirement of equality, and who show that the teachings of Islam prescribe neither worldly punishment nor stigma to the apostate.

On one hand the Qur'an forbids apostasy but does not recommend any worldly sanction to be implemented by human beings: "After their submission, they became disbelievers. . . . If they return, that would be better for them. If they turn their backs, God will punish them with a grievous punishment, here and in the next life, and they will find no ally or recourse on earth."[70] On the other hand several *ahadīth* reported by Muhammad ibn Isma'il al-Bukhari explicitly order men to punish apostates in this world: "He who abandons his religion [of Islam]: kill him" (*man badala dīnahu fa-uqtulūh*); or, "It is not permitted to endanger the life of a Muslim except in three cases: disbelief after faith, adultery after marriage, or murder without motive."

The representatives of official Islamic institutions in Egypt have tried to maintain a discourse that does not contradict any of the diverging opinions expressed by their members, while adopting a position opposed to punishment for apostasy. The era when al-Azhar promoted punishment seems to be over: in May 1977 al-Azhar had published a draft penal code in the paper *al-I'tisam*; the code would apply (in its articles 30 to 34) punishment for apostasy. On August 6 of that same year *al-Ahram* reported that the State Council had decided in favor of the draft's review by the relevant authorities. The Coptic pope and numerous intellectuals revolted against such an announcement. Notably, Gamal al-Banna railed against the draft's authors. The draft was never presented to the People's Assembly.[71] In 1982, however, the legislative committee charged with drafting a penal code to conform with shari'a devoted ten articles (178–88) to apostasy and outlined punishment except where the "guilty" repented, was a minor upon becoming Muslim, had retracted conversion to Islam, or had been coerced to embrace Islam. This draft, rejected by a parliamentary committee in May 1985, was never submitted for debate at a plenary session in the People's Assembly. During the controversy provoked by reconversion trials and the Higazi affair, several personalities affiliated with Islamic institutions—such as Grand Mufti Nasser Farid Wasil, Islamic theology professor at al-Azhar University; Dr. Muhammad al-Masir; and a member of the Islamic Research Academy, Shaykh Yusif al-Badri—reaffirmed the obligation to punish any apostate who publicly announced the abandonment of Islam. Shaykh Wasil explained that the reasoning for this was that every Muslim was tied to the *umma* by an implicit contract, the disruption of which disturbed the social order. In this view the Qur'anic suras "whoever wills—let him believe; and whoever wills—let him disbelieve [the existence of God]"[72] or "there shall be no compulsion in [acceptance of] the religion"[73] concern only whether non-Muslims are free to adopt Islam or not.[74]

Grand Mufti 'Ali Jum'a issued a ruling, in two stages, that appeared as a simple exemplar of the opinions of many jurists and 'ulama' but was actually radically different. He derived his argument from the well-known distinction between faith and the disturbance of public order that apostasy could engender: "Abandoning religion is a sin that God punishes on judgment day. If one leaves Islam, there is no penalty in this world. . . . If, however, in addition to the sin of apostasy, one undermines the foundations of society, then the case must be submitted to the courts, whose role is to protect societal integrity."[75] By affirming that the "case must be submitted to the court," the mufti withdrew the ruling from the religious domain, as long as this statement is interpreted side by side with the *fatwa* he had issued three months earlier, in which he ruled that

> these [reconverted] Christians are, from the view of *fiqh*, apostates, but the question of their civil and citizen rights after their apostasy . . . is a question that the administration must decide, in assessing the benefits and ills of each option, and in evaluating the compatibility [of these options] with the Constitution and applicable laws, and considering their impact on social peace and national integrity. All of these aspects are brought to bear on life in society, and therefore it is the administration that is responsible for whatever the verdict on religion may be.[76]

By asserting that religious norms and the laws of *fiqh* are invalid in the domain governed by the Constitution and substantive law in the name of public interest, Jum'a created a distinction between the religious domain and the political and legal one—between what is a sin, which only God can judge, and what carries citizen penalties and rights, for which governments are responsible.[77] Later on, he posits that substantive law is dispositive of any necessary referral to Islamic jurisprudence and independently of it, on this subject, that the latter is not integrated into substantive law.

Other theologians have attempted to demonstrate that nothing related to penalties for apostasy exists in Islam, whether through historical analysis to reveal the instrumental nature such a penalty would hold in the hands of a ruler anxious to get rid of those deemed undesirable; by annulling an old verse with a new one, in accordance with the exegetical principle of abrogation (*nashk*); or after a textual exegesis that found a circumstantial nature for the hadith referred to by those supporting worldly penalties for apostasy. In one recent work the doctor al-'Alwani follows the reasoning of Muhammad 'Abduh and argues that the hadith "He who abandons his religion [of Islam]: kill him," reported by Muhammad ibn Isma'il al-Bukhari, should be interpreted as a response to the attempts to sow strife that are evoked in the sura "al-'Imrān": "And a faction of the People of the Scripture say [to each other], 'Believe in that which was revealed to the believers at the beginning of the day, and reject it at its end, that perhaps they will abandon their religion . . .'"[78] Described as a tactical response to a particular event, specific to one place and one time, the validity of this language was also limited to these particular circumstances; the Qur'an itself did not suggest that apostasy must be punished in this world, leaving to God the power to judge and decide the penalty. Moreover, given a rereading of 'Ali 'Abd al-Raziq's *Islam and the Foundations of Political Power* (*al-Islām wa uṣūl al-ḥukm*),[79] al-'Alwani highlighted verses from the Qur'an that would prohibit the Prophet from assuming a political function.

(Re)Conversion in the Police and Judiciary Systems

As with most Muslim jurists and leaders, the Egyptian judiciary and police reserve different treatment for those converts who were Muslim originally and those Christians who were registered as Muslim but wished to change this (back) to Christian.

Although they had rarely attempted to officially change their religion, Muslim-born converts to Christianity were sometimes confronted by the Egyptian judiciary for infringement or the use of false papers stating their current religious affiliation.[80] After the introduction of Article 98-F in the Penal Code (by law 29/1982) these converts were more frequently drawn into the hell of a military-police modus operandi whose arbitrary workings seemed to be legalized by the state of emergency that endured for forty-five years almost without interruption. State Security forces would arrest numerous converts, referring to the article, which prescribed "a penalty of imprisonment for no less than six months and no more than five years, as well as a fine of no less than 500 EGP and no more than 1000 EGP, to be applied to any person who uses religion to propagate, orally, in writing, or by any other means, offensive ideas aimed to create strife, to ridicule, or defame heavenly religions or the communities that adhere to them, or to undermine national security and the social order." National security being at stake, the cases were referred to the State Security Court—Emergency Status (*maḥākim amn al-dawla—ḥāla al-ṭawārī*) under the Legislative Decree 162/1958, issued in October 1981 when the state of emergency was reinstated after a brief hiatus. These courts existed as long as the state of emergency was in effect.[81] The law governing the state of emergency (162/1958) allowed for provisional detention for an indeterminate period, at the discretion of the minister of the interior or State Security services. "Suspects" generally would undergo torture and humiliation during their detention. After six months of incarceration the detainees could have, theoretically, submitted bail requests to the president of the republic or to the interior minister. They could not, however, submit these to the State Council or the Supreme State Security Court, as the determination of the competent body to deal with these requests and the length of the waiting period before being allowed to present them had undergone several changes.[82] The verdicts of these courts were not subject to appeal, and the penalties handed down could not be changed by presidential decree. The minister of the interior would often refuse to release detainees, despite the courts' having issued decisions to do so.

The "reconverts," initially Christian, would be registered as Muslim when one parent had converted to Islam while the child was still a minor or after the child's own conversion to Islam. There were many reasons that, in an overwhelmingly majority-Muslim society, a Christian would be encouraged to convert: marriage to a Muslim, social pressure, desire to improve social and economic status, or desire to divorce.[83] Although law 143/1994 on civil status allows the modification of information written on official documents, including religion, officials in the Civil Status Department are reluctant to change "Islam" to "Christianity." These officials and those in the Ministry of the Interior, particularly the senior officers in the Civil Status Department's intelligence services (*mabāḥith al-aḥwāl al-madaniyya*), do not hesitate to use various forms of pressure on reconverts or Bahai so that they will register Islam as their religion, sometimes going as far as threats or maltreatment.[84]

In 167 cases studied by EIPR and Human Rights Watch individuals had furnished an official document, issued by the Coptic Orthodox church, attesting that they had practiced their Christian rites in a church. The document is presented to fulfill requirements in Article 53 of law 143/1994, which stipulates that a change in information concerning religion must be made upon presentation of a document from the competent body (*jiha al-ikhtiṣāṣ*). In the case of conversion to Islam the competent body is the religious institution representing the religion that the individual has adopted, al-Azhar. But neither the government nor the State Council commissioners responsible for giving an advisory opinion (which is generally followed by the courts) recognize the church as the competent body, arguing that an individual who had converted to Islam remains subject to the principles of shari'a. The church intervened as a party in the appeal proceedings brought in April 2007 by plaintiffs whose claims had been rejected.

Some four hundred people had brought cases to the State Council against the Ministry of the Interior, which contains the Civil Status Department. For the first time, one of the chambers charged with reviewing the cases, presided over by Judge Faruq 'Abd al-Qadir, issued twenty-six verdicts in favor of the plaintiffs between April 2004 and September 2006. After al-Qadir's retirement Judge al-Husayni followed the previous jurisprudence, and under his tenure, on April 24, 2007, the Court of Administrative Justice rejected the petitions of the Christian reconverts. They appealed. After several delays the Supreme Administrative Court presided over by Judge Nawfil accepted the plaintiffs' appeals on February 9, 2008. In the 211 petitions reviewed between 2004 and 2005, government lawyers pleaded for rejection, arguing that the principles of shari'a did not allow for the recognition of apostasy and so the plaintiffs had no case.[85] In an effort to show that the laws relative to apostasy did not contradict freedom of belief, they frequently argued that these applied only to Muslims who, in choosing to adhere to Islam, had accepted submission under these laws, leaving non-Muslims free to practice their religion. Following this reasoning which does not allow conceiving how a Muslim would change religion, they reached the conclusion that the plaintiff being Muslim, the church was not the competent body to certify religion and therefore judged the officials' refusal to issue new documents to be legitimate.

Certain judges and jurists evoke the maintenance of "public order." Yet Maurits Berger has shown how, in this type of reasoning, *public order* and *shari'a* are interchangeable: public order rests on the respect of the values and norms accepted by society and, consequently, the principles of shari'a are considered these foundational values and norms.[86] In case no. 24673/58, January 2005, the State Council Commissioners justified recourse to Islamic jurisprudence by the absence of legislation on apostasy in Egyptian substantive law, referring to Article 3, line 1 of law 463/1955, abrogated by 1/2001, which provides for the application of Hanafi jurisprudence where statutory law remains silent. Throughout their review of the same case state lawyers appealed to Article 2 of the Egyptian Constitution, as amended in 1980: "Islam is the religion of the state, Arabic is its official language, and the principles of shari'a are *the* main source of legislation" (emphasis added).

Article 2 of the 1971 Constitution states: "Islam is the religion of the state, Arabic is its official language, and the principles of shari'a are *a* main source of legislation" (emphasis added). In the twentieth century all of Egypt's constitutions have referenced Islam in the text. For example, the Constitution of 1923 already stipulated that "Islam is the religion of the state," though not in the early, core articles, but in Article 149.[87] Most constitutions in Arab or Muslim-majority countries refer to religion similarly, as do a good number of European and American constitutions. But as Baudouin Dupret noted, "In Egypt, the Constitution of 1971 marked a rupture, since it introduced a reference to the normativity of Islam in the institutional system for the first time."[88] In legal terms this article led to four questions: (1) What is shari'a and "principles of shari'a"? The wording is terribly ambiguous, and the preparatory work for the Constitution did not allow a clear idea of its authors' intentions. Does shari'a refer to the moral, religious, and social principles established in the Qur'an and the sunna? In this sense the jurists who believe the Egyptian legal and judicial system respect these principles argue, with 'Ashmawi, that shari'a is the current system. Or, do the authors adopt a broader concept of shari'a that also includes *fiqh*? (2) Does the mention of shari'a as a source of legislation call into question the unity and coherence of the constitutional articles? In other words, are only laws subject to constitutional review and, therefore, to conformity with Article 2? Or is there a "deliberate hierarchy between Article 2, which establishes shari'a as a primary source, while the other articles, being governed by substantive law, are therefore susceptible to being challenged for not conforming to Article 2?"[89] The Court of Cassation has repeatedly issued decisions that imply the submission of constitutional articles guaranteeing liberty of expression (Article 47) and belief (Article 46) to Article 2.[90] (3) Do Egyptian judges refer to shari'a? The preceding examples testify that they do. But the invocation of principles of shari'a is insufficient to legitimate a ruling, and the reference to Article 2 appears most often accompanied by another source from Egyptian substantive law, for reasons that the fourth and last question partially explains. (4) Does this formulation signify that the principles of shari'a represent an immediately applicable rule of law, abrogating anterior laws that do not conform to it? Contrary to such an interpretation, the Supreme Constitutional Court ruled in 1985 that Article 2 was not retroactive and was addressing the legislator charged with overseeing laws' accordance with the principles of shari'a. In other words the principles of shari'a are not substantive laws to be applied by the courts.[91] Consequently, were a judge to consider a law in violation of these principles, he could simply submit it to the Supreme Constitutional Court. Judge al-Husayni, who had ruled in the Higazi case, requested that the Supreme Constitutional Court review the constitutionality of Article 47 of law 143/1994 on civil status and decide whether modifying information relative to religion contravened Article 2 of the Constitution. As of this writing, the Supreme Constitutional Court has not decided on this request, submitted in July 2008.

Based on the fact that Egypt's legal and constitutional frameworks authorize conversion, (re)converts' lawyers and the judge 'Abd al-Qadir referred principally to the laws of the Egyptian Constitution, as well as international treaties, to plead in favor of liberty of belief and to prove the illegality of the Civil Status Department officials' refusal to make the requested change. In the reasoning of judgments issued on the process of reconversion, the Court of Administrative Justice, presided over by Judge 'Abd al-Qadir, expressed two concerns.[92] It based the reasoning on substantive law and international treaties. Although the details of the reasoning differed somewhat from that of the lawyers and the plaintiffs, the court referred to the same articles of the Constitution (notably 40 and 46), Egyptian laws (Article 47, 48, and 53 of law 143/1994 on civil status), and international treaties (Article 18 of the United Nations Universal Declaration of Human Rights) to prove the legitimacy of the plaintiffs' motion and to recognize the church as the competent body to produce the necessary document. It therefore refused to admit the legitimacy and legality of the Civil Status Department officials' refusal, which it qualified as an "unjust intervention and coercion of a citizen to choose an undesired belief and specific religion." The court reaffirmed that the administration was subject to a legal obligation to recognize the current religion of the petitioners and to prevent discrimination and protect freedom of belief. It mentioned, moreover, Articles 26 and 27 of the Arab Charter for Human Rights, approved in the Arab League by resolution no. 5427 on September 15, 1997. Moreover, the court took care to show that satisfying the plaintiffs' petition not only did not transgress the rules of Islamic jurisprudence but that the latter allowed a verdict in their favor. Islam, the court argued by citing verse 256 of the "al-Baqara" sura and verse 99 of the

"Yūnus" sura, preceded all international treaties in establishing the freedom of belief. Finally, the court proposed a definition of apostasy, judged to conform to Islamic jurisprudence, which applied only to those who denied Islam and delighted in impiety. This definition, it followed, did not allow for the plaintiffs to be considered apostates.

Thus, the references to Islam, international law, and freedom of belief are embedded in antagonistic arguments. From another angle, Nathan Brown observed how, since the beginning of the twentieth century, Egyptian citizens had learned to play on the existence of different normative and legal references, even within Islamic jurisprudence, to win in court.[93] Yet in the venues analyzed in this chapter, reference to Islam determines a closure of discourse and modes of exclusion. It became constitutive of the governmentality of the Egyptian state, and conferred legitimacy to overriding the rules of law and to the reign of the arbitrary.

2 PURITY AS AN EMBODIMENT OF SECURITY?

Through the analysis of historical, symbolic, and discursive processes I shed light, in this chapter, on the interplay between the renewed ideal of purity and the transformation of security into a normative concept, thereby pushing further the reflection on structural violence in Egypt's authoritarian situation.

During the nineteenth-century nation- and state-building processes religion became an identity marker, defining both nation and state in opposition to the occupying powers, which were considered "Christian."[1] By the same token, group representations—Egyptian nationalist, Coptic, or Islamist—became embedded in this logic of exclusion that governs the definition of the self and the other and that mobilizes fear. Both the expressions "umma qibtiyya" (Coptic nation) and "umma misriyya" (Egyptian nation) emerged at the same time, an obvious sign of the concomitant production of national and Coptic awarenesses, combined with the new state's modernization and partial autonomization from Ottoman rule.[2] Tied to the emergence of landowners, liberal professionals, and an urban population that was keen to be included on the national political stage, the promotion of a Coptic cultural "renaissance" (*nahḍa*) at the end of the nineteenth century was considered part of the national construction project.[3] But beginning in the twentieth century, noticeable tensions marked what had initially been complementary relations between national and community constructions. As the Egyptian nation was defined more and more openly in reference to Islam, Copts tended to give greater priority to their own community than to engagement in a national movement that had failed to deliver on promises made in the euphoria of the 1919 revolution. This is seen, for example, in Coptic political personalities' "strategies of insertion."[4]

COPTS AND PHARAOHS: THE COMMUNITARIAN UTOPIA

The changing contours of community spaces and the distinctive traits of each group emerged from these mimetic and exclusionary dynamics. Playing, turn and turn about, adversaries and enemies, rivals and collaborators, the Copts place themselves at the very center and origin of an Egypt whose society relegated them to circumscribed areas of national history and the margins of contemporary political life.

One saying, perhaps, provides the axis for these evolving representations between the late nineteenth and early twenty-first centuries: "The Copts are the descendants of the Pharaohs." The origin of this credo remains difficult to ascertain. According to the testimonies of European explorers, Copts professed it at the end of the eighteenth century. But the texts of the French scientists and thinkers who accompanied Napoleon on his Egyptian adventures made reference to the Copts' anchorage in the Pharaonic world, the first to my knowledge to have done so. If the French (who were known admirers of all things Pharaonic) harbored these assumptions, could it have been the same for Christian Egyptians? By introducing a taste for Pharaonic history to Egypt, could the French have contributed to awakening educated Copts to the idea that they were the "true" descendants of the Pharaohs? Or were the French just repeating what they had already heard from the Copts themselves?[5] The first Coptic texts to mention this idea appeared in the second half of the nineteenth century, but obviously the idea could have been present before having been written down.

In her remarkable text on the twentieth-century Coptic "renaissance," Dina El-Khawaga explains that "to observe a concrete, daily, religious bond between clergy and devotees, it was necessary to await the first signs of missionary presence and, therefore, a form of religious defense."[6] El-Khawaga emphasizes the Coptic Church's institutional disintegration throughout the centuries, drawing on missionaries' accounts of Coptic history. Then she develops her argument based on the postulate that confrontation with a third party stimulates identity formation, and she untangles the different stages of this community-making. Adopting a constructivist approach, however, leads her to assume that Coptic identity is basically a creation ex nihilo. How could the existence or absence of seventeenth-century religious bonds be assessed from 1990? Wouldn't the assessment necessarily be based on the absence of written documents or testimonies? Yet anything other than this absence would be surprising, given that written history is a recent practice. Nevertheless, other practices did exist, though they left no enduring traces. The devotees El-Khawaga mentioned lived, in large part, in the countryside. Before the works of Father Ayrout, Gabriel Baer, and the extraordinary monograph that Nessim Henein devoted to an Egyptian village,[7] there were few sources or studies of Egyptian peasants' customs, rituals, and practices. Study of village structures has specifically shown that religious practices shared by devotees and the local clergy persisted over time. In sync with the rhythm of the changing seasons and Nile floods, these practices transmitted a system of belief based on miracles and liturgy,[8] particularly in Coptic chants. Handed down from generation to generation, this process left ample space for improvisation. Beginning in the nineteenth century, endeavors to transcribe these songs became part of a process of the valorization of Coptic heritage, which has altered the musical practice itself.[9] The "renaissance" was first carried out under the auspices of a new, cultivated elite, and then the enlightened patriarchy under Cyril IV, and it was anchored to state-construction and changes in rural organizations. It was defined in part as the nascent urban elites' transcription of practices they deemed "backward" in a discursive and symbolic system that involved self-representation as a unified group. In other words the emergence of a Coptic identity depended on the appearance of a narrative, visual, theatrical, and political *dispositif*: representation. The communitarian fact was not forged thanks to the "bonds" between individuals. It took shape in a system of sense and values, signs and codes, and in the institutions that embodied them, as Dina El-Khawaga precisely and brilliantly noted in her dissertation.

"The Copts are the descendants of Pharaohs." The significance of this and other similar declarations is worth examining. It summarizes the story of a gap between the Coptic and Muslim symbolic configurations, despite an enduring common national code. Initially, the statement had a corollary: "We Egyptians are all Copts." This formulation had an alleged etymological justification: "because, 'Copt' at its origins simply means 'Egyptian.' Since the Islamic era, the term, developed from the Greek 'Eguptus' through an Arabic transcription 'al-Coht,' has designated the Christian Egyptian."[10] From the mid-nineteenth century the Coptic elite devoted themselves to representing the history of the church and promoting Coptic culture; they conceived of national history and Coptic history as inextricably intertwined, as one single history. The Coptic Church, a national church, was rooted in the Egyptian soil—albeit the soil of a reimagined Egyptian geography. National and community narratives were outlined simultaneously, like two sides of the same coin. Despite Christian authors' insistence on their Pharaonic heritage, throughout the first decades of the twentieth century the valorization of Coptic cultural and religious specificity did not appear incompatible with an Egyptian identity. It was unfolding in continuity with the Coptic Church's renaissance, as well as with the Copts' integration into the nascent nation's social and political life. It could even have sat alongside Arabism as long as the Islamist discursive framework did not prevail. In other words Coptic cultural specificity was tied to the emergence of Egyptian nationalism, insofar as the latter borrowed its main characteristic from its deep connection to the Nile Valley. In this way Coptic culture would bind its glorious past to contemporary Egypt. This representation inverted the image of the official *Weltanschauung* enunciated in the scholarly manuals and the vision described in Islamist narratives of all stripes. It positions "Coptitude" as the foundation, or quintessence, of the Egyptian nation, going so far as pretending to represent the nation in its totality. Coptic sensitivity to being termed a "minority" might be related to an unspoken assumption: Copts cannot be a "minority," reduced to one part of the nation, because they represent its totality, its essence. Do Copts represent 6, 10, or 25 percent of the total population of the country? The exact percentage is not at stake here; it is not a real political concern anyway, as sectarian power sharing did not, and does not, seem feasible in Egypt. It is the essence—the origin—that is at stake and that supersedes any possible number, and, consequently, no number can account for it.

Nevertheless, these latent representations did not become widespread and, later, publicly expressed until the myth of sacred unity was shattered for the Copts and the definition of the Egyptian nation increasingly referred to Arab and/or Islamic identity. Two antagonistic tendencies thus worked to disentangle the Coptic worldview and the dominant national narrative. While still drawing on folkloric Pharaonic representations, divorced from Egyptians' daily concerns, the national narrative mobilized Islamic signs and symbols to a greater extent and integrated Egyptian history into the framework of "Islamic civilization." Correspondingly, but counter to this tendency, Coptic authors traced a genealogy of Coptic history—hence, in their view, of national history. At the forefront of this history were "heroes" and *topoi* that, at best, did not mean much to the Muslim majority and, at worst, were given characteristics antithetical to those the Copts assigned, as in the case of the figure of General Ya'qub, who raised an army under Kléber's orders.

Furthermore, this splitting in two of memories initiated in the 1930s combines with the contemporary ethnicization of community identity.[11] The axiom "Copts are the descendants of Pharaohs" has thus turned round, the inclusive becoming exclusive, until henceforth it means "We (the Copts), alone are the true and pure Egyptians. The others (Arabs, Muslims, Bedouin) are invaders." One of the first Coptic activists in the diaspora, Shawki Karas, contributed to disseminating and promoting this image: "The ethno-religious Coptic people, descendants of Pharaonic Egypt, are exposed to systematic persecution and ethnocide by Egypt's Arab Muslim government. The goal is to destroy the Copts—who account for twenty percent of Egyptians—socially, economically, and politically."[12] In 1985 Karas published a text entitled *Copts in Egypt: Strangers in Their Own Land*, a scrupulous mimicry of the 1908 Shaykh 'Abd al-'Aziz Jawish article that had marked the beginning of hostilities between Christians and Muslims in the press at that time: "Islam, Stranger in Its Own Country."[13] Hence, the demands for ethnic distinction combined the affirmation of Coptic cultural and religious specificity with the more or less vehement rejection of Arab identity. The Coptic diaspora activists' discourse was the first to highlight the difference between Coptic and Muslim Egyptians. Disseminated over the Internet for several years, their rhetoric crystallized a previously diffuse imagery that had circulated in Coptic (and Muslim) circles and rose to the surface, once again, during a period of crisis. Hence, the lawyer Maurice Sadiq suggested celebrating the anniversary of the *Reconquista*, and the website Amcoptic (heir to Karas's work) displayed a Coptic flag chosen by activists in 2005. They justified the initiative as the denial of Arab identity as symbolized in the Egyptian flag and mentioned in the state creed of the "Arab Republic of Egypt" (*Jumhūriyya miṣr al-'arabiyya*). Print literature and ranting from new satellite television stars (like Zakariya Butrus) also helped to promote this discourse. Moreover, senior members of the Coptic clergy had publicly endorsed these long-marginalized representations, a sort of Internet *creation ab nihilo*. Anba Bishuy, who, in 2009 and 2010, was the most powerful man in the church after Shenuda III, extolled the benevolence of Copts who welcomed Muslims on "their" earth. On July 18, 2008, Anba Tuma, the head of the diocese of al-Qusiyya in Assiut, delivered a lecture at the Hudson Institute under the title "The Experience of the Most Important Christian Community in the Middle East in an Era of Accelerated Islamization," prompting an outcry in the Egyptian press. In his presentation Tuma affirmed that

> Egypt is our identity, our nation, our earth; it is our language and our culture. But some Egyptians converted to Islam and, turning away from their language and their culture, they began to look toward the Arabs, Arab identity becoming

> the principal object of their attention. If you tell a Copt that he is Arab, you have insulted him. . . . We are not Arabs, we are Egyptians. I am very happy to be Egyptian and I do not accept being an "Arab," because from an ethnic point of view, I am not one. Egyptians have turned toward Arab identity, have claimed Arabism, and have integrated into the vast Arab landscape, and this has altered the identity of the nation. It is a great dilemma for Copts who have preserved their Christian identity, or, I should rather say, who have preserved their identity as Egyptians, who have their own culture, who try to preserve their language, music, and Coptic calendar, all the heritage of ancient Egypt. And yet, our compatriots have abandoned it for another culture. Today, when you see a Copt, you see not only a Christian, you see an Egyptian who strives to protect his own identity against another, imported identity. These two processes are still ongoing. The process [of Arabization-Islamization] has never ceased, as in their minds Egypt is not completely Islamized or Arabized and so the process must continue.

THE FIGURE OF THE YOUNG KIDNAPPED GIRL, "CONVERTED, AND MARRIED BY FORCE"

The image of the young kidnapped girl, "converted and married by force," has become the object of strong emotional investment on the part of the Copts.[14] The figure crystallizes the contemporary representations of community boundaries in a period of rapid societal and familial changes, although it unfolds in continuity with several discursive and symbolic networks from the present day or deeper in the past. By examining these reconfigurations, this analysis points to their dividing lines and the new rules of coexistence that they establish and reveal.

Religious conversions regularly attracted the attention of religious and political figures during the Ottoman Empire and in Egyptian society under British rule. Throughout these periods the issue mainly challenged the power relations between the occupying powers and the occupied countries.[15] But young Christian girls appear as a central *motif* in discussions around conversion after the 1970s; at the 1976 Conference of Alexandria, Pope Shenuda evoked the disappearance of young girls. But it was not until the 1990s that Christian emigrant activists elaborated on this theme, and their discourse focused on the girls' abduction and forced conversion. Then, at the beginning of the twenty-first century, a third type of participant joined the debate: European and American (non-Coptic) Christian organizations.[16] The structure and vocabulary of the families' narratives were similar to the activists', attesting to the complex information-sharing relationship between the two. The latter would pass on information provided by the families, who would deliver remarks in tune with the activists' point of view. They sustained one another based on at least one common objective: to attract third-party attention to the cases and engage an audience. To this end they both knew which elements to highlight and, conversely, to omit. Possible family tensions, the behavior of brothers or the father, a marriage proposal undesirable to the young woman—these were issues to be avoided.

Instead, the language would be immersed in the youth and innocence of the young girl, victimized and pure. A supposed enemy—individual or organization—would have forced the girl to convert and marry a Muslim, with the complicity of state institutions and their agents.[17] Magdi Khalil, in one of the numerous texts he has written on the subject, had set out a broad definition of coercion: "Bait, lure, mystification, seduction, pressure or physical and emotional temptation, blackmail, compulsion, abduction . . . all these mechanisms fall under forced Islamization, in the clear sense that these young women do not obey, in most cases, their free will. . . . Of course, in the case of an underage girl, she does not have any free will."[18] Khalil has attempted to establish that, these girls having been targeted for abuse, such coercion falls within the legal category of "organized crime." But he abandoned this argument (undoubtedly because to support it requires the existence of a criminal organization) in favor of another legal category: "forced disappearance." "Forced disappearance contravenes the *Universal Declaration of Human Rights*, the *International Covenant on Civil and Political Rights*, and the *International Covenant on Economic, Social, and Cultural Rights*. It violates the *Convention Against Torture* and the *Declaration on the Protection of All Persons from Enforced Disappearance* adopted by the United Nations on December 18, 1992. According to Article 17 of this declaration, 'Acts constituting enforced disappearance shall be considered a continuing offense as long as the perpetrators continue to conceal the fate and the whereabouts of persons who have disappeared.'"[19] He makes an effort to show that the Egyptian state not only transgresses its own laws relative to the conversion of minors, but it even acts as an accomplice to the crime whenever state agents support the disappearances and refuse to furnish information to the families regarding the location of the disappeared. But this argument remains tainted by the absence of rigor in establishing the facts of the allegations. In case after case it yet remains to be proven that the disappearances are indeed "forced."

In this regard some activists changed their tune for several possible reasons: they took the time to verify the given information; they realized that this image was not as great a mobilizing force as they had hoped; nor did the figure mobilize the desired allies. Actually, as Grégoire Delhaye has noted, only the Christian or Zionist (and, at times, Islamophobic) organizations would integrate this figure into their rhetoric. Anxious to identify what they considered cases of persecution against Christians or Christianity worldwide, they were liable to ignore local peculiarities or power structures. Yet the activists' traditional supporters within the "American establishment"—advocacy groups and those connected with the State Department on the freedom of religion—did not mention, or no longer mentioned, the kidnapping and forced conversion of young Christian girls.[20] Organizations and Copts living in Egypt criticized the media's exploitation of these affairs. Asked in private, several Coptic activists offered a more nuanced explanation of their position. William Wissa, for example, who in several articles referenced an organized network along the lines of Magdi Khalil's suggestion, used the expression "network of friendship and solidarity" in a conversation with me, which proves closer to reality.[21] He pointed to the fact that a Christian girl leaving home to marry a Muslim man faced no obstacles in carrying out this endeavor. The protagonists involved at each stage of the process would facilitate it. According to law, a minor cannot convert without the consent of her legal guardian. But a member of the young Muslim man's family usually plays this role, while officials in charge of the conversion and marriage procedures consider it acceptable to modify information (age, first and foremost), close their eyes to the fact that the candidate for conversion did not follow the required steps, and leave the family with no news of their relative.[22] Until 2011 no reports had verified the kidnappings of any "criminal organizations" at the national, regional, or global level that might have encouraged the abduction of young Christian girls. In a survey conducted on the controversial issue, Janique Blattman noted that "the facts actually suggest a 'runaway' situation, usually for love."[23] Yara Sallam (EIPR), who has heard the grievances of many Coptic families, also did not count any cases of abduction.[24]

Integrating Febe Armanios's conclusions on women's role in the contemporary Coptic community into a study of diaspora activists' discourse, Delhaye remarks that these romantic relations often expressed a desire for emancipation from an oppressive family structure[25] and, as Tewfik Aclimandos adds, a "suffocating community environment."[26] Young Coptic girls live under the supervision of their family, not only of their father but also of their brothers. In addition to these constraints they shoulder the burden of the daily chores incumbent on women in family life: "Although the strong social control exercised by men in Egyptian families is not specifically Coptic, Febe Armanios has shown how the effects of clericalization characteristic of the Coptic revival came to give masculine domination a Christian religious justification, and how in this context 'to dispute the position [of a father's dominance in the family] has almost become a sin.'"[27] The tendency toward a clericalization of the laity placed women in the center of a "mechanism of parochial reproduction, not only in biological terms (by procreation) but also spiritual (by religious education)."[28] But the strengthening of paternal authority and the centrality of the woman's role partially appeared as a reaction to the propagation of new models of feminine emancipation, at a moment when Coptic and Muslim bigotry has hardly hindered the disintegration of the family unit. The first cases of young women's disappearance were conjured at the end of the 1970s, at the precise time when these two conflicting models also spread in the middle and lower classes of the Egyptian population. However, women in these less-fortunate social categories could not count on their family relations to emigrate and so had to satisfy their desires for emancipation from the Coptic familial straitjacket in an Egyptian context. They saw in Islam and in marriage a means to flee the authority of their father or an oppressive family situation, to escape a quasi-minority status evident even in the most intimate perceptions, and to discard a self-hatred instilled in their Coptic bodies by the multiple signs of Christian inferiority in collective spaces. The indisputable authority of the father and the central role of a woman pressed families to save face. Whether the young girl, disappointed, wanted to return to her Christian family after an affair, or a marriage, or whether the parents had no news from her, neither the families nor the young girls were willing to publicly admit that the conversion was voluntary. Deep down, did they know it? The truth is highly uncertain, as the radicalization of sectarian antagonism fuels an entrenched bias, as is the case with both Muslims and Christians. A member of the community could not possibly adopt a "false" religion, unless under the influence of madness, drugs, or ill-intentioned individuals. Denial that voluntary conversion might be possible is so strong that, for example, after the disappearance of Camelia, the wife of a priest, in the summer of 2010, hundreds of Copts mobilized once again at Saint Mark's Cathedral in 'Abasiyya, the seat of the patriarch in Cairo. The announcement of her return and the knowledge that she was not in fact kidnapped did not calm the demonstrators: they continued to protest against kidnappings, despite their knowledge that neither Camelia, nor Wafa' Qustantin—another priest's wife gone missing—had been abducted. The specific event—the disappearance of a woman—functioned simply as a trigger for an affective dynamic; establishing the facts was not enough to mollify a sense of injustice that was fed by several centuries of historical experience. Additionally, the confrontational nature of the situation made the crowd, as an active force, adopt a more radical position than any of the members that composed it.[29]

Three types of discrimination work to produce this sentiment of injustice, further overdetermined and intensified by the socioeconomic factors that affect Christians and Muslims. First, the agents of state institutions favor conversions to Islam but hide the fate of Christian women from their friends and families. Second, religious conversion is possible in one sense—toward Islam—but not in the other direction. Third, according to Muslim personal status laws, a Christian woman can marry a Muslim man without converting, but a Christian man cannot marry a Muslim woman unless he embraces Islam. Marriage is a pivotal event in Egyptian society, focusing families' attention and long-term economies. This third discrimination seems all the more unjust in the eyes of young Copts for whom the high cost of marriage presents an obstacle to its realization, condemning many urban Egyptians to celibacy until the age of thirty, or even forty, even when they have met their soul mate or the spouse their families intend. Whether unmarried or in the unfortunate case of being in love with a Muslim woman, young Copts have difficulty accepting the fact that Muslims can, for their part, draw happily from a pool of Christian women. At the forefront of protests against disappearances, they chanted at the demonstrations organized to demand the return of Wafa' Qustantin: "First they took our wives, now they take our *Tasoni* [in reference to her status as the wife of a priest]."

• • •

The figure of the young woman converted by force constitutes one of the last avatars in a war between Christians and Muslims that has played out on different fronts and where the protagonists deploy a varied arsenal to attest to the strength of their religion.

Christian activists' advocacy efforts appear to be a mirror image of the Egyptian opposition to the Sidqi government, which launched diatribes against missionaries' activities in the 1930s.[30] In attacking missionaries, the opposition denounced the weakness of the Sidqi Cabinet, which they believed had failed to defend the Egyptian nation's specific values—religion and Islamic civilization[31]—

against foreign intrusion. The Muslim Brothers made the struggle against the missions their first rallying cry,[32] and the opposition parties did not pass up any opportunity to incriminate the missionaries. Rumors circulated on the tactics they deployed to attract young people: corruption, money, "occidental" charms . . . the use of hypnosis and drugs to obtain victims' consent appeared as preferred motifs. The idea that the "victim's spirit and desire"—innocent whether male or female—had been subverted was a recurring and compelling theme.

From the 1950s, writing hostile to Christian proselytism came to form its own literary genre, highlighting how missionaries would insidiously subvert and destroy Islamic religion and "culture."[33] In this regard missionary activity has been seen as the accomplishment of a project of religious and political domination to continue the Crusades, and then the colonial enterprise, under the guise of educational or charitable works. Furthermore, in his thesis "Christian Action in the Arab World" (*al-'Amal al-tanṣīrī fī al-'ālam al-'arabī*), the scholar 'Abd al-Fattah Ghurab suggests that any secularization or imported or concurrent doctrines were in service to the project of domination and thus implied "de-Islamization" without necessarily targeting the conversion of Muslims to Christianity. From such a perspective, secularization was equated, in good or bad faith, with "Christianization" (*tanṣīr*, which Ghurab distinguishes from *tabshīr*, or "evangelization").[34]

> Conversion . . . took center stage at a moment that is difficult to situate with precision, between the end of the 1970s and the second half of the 1980s. . . . One of the most deplorable aspects of the renewed religious fervor was the increasing dissemination, using all privately available means of communication, of delusional speeches on the religion of others, denigrating and insulting them. These speeches were often, but not always, produced by religious figures. For my purposes, the crucial variety of these was that of the "battle" between a priest and a Muslim cleric, sometimes scoring points using relevant arguments, but also often stupid ones. In the Coptic videotapes, the priest crushes the cleric; in the Muslim ones it's the opposite, and the discomfited priest converts.[35]

While these types of recordings still circulate in the market, Christians and Muslims now deploy a more powerful arsenal. The rise of the Internet and amateur videos has provided the technical support to rapidly disseminate images to the entire world. The form and tone of the remarks has partially changed. The priest or the shaykh are no longer the only figures and the "man without qualities" lies at the core of a new discursive system. Theological arguments are now embedded in a new matrix of meaning, one that implies a new subjectivity and a reconfigured system of references that gives priority to the welfare of the novice, morally and physically. Individuality has become central while at the same time lacking any singularity. Thomas Brisson has analyzed with finesse several video series and shown how the content and presentation vary depending on the intended audience. In the films addressed to an Arab and Muslim public, the argument employed by the narration of the Christian convert takes into account the difficulty of converting and includes a critique of evangelical activity, all the while presenting conversion as a simple act, a deliberate decision, deliverance, and a social promotion. Justly, Brisson points to the different steps in the process of conversion as they are presented in these stories and identifies two moments in the recognition of a new theological truth: the future convert first pronounces the phrase "Christ is the son of God," without having a clear understanding of what the phrase implies, then, usually following a period of revolt, repeats the phrase, "but, this time, with a convicted tone, as a recognized and accepted truth . . . in an act of free will."[36] According to the videos' producers, it is the proximity to Christ, precisely the presence of this intermediary between divinity and humanity, which establishes the superiority of Christianity over Islam. This theological argument does not follow reason but rather an individual experience of spiritual and physical deliverance. Brisson puts this motif into relief with two videos of this type: The individual talks alone, with neither interlocutor nor questions. He starts by recounting how he was raised in the Muslim faith but had had doubts and felt a certain discomfort about the nature of true faith. Layla confesses her previous hesitations. At adolescence, these torments affected her physically; she suffered from crippling headaches and considered suicide. The physical dimension that traverses these stories is surely far from coincidental: the implicit equivalence of the salvation of the spirit and body is present in a number of these videos. Often, a pharmacist offers a Bible to future converts for the first time, going as far as to say in one video, that the sacred book "offers a relief that cannot be found in medicine."[37]

The cases of young Christian women's abduction have benefited from new media that allow the viewer to witness the magical reappearance of the disappeared onscreen. Christian journalists close to emigrant Egyptian activists released interviews on YouTube with families of young converted women. In the case of "Marianne and Christine" the response was twofold. Shortly after the disappearance of Wafa' Qustantin, a Christian mother alerted Egyptian authorities to the kidnapping of her two daughters. State Security and the president of the republic offered a blistering denial of the allegations, for once finding the two girls without delay. Invited to speak during prime-time hours on the *Dream TV* channel, Marianne and Christine, both married and both mothers of a family, affirmed that they were happily living with the men of their choice. Websites moderated by Islamist activists outdo each other by putting out several online videos. In one of these Marianne and Christine have become Habiba and Asma', wearing thick *niqabs* that they consent to remove for a few shots, and are shown in their adopted Muslim family with their husbands and children. The video confronts the assertions of the Coptic family and the priests, that the girls were minors, were abducted, raped, and forced to marry Muslims; the women's testimonies claim that they were adults, had been neither kidnapped nor raped, and had married for love.[38] Other videos feature young veiled women, who had been Christian but converted to Islam.[39] In one of these the young woman seems to come from a modest background but expresses herself with clarity in a polished Egyptian Arabic, clearly different from Marianne's strong, coarse accent punctuated with trivial exclamations. The conversion appears synonymous with social promotion and education. These videos present two types of emancipation. In both cases they paint the picture of determined and sane young women, happy in their choices, clearly affirming that they harbor no regrets, and in no way desire a return to—nor even a reconnection with—their families.

SPATIAL AND SOCIAL SEGREGATION

The closure of private space to members of the other religion sharply signals the deterioration of the relations between Christians and Muslims over the last forty years.[40] From the top of the social ladder to the bottom, Christians and Muslims rarely visit one another's homes any longer (with exceptions, of course). This physical separation also became established in collective spaces, in various ways and depending on criteria that are not easily discernible. A Muslim buys bread at the Muslim's bakery rather than the Christian's; Christians forget to offer well-wishes for the end of Ramadan, and Muslims forget at Easter; a Muslim building owner refuses to sell to a Christian for fear the latter may reserve usage for Christians. . . . Over time, these repeated practices erect a growing number of barriers and, even, establish rules.[41]

On university campuses teachers notice the formation of zones exclusively dedicated to Coptic students organizing activities that are off-limits to Muslims. Alarmed, the teachers raise their concerns to the clergy. The Youth Bishopric gathers student testimonies in a video report and invites Christian as well as Muslim students and teachers to several brainstorming sessions to address the problem.[42] Campus segregation has seen a marked upsurge since the late 1990s. But the phenomenon actually began in the late 1970s / early 1980s, when the church expanded its influence at universities as a response to Islamist activism and Muslim Brotherhood organizing that had become prevalent there. The Youth Bishopric had then encouraged the creation of the first Christian "families" (*'usar*), an indication of retreat into community space, while simultaneously expanding its signs and practices outside of ecclesiastical walls. Yet the activities organized by religious groups used to, and still do, constitute the only extracurricular activities available on campus.

At present, Islamist activists strive to spread Islamic symbols in shared spaces and to disseminate pamphlets hostile to Christians and Christianity. During the past three decades some Salafist groups, as well as preachers holding various views, have massively propagated teachings that purport to define possible relations with Christians. It is unclear to what degree these teachings are followed, although it is clear that actual practices comply with some Salafist "commandments" on forbidden behaviors. Greeting a Christian is prohibited, or at least requires a different greeting than that used with a Muslim. Meals, particularly, are the object of some attention. To share a meal with a Christian is disallowed, as is even tasting a meal that a Christian has prepared. Several accounts testify that these prohibitions are not followed by some Muslims alone but also by some Christians, although no biblical text supports them.

Hence, the contemporary pervasiveness of purity creates new boundaries, overdetermines social practices, and reactivates latent representations.[43] Furthermore, purity's pervasiveness could be described as a hystericization of the sectarian variable, especially when one observes the transition from fear of impurity to dread of defilement. In media coverage, for example, fear and rumored rape are now presented publicly as the reasons for an outbreak of attacks against Christians: on November 18, 2009, in the city of Farshut, Qena Province, a Muslim family accused a Christian of having raped a family member. The arrest of the suspect did nothing to stem reprisal, and violence spread from village to village, day by day, until on January 6, 2010, six Christians were murdered in Nag' Hammadi. In another rumored scenario that year, a gang of Christian boys were said to have filmed Muslim girls in compromising situations.[44] Omnipresent in diaspora Coptic activist discourse, the theme of rape is embraced by the media, which has correspondingly devoted close attention to sexual harassment of late. Yet, ironically, this underscoring of sectarian borders happens contemporaneously with their ever more visible transgression and demands to abolish them. In a television series broadcast during Ramadan in 2000 (the same time that *Hassan and Marcus* was released), the writers told a love story about the romance between a young Christian man and Muslim woman. Far from placing blame, the series suggested that those rules preventing the young lovers from realizing their desires should be changed.

The rules that adjudicate purity and impurity extend to all physical relations with members of the other religion. In discussions on the protocol for organ transplants in July 2008, the president of the Doctor's Syndicate, Hamdi al-Sayyid, declared that he would prohibit transplants between Muslims and Christians. Such a decision would have no impact on organ donation, already limited to fourth- or fifth-degree family members and thus already generally excluding the possibility of "interreligious" donation. Presumably, al-Sayyid was searching for a way to pander to his Brotherhood clientele, and a Brotherhood-affiliated parliamentarian proposed to regulate blood transfusions in a similar way. Al-Sayyid justified his proposal by arguing that he simply wished to limit the possibility of black market organ sales, particularly that of poor Muslims' organs to wealthy Christian buyers.[45] Far from coincidental, this remark reactivated the fantasy of presumed Coptic wealth and revealed contemporary phobias.

Several months later, when the Egyptian government ordered the slaughter of pigs in response to concerns about swine flu, news media issued scandalous "reports" and divulged the names of supermarkets that were allegedly selling their pork products by another name. Photographs of grim-looking supermarkets "certified" the story. People on the street warned each other: "Careful, now, don't buy *maḥshi* [meat mixture], because Christians are trying to get rid of their pork in the markets." Anxieties over ingesting pork were doubled because of the fear of contracting swine flu, despite the fact that scientific reports found it could not be passed from pigs to humans. A potential cause of the spread of the disease, Christians again appeared as a virus in the figure of the pig, rivaling Jews, who, according to local folk-genealogies of "human races," descended from pigs.

Egypt's swine flu episode and the pork slaughter revealed with unusual clarity the pervasiveness of the logic of exclusion throughout social, discursive and symbolical practices. Rather than a causal factor that would impact on the main participants' intentions, this logic overdetermines the sense of every decision and event, and constitutes an underlying principle of intelligibility.[46] The decision to carry out the slaughter was made on April 29, 2009; it was presented as a preventative measure against the diffusion of the H1N1 virus (swine flu) on Egyptian soil and a preliminary effort in the reorganization and sanitation of pig farms. On the day that the People's Assembly voted in favor of the decision, April 28, and on April 29, the day that the head of state consulted the Health Minister, Hatim al-Gabali, the World Health Organization (WHO) had not documented any cases in which a human had contracted the disease from a pig. On the contrary, the organization rejected the hypothesis that the disease could be spread in this way. The only two people to have contracted the disease in the Middle East were two Israelis returning from vacation in Mexico. No other state adopted such draconian measures. The three largest livestock owners, all Christians (one of whom is related to the Sawiris business family), tried in vain to convince officials to abandon their plans, offering to finance the transfer of their farms to the Cairo suburb of Helwan.[47] Egyptian debates focused, in part, on whether the government's decision had "sectarian" motives. In a televised speech on government channels, the minister of Awqaf, Mahmud Zaqzuq, incidentally addressed the subject by expressing his surprise at the idea that rumors of this nature could be circulating.

In fact, the "sectarian" dimension of this event did not explain the government's decision—even if it is probable that, at the level of the People's Assembly, the imagery associated with pork in Egypt had steered the request for some of the parliamentarians. But the decree was ultimately issued by Mubarak, after discussion with the ministers of health and agriculture (al-Gabali and Amin Abaza). According to a cardiologist close to the health minister, al-Gabali was surprised that Mubarak had chosen to slaughter the animals and explained the decision primarily as one of panic. Evidently, the president of the republic had received contradictory reports as to the possibility of the virus's transmission from pig to human at the same time that alarmist rhetoric about the sickness and its imminent spread prevailed. In the first half of 2009 Egypt suffered the highest number of bird flu cases because, according to information provided by the Ministry of Agriculture, Egyptian research institutes failed to develop an Egyptian vaccine, and the method used was unsuccessful to stem the spread of the virus in the country. Without a doubt the president was afraid that in facing the spread of swine flu (or a mutant form of it) from pig to human, Egypt would not be able to combat the scourge, neither its health consequences nor its symbolic significance. The possibility of such a scenario, as well as the Muslim Brothers' denunciation of government incompetence, however, could have oriented anger toward the Copts. In this sense, perhaps, the presidential decree could be explained by "sectarian" motives. Finally, while there might be some economic benefits from the decision (those close to the president may have profited by redeveloping the farms, for instance), this factor is insufficient to fully explain the rationale behind the president's decision.

The decree provoked strong emotions in Christian circles, although several Christian personalities had consented to publicly declaring its merits, and Pope Shenuda neither fully disavowed nor supported it. It was explicitly fashioned as a metaphor for Christian extermination and exerted a physical sort of violence. Was there a single Christian in Egypt who was not wounded the moment the decision was announced and, even more, during the fifteen days of its application, when the Egyptian daily newspapers showed heaps of pig corpses on their front pages? Souad Ferrié reported that the pig farmers of the Manshiyyat Nasr neighborhood echoed the cries of their wards: "These are our children that are being killed." The farmers' grief, their anger, and the resistance that they put forth against the teams that came to carry out the mission could not be explained simply by the loss of their principal, even their only, source of revenue. (They were either poorly compensated or not at all, contrary to government promises.) Other Christians, left to their own misery in villages or Cairene neighborhoods, expressed the feeling of having been slaughtered themselves, even without the subject being raised. In December 2009, in the church in the al-Waraq neighborhood of Imbaba, Giza, several witnesses ascribed visions of the Virgin Mary not to any vague legacy of persecution but to this specific event, in which they read the story of their own worthlessness in the eyes of their rulers. Throughout those first two weeks of May 2009 Egypt showed an image of violence that was all the more terrible given the extreme savagery (termed as such by an MP) with which the beasts were dispatched and the spectacle in which their images were broadcast, as if through some morbid fascination.

Those who debated the issue sought to prove (or disprove) a sectarian dimension by questioning the causality of the decision and thus the intention behind it. But the sense of an act, of a text, or of an image is formed independently of the intention of its authors, though this does not imply that it can be assigned any meaning whatsoever. This event has been seen as a metaphor. But why was it understood as such? A metaphor for what? What did the image show? Did it allow Egyptian society to face its fears while, at the same time, exorcising them? Did it occur as a sacrifice, a pagan sacrifice, the sacrifice of a scapegoat for pain yet to come? Or was it a tragedy, an exercise in catharsis at the national level? This image crystallizes the structural violence that operated in Egyptian social and political relations through a rhetorical device—*catachresis*, a figurative term for a literal one: pork, regardless of any decision, has denoted Christians in Egyptian symbolic configurations from the nineteenth century to the present day.[48] But this rhetorical device does not reveal a play on words; it offers a vision of the physicality inherent in every symbolic act. In this image security and purity fold into each other.

3 THE COPTIC CHURCH AS SPACE OF RESISTANCE AND ALLY OF THE REGIME

Intracommunitarian dynamics have also buttressed the production of a Christian minority. The transformation of the ecclesiastical space under Shenuda III fueled the logic of exclusion working at the national level. Stimulated by internal dynamics in the Coptic world and by nationwide processes of minoritization, the creation of a closed community space—although partly formed as a resistance to these processes—has nevertheless fostered the production of Coptic sectarian discourses. Thus, the subjugation of Copts to the church order, as well as their withdrawal into a space considered by most of the community to be a refuge, has reinforced their marginalization on the national stage. The mutation in the ecclesiastical institutions under Shenuda III and the contemporary politicization of the minority phenomenon influenced each other, and they both depended on the relationship between the church and the presidential regimes.

In this chapter I analyze the foundation and engineering of Pope Shenuda's authority and power in order to highlight the apparently paradoxical consequences of his rule. Indeed, the pope only partially achieved his fundamentalist project, which implied total control over the production of meaning and values. Paradoxically, its realization could not prevent the disconnection between community belonging and individualized religious practices, and it contributed to a "secularized" redefinition of patriarchal authority.

WAFA' QUSTANTIN

On November 27, 2004, Wafa' Qustantin disappeared.[1] A forty-seven-year-old mother of two children who had recently finished their studies, Wafa' was working as an agricultural engineer and enjoyed an excellent reputation in her community and at work. One day, she left the village of Abi al-Matamir, in Bahaira Province, where she had lived from the time of her marriage to a Coptic Orthodox priest who had lost both his legs to poorly treated diabetes. She presented herself to the police in the Dar al-Salam Prefecture of suburban Cairo, accompanied by a Muslim woman from her home province of Minufiyya. She filled out and signed a form to convert to Islam.

Murmurs started in Christian circles that Wafa' had been abducted and forced to convert to Islam or, alternatively, that she had succumbed to the nefarious influence of a Muslim colleague and fled with him. On December 2 Copts began to gather in Abi al-Matamir near the village church. At this first, local stage of protest the clergy and Anba Bakhumyus, bishop of Bahaira, did not discourage the crowd that had formed near the church. Simultaneously, the pope, who had flown into a rage on learning about the disappearance and conversion of Wafa', attempted to negotiate for her return with the local authorities, receiving assurances from State Security forces. Having been informed of the suffering that Wafa' had endured in her married life and her desire to be free of it, the clergy had nevertheless not waived Shenuda's ruling, according to which only adultery justified breaking the sacrament of marriage. And Bishop Bakhumyus had not acted on the request to provide counseling and guidance sessions (*jalasāt al-nuṣḥ wa-l-irshād*), after which Wafa' had begun the administrative conversion process.

Two incidents exacerbated tensions. State Security agents did not keep their promise, while the only information provided regarding the flight of Wafa' fanned flames among the Copts: 'Abd al-Rahim Shihata, from the local Ministry of Development, coming to meet the clergy and official representatives in the village and province, announced that Wafa' Qustantin had already converted and that her file was closed. The daily paper *al-Ahram* relayed the message from the deputy minister. Copts, however, refused to recognize the validity of the conversion since the counseling and guidance session had never taken place. The Coptic weekly *Watani* published a communiqué from the Majlis al-Milli of Alexandria that denounced Shihata's remarks, which were disseminated in a government paper.[2] Radicalized demonstrators traveled, en masse and in church-sponsored buses, to the Cathedral in 'Abasiyya, the seat of the patriarch in Cairo. That the heart of the protest moved from the local church to Cairo signaled a passage to the national level.

A sit-in followed at the Cathedral, and in the continued absence of Wafa' tensions mounted between December 3 and December 8. Demonstrators took advantage of an unexpected opportunity to make their voices heard in high places: the funeral of writer Sa'id Sunbul, in one of 'Abasiyya's churches, brought together the political elite, and well-known personalities. Young Copts brutally assailed them, injuring Usama al-Baz, an adviser to President Mubarak. After the incident the media devoted increasing attention to the Wafa' Qustantin affair while part of the intellectual elite gingerly stepped into the limelight. The pope negotiated with the highest-level officials in the executive branch, directly or through more or less neutral channels, such as Mustafa al-Fiqi. As the talks continued without result, Shenuda III canceled his weekly Wednesday sermon and announced his retreat into the Saint-Bishuy monastery in Wadi Natrun. The young demonstrators took to the streets, and when security forces tried to contain them, the infuriated youth threw rocks at them. Thirty-four arrests were made. The demand that Wafa' be returned to her family changed, and, at Bishop Bakhumyus's instigation, the crowd insisted that she be returned to the church. Hosni Mubarak personally gave the order to return Wafa' Qustantin to the church.

Anba Yu'annis informed the protestors that their demand would be granted and encouraged them, unsuccessfully, to put an end to their sit-in. Talks then revolved around where to bring Wafa' Qustantin. State Security officers and the clerical hierarchy finally opted for a canoness monastery in the Ain Shams neighborhood, which, under the circumstances, was placed under heightened surveillance. The most eminent clergy members—Anbas Mussa, Armya, Bishuy—accompanied Bishop Bakhumyus to pay Wafa' her first visit. They invoked the shock that Wafa' must have endured as a reason to prolong her stay at the convent until she was able to engage in a fully comfortable dialogue.[3] She stayed for one week. State Security agents have always maintained that Wafa' was in good spirits and seemed in perfect health when they brought her to the convent. And, according to others, Wafa' had initially refused to renounce her conversion.

On December 15 she appeared in the office of the Prosecutor General, escorted by six or seven religious figures. The judge declared that, according to the laws regulating the process, her declaration could not be made in their presence. After some discussion, only two of them remained. Wafa' Qustantin's statement was recorded and published the following day in the press: "I was born a Christian, I remain a Christian, and I will die a Christian." Then Wafa' disappeared again, and presumably she remained under strict surveillance in one of the monasteries of Wadi Natrun, where she would exercise her profession as an agricultural engineer, far away from her husband, who has since died.

Still in retreat in Wadi Natrun, Shenuda declared that he would not emerge until the young Copts arrested during the protests were released from custody; he wanted the crisis resolved before Christmas. The detainees' parents addressed letters of grievance to President Mubarak to plead that their children be set free. And they were.

REVIVAL (*IḤYĀ'*) OR REFORM (*IṢLĀḤ*): THE VICTORY OF THE CLERICS

The very origins of Christianity in Egypt remain subject to significant uncertainty. According to a nineteenth-century tradition, Mark the Evangelist, considered the founder of the Coptic Orthodox Church and the first bishop of Alexandria, had introduced the new religion to the cosmopolitan city, the home of an important Hellenized Jewish community from which Egyptian Christianity probably developed.[4] A hub of Neoplatonism, the city became a vibrant center of Christian theology thanks to the activities of several important personalities like Clement of Alexandria, Saint Athanasius, and Saint Cyril, each of whom played a crucial role in the formation of Christian theology. From the beginning of the fourth century, Egyptian Christianity developed distinct traits, and especially its particular spiritual orientation, monasticism, which imposes the retreat in the desert, where were built the first monasteries from which the Egyptian *fallāḥīn* were evangelized.[5]

Despite the persecution that Christians suffered under Roman authorities, particularly during the reign of Diocletian (284–324), the number of the faithful continued to grow, until even the pagan-born emperor Constantine (324–37) embraced Christianity—presumably for political reasons.[6] In a Roman Empire weakened by new powers like the Persians, the Nile Valley had to redouble its efforts to provide the required supplies and men. Political rivalries weighed on theological disputes, as evidenced in the history of councils. At a time when the theological vocabulary was not yet settled, disagreements on the mystery of Incarnation triggered the Alexandrine bishops' rejection of Byzantine power. Together, these led to a schism between the Patriarchate of Constantinople and the pre-Chalcedonian or "monophysite" Coptic Orthodox Church, though this term was incorrect, as the Copts *do* recognize the dual nature of Christ.[7] Two churches would therefore compete in Egypt: the church of the occupying power, which reported to the patriarch of Constantinople and was found in the large cities where Greeks remained; and the schismatic, Coptic, Egyptian church, which was largely established in the monasteries of the countryside, far from the central power.

Between the Arab armies' conquest of the Nile Valley and the beginning of the nineteenth century, the Coptic Church saw an institutional, economic, and cultural decline, as well as a continuous fall in numbers due to conversions to Islam.[8] From the establishment of Muslim rule, Copts were submitted to *jizya*, a tax in exchange for which, according to the *dhimma* pact, the sovereign was required to ensure the protection of their lives and property and guarantee them the right to practice their religion. In the eighth and ninth centuries, after Coptic revolt against the tax, which had by then extended even to the previously exempt monks, the leadership ordered that numerous monasteries be dissolved, weakening Coptic religious institutions and the entire Christian population. In the ninth century Copts had become a minority.[9] After the reign of the Sultan al-Hakim (996–1021), a period of particular torment for the Copts, the loss of monasteries continued. They had dwindled to such a degree that, on several occasions between the eleventh and thirteenth centuries, it became necessary to select a patriarch from the lay elite rather than from among the monks—contrary to the canon of the church. From the beginning of the Mamluk era, trains of popular opinion hostile to a Coptic population that was viewed as the Crusaders' ally began to emerge in the attitude of the rulers. Up to that time the rulers had not systematically adopted anti-Christian policies despite several episodes of conflict and repression. From that time on, discriminatory measures were applied more scrupulously, while churches and monasteries were destroyed. By the fourteenth century Copts did not represent more than 10 percent of the population, a figure that has fallen to 6 percent today.[10] "The Coptic language had completely disappeared from monasteries, and Arab-Christian literature dwindled to a trickle. The decline of the community could be measured by the accelerated decline of the churches and convents."[11] But most of the Copts' social, cultural, and professional activities took place outside the religious sphere. Although rank, wealth, profession, and sect had drawn boundaries among the different neighborhoods of Egyptian cities,[12] the Copts from various social strata interacted with Muslims and with other minorities. An educated Coptic elite class had existed since the Byzantine era, and its members often held positions as tax collectors in the successive empires' Egyptian provincial administrations—positions that were certainly held in low esteem. Representatives of Ottoman power in the Nile Valley also frequently solicited opinions from the laity on the choice of pope. Outside of professional exchanges and individual relationships, practices and beliefs bound together lower-class Christians and Muslims, as the studies of Kurt Werthmuller, Febe

Armanios, and Catherine Mayeur-Jaouen have admirably elucidated for the Ayyubic, Ottoman, and contemporary eras, respectively.[13]

Coptic laymen, joined later by the clergy, initiated an institutional and cultural "renaissance" (*naḥda*) in the nineteenth century.[14] The project was forged under the combined impact of the construction of the Egyptian nation-state and the ambivalent relations of rivalry and cooperation between the Coptic Orthodox Church and first Catholic, then Protestant, missions.[15] As in other provinces in the Ottoman Empire, the establishment of a Majlis al-Milli in Egypt institutionalized sectarianism by according the church a certain controlled legislative and judicial autonomy. A law established by khedivial decree in 1874 further defined, in 1883, the relationship between this council and the pope. It granted the Majlis al-Milli all prerogatives that were outside the strictly religious domain—namely the management of endowments; administration of welfare institutions; and maintenance of records for baptisms, births, marriages, and deaths—and a jurisdictional role in the personal status of the Copts. Any change in the law regulating the powers of the council would have to be previously approved by government authorities; this distribution of powers is still in force although the government bodies responsible for reviewing draft amendments to the law have changed. The institution of the Majlis cemented the rivalry that already existed between the clergy and the laity. Two socioreligious projects were born.

The product of Coptic elite initiatives seeking active engagement in the church administration and nascent national political life, the Majlis al-Milli became the forum for expression of the reformist trend. From its long-delayed creation it faced opposition from the clerical hierarchy. Supporters of reform (*iṣlāḥ*) desired "to democratize the Church by introducing people's representatives (that is to say laymen) into its institutions, thus enlarging the electoral college of the patriarch, and offering wider opportunities for candidature for the supreme head of the Church, traditionally limited to monks."[16] Indeed, they aimed to reorganize the church, while distinguishing between religious and secular powers, and to reconcile a sense of community with political and social modernity. In 1908 and 1912 Cyril V managed to enact two laws restricting the powers of the council, including taking away its management of endowments. In 1927, however, in a context more favorable to the secularity of religious institutions and in the absence of strong clerical elites, Suryal Jirjis Suryal successfully petitioned for the law's repeal and the adoption of a new law that restored the same powers given in 1883. The attitude of the government with regard to the Majlis al-Milli depended on the margin of action enjoyed by the Wafd Party and other organizations favorable to the reformers, while the king remained hostile toward them. The council's fate was similar to that of the Wafd Party during these two decades, which were marked by increasing corruption and violence on the social and political scene. Both lost their prestige because of the personal rivalries that divided and distracted them from their political work.

For their part the actors of the revival (*iḥyā'*) promoted a fundamentalist project: they endeavored to rebuild a contemporary community of believers by reviving the Coptic Church's supposed original principles and values, updated in accordance with modern ideals. This revival was only ever partially achieved. The first Sunday school graduates succeeded for a brief moment in reconciling these two antagonistic trends around the leading figure of Habib Guirguis. In 1918 Guirguis had founded the Sunday schools on the Protestant model and launched pedagogic and educative projects.[17] From the 1940s the expansion of Islamic religious slogans in sociopolitical life and the communitarian preuniversity education for Copts, combined with the loss of influence of the Majlis al-Milli, besmirched reformist values. Revivalist values predominated, and young graduates joined monasteries and the clerical body, climbing its ranks by adhering to such an outlook. The creation of the state of Israel should be factored into the turn to communitarian attitudes, but the analysis of its impact on interreligious relations in Egypt remains to be explored. Certainly, Nasser's attitude with regard to the Copts favored the success of the revivalist trend. Indeed, by restricting any expression of a sense of community to the religious sphere and, for example, by delaying the Majlis al-Milli elections, Nasser allowed the rising clerical elites to transform the ecclesiastical space into a communitarian one, integrating a growing number of nonreligious activities. Anbas Gregory, Samuel, and Shenuda III were among the young elite who would climb to the top of the clerical hierarchy.

THE POLITICAL THEOLOGY PROJECT OF SHENUDA III

On his coronation day Nazir Gayid took the name of "Shenuda," thereby making a symbolic and programmatic choice. A 1960s hagiography praises this saint, activist, and builder; "his battle against Nestorian heresy and idolatry and his fight for Monophysite doctrine are exalted, as well as his political action as the leader of monks: 'Shenuda's life,' the hagiographer notes, 'is the life of a people who struggle and mobilize for the freedom of religion and country, as well as for social justice. The Copts revolted against idols, occupation, and heresy. It was a revolt for the Copts' religious, national, and social rights."[18] A prudent politician, Shenuda III fought on all these fronts.

The patriarchal function has always been a political one, and the pope was never solely the representative of a religious group. He often wore the hat of official ambassador for the Nile Valley provinces with the leaders of other Christian regions, such as Ethiopia, which had long been attached to the Coptic Orthodox Patriarchate.[19] Cyril VI (1959–70), described as a saint hungry only for spiritual nourishment (some going as far as to reproach him for praying too much), led several key actions in the contemporary politicization of the role of the pope and the centralization of power in his hands. Breaking the relative isolation of the Coptic Orthodox Church, he integrated it into the World Church Council, while Christians, beginning a massive migration, founded the first overseas Coptic churches in New Jersey in the 1960s. He served the foreign policy of the July regime in East Africa and aligned with Nasser's position concerning the Palestinian question.[20] Nasser adopted the habit, maintained by his successors, of dealing with the pope as the representative and spokesperson for any complaints or wishes of the Copts, who were viewed as a single monolithic bloc. Marginalized in the community scene, Coptic laymen—as with their Muslim counterparts—had difficulty finding a role to play in a national politics restrained by the state apparatus. Although Nasser sometimes resorted to lay personalities to pass a message to the clerical hierarchy, his preferred interlocutor remained the pope, with whom he developed a "millet partnership."[21] Nasser and Cyril VI forged a political friendship, which was cleverly orchestrated in the media, with several episodes becoming the subject of controversial stories.[22] This privileged relationship allowed Cyril VI to sideline some Coptic figures, particularly laymen who opposed some of his decisions or hindered his projects. Finally, he effectively mobilized the community by virtue of his efficacy as an intercessor, through his charisma, and he encouraged the promotion of his image as a holy arbiter and healer.

Just like his predecessor, Shenuda III understood perfectly well that the law was the main pillar of his authority. At the end of the 1970s he protested against Azhar-backed efforts to codify and apply shari'a law and imposed his interpretation of confessional laws. Thus, he set his vision against all other interpretations of biblical texts, against the law of the Muslim "others," and against substantive law in those cases where it impeded the implementation of communitarian law or encroached on areas where the pope felt he had absolute dominion. A few weeks after his coronation, Shenuda III declared the 1938 personal status laws null and void and reduced the number of cases eligible for divorce. The papal order stipulates that divorce will only be granted for proven cases of adultery and remarriage only permitted where divorce was issued because of adultery. The Copts' personal status regulation had been adopted on May 9, 1938, by General Majlis al-Milli. At this time laymen had played a more important role in the clerical administration, and those who sat on the council had not been elected for their allegiance to the pope. The *Collection of Laws Relative to the Personal Status of Orthodox Copts* (*majmūʿa qawāʿid al-aḥwāl al-shakhsiyya li-l-aqbāṭ al-urthūdhuks*) contained nine articles (50 through 58) that addressed entitlement to divorce.[23] The pope revoked these, arguing that the Holy Synod (*al-majmaʿ al-muqaddas*) of the Orthodox Church, the only authority competent to legislate, had not ratified the choice of this corpus on personal status regulations and that they violated the teachings of the Gospel. He held that the 1955 adoption of a new law with the Holy Synod's approval had abrogated the law of 1938. Although Parliament failed to vote in favor of either of these texts, the Court of Cassation ruled that the 1938 corpus was considered "legally binding."[24] But since the time of Nasser's judicial reform in 1955, state courts, and not denominational courts, have held the power of arbitration. Also, when the State Council required the pope to authorize the remarriage of ʿAtif Kirillus, Shenuda not only refused to submit to a judgment considered as an interference in church affairs and contrary to the Gospel, but, further, he orchestrated the amendment of the 1938 regulations. In June 2008 a Majlis al-Milli aligned with the pope adopted a new regulation. The articles (52 to 58) that stipulated any cause for divorce outside of adultery and the change of religion were suppressed, conforming to the 1971 papal decree. However, council members formulated a more comprehensive notion of adultery and added both adultery in literal fact (*faʿlī*) and virtual or presumed adultery (*ḥukmī* adultery).[25] Pending an overhaul of the regulations, nuances of this sort allow judges a relatively wide margin of discretion without requiring them to contravene the pope's wishes. In June 2010, during a period of sustained public criticism over the administration of community affairs, and his political positions favorable to the regime, Shenuda managed the feat of mobilizing the quasi totality of Copts behind him in the name of respect for the personal status laws. A similar case to that of ʿAtif Kirillus had arisen, and Shenuda once again refused to apply the court decision requiring him to grant a remarriage to the complainant, who had legally obtained a divorce in conformity with the 1938 laws applied by the courts but not by the church. It was a Pyrrhic victory insofar as the circumstantial unanimity poorly masked conflicting intracommunity views on the personal status laws and the role of state institutions. Believing that the state authorities would not override shariʿa-based sectarian laws, Copts massively opposed the idea that the state could sanction the pope or force him to bend to the judgment of the courts. The repeated analogy indicates how the normative, political, and social pressures of the "majority" determine the changing formations and characteristics of the minority, even the development of modes of individualization and resistance.[26]

Shenuda III endeavored to defend Orthodox dogma, as he interpreted it, against a variety of internal and external "heresies." Conscious of preserving national unity, he never attacked Islam nor publicly criticized the Presbyterian, Egyptian Anglican, or Catholic churches, although he did not prevent his secretary, Anba Bishuy, from doing so. He penned several pamphlets against Adventist and Jehovah's Witness doctrines.[27] Yet the pope's strategic-theological battles were primarily directed toward the Copts themselves: Shenuda III purged the clerical apparatus. In addition to drastically reducing the role of the laity, Shenuda sidelined those whose theological visions did not coincide with his own or whose talents threatened to undermine his prestige. Though it was achieved without the bloodshed and violence that typically accompanies revolutions and coups, the patriarch's project similarly erased his enemies' names and faces from the historical record. At the head of his list of rivals was Matta al-Maskin, who was exiled to his monastery (which he incidentally turned into a prosperous spiritual and economic center), his name and works banned. On October 6, 1981, stray bullets, destined for Sadat, decided the fate of Anba Samuel. The priest Zakarya Butrus, after having first been relieved of his leadership at the Misr al-Gadida church and then imprisoned when Sadat ordered a wave of arrests in 1981, fled Egypt for Australia in an agreement between Shenuda and State Security.[28] Shenuda saw in the priest a figure of charisma and popularity rivaling his own. For their part the authorities wanted to get rid of a character who not only directly took on Islamists on their own ground with his personal interpretation of the Qur'an and Christianity but who openly called (and still calls) for the conversion of Muslims. Nevertheless, Butrus returned to the media scene with the advent of satellite channels, regaining a large audience.[29]

• • •

Shenuda III was not a grand theologian but rather a remarkable administrator and one of the most skillful players on the Egyptian political scene. He engaged in twin operations, to simultaneously centralize and expand the Coptic Orthodox Church, and he knew how to mobilize the community to achieve these goals.

He was not content to simply impose his interpretation of biblical texts but committed himself to control the workings of the clerical institutions.[30] He directly supervised all the key bodies in the clerical administration, in particular the management of the Holy Synod's endowments, restricting again the role and powers of the Majlis al-Milli. Moreover, he reined in the Majlis's authority in matters of personal status. In commissioning the General Council of Clergy, he ensured that any requests touching on personal status would be reviewed by a carefully selected team of members. Anba Bula, who served as head of the council, followed the pope's law with blind obedience, as was evidenced in an exchange between Anba Bula and one woman, frustrated at his refusal to grant her demand for divorce: "You are inciting us to change our denomination or to embrace Islam!" the woman proclaimed, exasperated. Anba Bula responded, calmly: "We will put buses at your disposal, at the corner of the Cathedral, for those of you who wish to convert with the Shaykhs at Al-Azhar."[31]

Shenuda proceeded to overhaul the clerical institutions, "expanding the Eparchies in Egypt from 23 in 1971, to 49 in 2001 . . . and raising the number of bishops by the same proportion. He also developed monastic life, with the nine male monasteries in 1971 growing to 21 in 2001. Monks, no more than 200 at the time of his enthronement, now number more than 1,200; the majority of them former academics."[32] Nevertheless, he ensured that this unprecedented expansion of the clergy did not result in a corresponding multiplication of centers of power. He placed men in the diocese whose loyalty—or obedience—he had acquired, to serve alongside an older generation of bishops who might not cooperate as he wished but whom he could not force to retire without just cause, their attachment to the diocese being a sacrament and not a mere nomination.

The pope integrated the lay community into clerical activities at the same time as he extended the ecclesiastical space into the secular spheres of life. Priests visited Copts more frequently, paying special attention to community members who had left the church, encouraging them to take part in newly organized church activities.[33] The figure of Shenuda thus crystallized a sense of community while new, nongeographic dioceses fostered and supervised the creation of cultural and educational activities. Anba Musa, in charge of international relations, handled a diocese dedicated to youth.[34] At the initiative of

Anba Samuel, the church instituted a network of social services and aid to the poor,[35] a favorite task of a laity that had founded the first charity organizations at the end of the nineteenth century. Priests got involved rather late in this area, and not content to work in bodies dependent on the church, they partook in a growing number of cultural and charitable organizations previously run by laypersons.

Hence, the near totality of secular spheres has been embedded in the signifying and normative logics of an ecclesiastical space that has become the principal and perhaps only "producer of meaning and value" in a national environment increasingly—and often justly—perceived as hostile. The pope's project appears as the mirror-image of the Salafist and Muslim Brotherhood's *shumūliyya* (totalitarian) project that aims to expand supposed Islamic norms and behaviors into public as well as private spaces. Unable to imprint the emblems of Christianity in Egyptian homes and streets, the church incorporated other areas of life. In creating this total space, Shenuda, as he was accused by many observers, encouraged the Copts' withdrawal and isolation behind the "walls of the Church," discouraging their interest in national political life, or anything not directly concerning their own community.

However, the reconfiguration of the Coptic Orthodox Church in Egypt and the construction of Shenudan power rested principally on the pope's foreign policies. Cyril VI had broken the church's isolation by associating with the World Church Council; Shenuda continued this effort and accepted dialogue with Rome on the question of the nature of Christ. The *Common Christological Declaration of Faith* between the Roman and Alexandrine churches, signed by Paul VI and Shenuda III on May 10, 1973, set the first stone in a winding road that led to the *Common Declaration on the Mystery of the Incarnation*. In parallel, the resumption of theological discussions with the Chalcedonian Church, and the dialogue established with the Anglican Church throughout the 1970s, was cemented in a *Common Christological Declaration of Faith*, signed with the former in 1989 and the latter in 1987. Despite the difficulties encountered in the ecumenical dialogue—particularly with the Protestants—the Egyptian church's integration in the network of Roman and Eastern churches allowed the Coptic patriarch to establish direct relations with the religious and political representatives of most countries in the world and to gain thereby an unprecedented international visibility.

Above all, Shenuda transformed the Coptic Church itself into a transnational organization. He actively engaged in policies that facilitated the church's expansion into countries with an Egyptian Christian immigration: the United States, Canada, Australia, Mexico, and in the countries of Europe, where, in France, he founded the first Eparchy in 1973. The church's international prosperity represents, by Shenuda's admission, his proudest accomplishment.[36] The multiplication of churches abroad provided the mother church with a source of revenue that permitted it to complete its Egyptian development project and notably contributed to the enrichment of the monasteries. The transnational stature of the church reinforced the pope's prestige in the community and conferred an unprecedented international political dimension to his see. This was especially the case given another unexpected consequence of the growth of a diaspora population that enjoyed freedoms of expression and association that were restricted for their Egyptian counterparts. Emigrant Christians formed advocacy groups that would relay information from Egypt on the subject of attacks perpetrated against Copts and could exert various pressures on the Egyptian authorities. This activism, led by a tiny Coptic minority and officially disavowed by the church, formed a double-edged sword for the pope in his relations with the Egyptian regime. Shenuda's political success was primarily due to his intelligence around the dynamics that link the community, national, and international scales, and his capacity to pass from one to the other in the appropriate register—confrontation or conciliation—at the opportune moment.

REPRESENTING THE COMMUNITY

The politicization of the patriarchal function is not due simply to the transformation and internationalization of the church. It also relies on the extension of the patriarchal monopoly on the representations of the Copts, while Shenuda combined different types of political and religious representation.

Incarnation and Representation: The Charismatic Process

Elected by censitary (partial or qualified) suffrage,[37] the patriarch serves the Copts through a single term of office—but this is an *ad vitam* term—and his legitimacy is endorsed by the community or, more precisely, its economic, intellectual, and political elites. Following this modern political logic, the pope represents the community insofar as it has granted him the power to decide the religious affairs of the community in its name and has ascribed to him the function of spiritual guide. But the authority bestowed on the pope comes by the virtue of divine choice or, at least, divine assent. This assent is accorded when a name is drawn at random from among three candidates determined by electors. According to religious logic, the patriarch is the image of God on Earth and the intercessor between the divine and the faithful.

The regulation in force, enacted in 1957, fixes the conditions for a candidate's eligibility, the modalities of constituting the electoral college, and the steps in the electoral process, including the final name drawing. Conditions to accede to the papacy include being at least forty years old and having spent at least fifteen years in a monastery. The Holy Synod and the Majlis al-Milli have seven days to convene after the patriarchal seat has been vacated before choosing a kaimakam, who is charged with the management of church affairs until the sacrament of a new pope, and whose nomination has to be endorsed by presidential decree. Within one month of the Patriarchal See's vacancy, the Holy Synod elects eighteen members of a committee tasked with creating a list of candidates. Presided over by the kaimakam, this committee comprises nine bishops and archbishops and nine members of the general Majlis al-Milli. In a third step this committee reviews the candidates registered in the two months following the vacancy of the seat, then lists those deemed admissible. It makes the list public, testing it in this way for potential complaints from any voter, and then establishes a definitive list of candidates (between five and seven). Throughout a fourth step a committee that includes three clergymen and three members of the Majlis, chosen by the kaimakam, registers the hundreds of names that will form the electoral college. The electors have to satisfy several criteria relative to their age (at least thirty-five years old at the time of the seat's vacancy), their income and/or profession, their morality, their level of education, and they are registered in eight categories (three for clergymen, five for laymen). For the fifth step this college then elects three names from among the accepted candidates. Then, in a sixth and final step, these three names are submitted to a drawing. A young child grabs one of the papers, on which are written the names of each candidate. Church tradition holds that a white paper is added to the other three. If the blank paper is drawn, this is interpreted as a divine refusal of the three selected candidates. In this case the draw is performed again using the names of the next three from the approved list of candidates.

Debates on the election process and its possible reform further complicate the entanglement of political and religious registers, raising several questions about the source of patriarchal authority. Kamal Zakhir and others in the Coptic laity wanted the electoral college to be expanded to include all Copts. Adel

Guindy, who first leaned in favor of this "democratization" of clerical institutions, later made a U-turn:

> An election by universal suffrage, what would that mean? That patriarchal candidates will hold election campaigns? This is a complete misunderstanding of the patriarchal function, which is a religious function. The patriarch is not chosen by the community. In the Catholic Church, does the congregation choose the pope? No! Kamal Zakhir, who himself criticized the pope's political interventions on the national scene, argued that political interference in political life places him in a field of relative truths, lies, and corruption, when he should hold the role of spiritual and religious leader. Does Kamal Zakhir not understand that the idea of universal suffrage for the pope totally contradicts his own rejection of a political patriarchal function!?[38]

The representative of God on Earth and the intermediary between the faithful and the hereafter, the pope, from this perspective, is invested with the divine authority at the moment of his coronation. He becomes the image of the divine authority. Thus, his authority is neither founded in, nor even endorsed by, popular majority, and the electoral process simply allows the community to recognize the divine choice.

Like his predecessor, however, Shenuda III understood perfectly well that, in order to reign, he had to gain popular support; the authority vested in him through coronation would remain merely formal were it not sustained by the faith of the community. The mystery of authority resides in this "supplement."[39] Shenuda's case invites us to further reflect on the type of authority, which, from a Weberian perspective, is founded on devotion; "charismatic authority" nevertheless pervades the rational and traditional types of authority.[40] Charismatic authority merely characterizes a religious authority whose source lies in a transcendent order. Yet religion, faith, and devotion grow out of desire. Charisma is thus defined by an economy of desire and a logic of incarnation.[41] Charisma does not arise from a personality, although the leader also qualifies, by derivation of a sort, as "charismatic." Rather, it is a process: at some moment under specific circumstances one person is viewed by a multitude as the incarnation of a "community desire."[42] This person does not simply embody the transcendent order—God or Law, in Kantorowicz's model of royal authority. The charismatic process is twofold, consisting of the incarnation of the transcendent order and the incarnation of the people, hence a bottom-up movement from the multitude toward the "charismatic leader." In this process the multitude forms a "people," an "emotional community," and the leader appears as such, as a leader, insofar as he embodies the desires of the community. Thus, the process of incarnation does not replace, but crystallizes in the worldly and emotional realm, the leader's formal authority as the representative of law and of the divine. This is the schema of the charismatic process, elaborated through case-study analysis. Thus, the charismatic process inherent in Shenuda III's religious function operates in the political sphere and combines three types of authority: his authority as divine intermediary; his authority as embedded in tradition, in the age-old continuity of the Coptic Church; and his rational authority conferred by his election in the electoral college.

Three forms of physical expression put the charismatic process to work: mise-en-scène, language, and pantomime. The leader embodies the desire for group belonging and integrity through a staging that allows this desire to be formulated and communicated. To be sure, from the outset, the church's institutional *dispositif* sets the scene, and the liturgy defines the rules of the game. But the success of the mise-en-scène and, thereby, of the charismatic process also depends on the personality and talents of the leader, on his capacity to attract support through emotional transfer. Let us consider one example among many: in addition to religious ceremonies, Shenuda III would preside over two types of public assembly. In one he would discuss theological problems and issues of interest in the community. In the second he would respond to questions from the audience. Expressing himself in the colloquial Egyptian dialect, he joked readily and provided advice and warnings. Contact was not established so much through the content of expression but rather through the form of expression, especially the material quality of the language: employing the dialect, intonations, and individual interpellations set the scene to establish closeness between the pope and the audience. Yet this close relationship is established in perpetual tension, rooted in the irreducible gap that separates the one from the other. And the pope would play with this tension sometimes, the desire to be blessed by touch: a meeting devoted to theological discussion opens with greetings. The pope takes his place on the platform. One by one, the bishops march by, genuflecting, kissing his hand, embracing him. Several try to murmur a few words in his ear—requests, denunciations, compliments—taking advantage of this moment when, usually distant, he is within earshot. The final bishop hurries, bends down, and places his lips to the hand. The crowd watches, shaken, moved. The pope delivers his brief address. The meeting ends, and Shenuda announces: "Now, you may come and greet me." A wave traverses the hall, the muffled commotion of the crowd rising and moving toward the platform, happy at such a rare opportunity.

A young woman, around twenty-five years old, fidgets at my side and grabs my arms: "Oh yes, already once we were able to greet the Baba, come on, let's go!" At the penultimate row of the spacious mezzanine, as well as in the room below, around two thousand people initiate a confused motion to approach the pope, who, after contemplating this spectacle for several moments in silence, declares, "Here is one thing that I am going to teach you: order (*al-niẓām*)."

This tension between distance and proximity regulates the second register of charismatic authority, which cements the intermediary status of the pope or, as it were, the dual nature of the patriarchal body, not only in the supposedly secular domains of community life but also in national politics. The pope's movements and silence mark his disapproval and anger around several confrontations with the regime and the president. His retreats into the desert, to the monastery of Wadi Natroun, often indicated his disagreement with the leadership's decisions or its failure to make them. If the pope's official discourse was characterized in general by conciliation and temperance, Shenuda showed his discontent and his anger by silence and retreat—negative violence in response to violence.

A third form of expression, the full gamut of facial expressions complemented the grammar of speech and gesture. In the eyes of the community the pope's drawn face or his tears were bodily signs of their own anger, sadness, or revolt and thus made them public and visible. For the charismatic process consists precisely of the affective mobilization of the community and of the embodiment of emotion. Perhaps it is in such moments of emotional mobilization that the totality of the diffuse representations and practices that are called "community" become perceptible to its members. Furthermore, the episodes of confrontation between the Copts and the regime constitute some of the decisive moments in the formation of communitarian sentiment and the personification of the political power of the patriarch.

Through the transfer and the expression of the "community desire," the community and the patriarchal authority appear endowed with tangible and visible reality. Not content with being the image of the divine and of the Coptic "people," the pope extended his monopoly over the entire image of the Copts and the church.

The Patriarchal Monopoly on the Representation of Copts

Having become the Copts de facto political representative, the pope still claimed to oppose any depiction of the Copts that did not conform to the officially authorized image.

The lawyer Ahmed Sayf al-Islam (of the Hisham Mubarak Center)—who might not be suspected of having sympathies toward Islamist trends—affirmed that the church is the body that submits the greatest number of censorship demands.[43] Indeed, the pope's lawyers have stigmatized several works that did not contain any disdain for Christians or Christianity. To be sure, determining insult or prejudice in a text that does not explicitly call for murder is a delicate task, and more delicate still is that of judging the merits of penalizing the insult.[44] Yet the church has criticized works even when the authors express no contempt against Christianity or Christians and where they satisfy artistic or scientific criteria in their discipline. They opposed, for example, the reprint of Jacques Tagher's *Christians in Muslim Egypt: An Historical Study of the Relations Between Copts and Muslims from 640 to 1922*, taking the reins from the Muslim Brothers, who led a campaign against the text's initial publication in Arabic in 1951. According to several observers, the fact that Tagher is Catholic and Syrian would have inspired distrust more than the content of the text itself. Religious identity certainly did not work in the favor of Ahmad al-Sawi and Yusef Zidan as far as the church was concerned: both were Muslims, and the respective authors of the study *al-Muʿallim Yaʿqub bayn al-usṭūra wa-l-ḥaqīqa* (The teacher Yaʿqub: between truth and legend) and the novel *ʿAzāzil*. The tone and subject matter of the works was enough to rouse the ire of clerical bodies and of numerous Copts. In the novel, which takes place at the birth of Christianity in Egypt, Zidan relates episodes in which the church and Christians do not assume the role of the Martyr but of the executioner.[45]

Al-Sawi undertakes a comparative analysis of the texts written on Yaʿqub, the Coptic general who raised an army under Kléber. He claims to finally untangle the truth from the falsehoods that surround this intriguing personality, whose actions have always been the subject of diverging opinions. Al-Sawi concludes that, far from being the "first true Egyptian,"[46] as writer Louis ʿAwad (1915–90) would have liked to believe, Yaʿqub had acted principally to satisfy selfish ends. Al-Sawi draws on a reading of historian Shafiq Ghurbal's text although he removes all the ambiguities involved in Ghurbal's hypothetical historical reconstruction.[47] From the outset al-Sawi evokes the open manner in which the Copts greeted the Napoleonic army,[48] and he seems sympathetic to this attitude. Like so many other discussions on Egyptianness, the debates on General Yaʿqub unfold in the conceptual and idiomatic realm, defined by an "identitarian articulation of meaning."[49] Some consider Yaʿqub a visionary, the first Egyptian nationalist, whose only shortcoming was having relied on the French to help him achieve his goal. Others paint the picture of a traitor to a nation that *had yet to come into existence*, which is not the least of the anachronisms that the debate's protagonists fall into, and from which few have tried to extricate themselves.[50]

Consider two other examples, one from the domain of cinema, the other from news, or more precisely, from scandal. In the month of June 2005 a Christian filmmaker released a film about a Christian family living in the working-class neighborhood of Shubra at the end of the 1960s (in 1967 specifically: in the second half of the film the characters listen to Nasser's famous speech after the defeat in the Six Days' War). In a neighborhood otherwise known for friendly relations between members of the two faiths, at the time of the film a sectarian mistrust had taken root. The characters were, quite simply, ordinary men and women, each carrying their burdens and anxieties, their faults and daily worries. The ordinary is not exemplary. These men and women did not make sacrifices for the well-being of the Coptic people; they ate and they laughed; they told lies and they had desires. The pope's lawyers launched an assault against the film and accused its creator of presenting a deplorable image of Christians.[51] At the time the film was released, a videographer friend of mine interviewed the audiences, most of them surprised to see "themselves" (if Christian) represented onscreen in their most stripped-down form, so to speak. The individuals interviewed rarely expressed reservations about the subject of the film or believed that Christianity or Christians had been denigrated. Rather, several said they preferred this realist and "human" picture (the term featured in several interviewees' reactions) of daily life as opposed to the rare figure of the Coptic stereotype in Egyptian cinema. Nonetheless, hundreds of Copts demonstrated at the 'Abasiyya Cathedral to demand the film's withdrawal and call for sanctions against the filmmakers.[52]

The image of the Copts finally caught the pope's attention in the case of Wafa' Qustantin, although this was not the decisive factor in Coptic engagement at the time. As the wife of a priest, Wafa', more than any other woman, should not have flouted the rules, be they written down or unspoken—for the sake of the church and for the "community." She should have adopted exemplary behavior. Dina El-Khawaga and Febe Armanios have shown how the clericalization of the faithful—a means of institutional control and a way to engage in the project of rebuilding the church—consisted, in one part, of sensitizing priests' families to the moral and ethical implications of their behavior that their status demanded.[53]

These four examples signal simply and unequivocally that the pope opposed the publication and public representation of any figure of a Copt or the church that was not *exemplary*. But, according to the pope, he alone was competent to know what counted as exemplary and which cases might satisfy his criteria.

Mobilizing the Community

Copts have been publicly formulating demands since the 1911 Conference in Assiut, organized by laymen during one of the tensest periods in the history of Christian-Muslim relations. The conference called for Sunday as an official holiday, at least partial state funding for Coptic schools, and an end to discrimination against Copts in the workplace, as access to management posts in the state apparatus remained tacitly prohibited. They had already made demands on the law regarding the construction of places of worship and on the definition of state and church prerogatives regarding personal-status laws. The demands remain, but their number and means of expression have varied as the number of supplicants rises.[54] For instance, the recommended solutions to address Coptic underrepresentation in elected assemblies or to remedy problems with conversion or divorce have never been unanimous. Coptic activism did not form, however, until the beginning of the 1970s, with the exception of the brief and emblematic experience of the Umma Qibtiyya, in 1955, when Ibrahim Hilal organized the first collective Coptic action against the Nasserist reform of confessional tribunals. Coptic activism emanated almost simultaneously from two poles: from the elite Egyptian clergy, with Shenuda III at its head, and from emigrant Christian groups in the United States and Canada. At this time these two principal currents of Coptic dissent neither mobilized the same resources nor planned any coordinated actions. Similar motifs have triggered Coptic anger since the 1970s: an attack on the church—its laws, symbols, members, or buildings—and the denigration of symbols of the Christian religion, or attacks against places of worship and violations of Coptic personal-status law. Other, more directly inflammatory, situations might be attacks against Christians, on their property, or their land, pressures exerted so that young women convert, or interreligious romances. Coptic dissent from the clergy primarily used religious symbols, spaces, and rituals as a sign of anger and protest. At the behest of the pope, the first major Coptic mobilization occurred on November 12, 1972, at Khanka, in the Nile Delta region, at the ruins of a church that had been burned six days before. The leader of Coptic dissent in Egypt in the 1970s and the beginning of the 1980s, Shenuda adopted a more accommodating position toward the regime at the end of his forced exile from 1981 to 1985.

Serious disagreements arose between Sadat and Shenuda. Though Shenuda managed to avoid the prison where Sadat had dispatched a not insubstantial portion of the Egyptian population, he did not escape the destitution that was arbitrarily decided by the Presidential Decree of September 3, 1981.[55] The existence of personal differences (which Shenuda constantly denied) are not necessary to understand the heightening of tensions that led Sadat to banish the pope to a residence at the monastery of Anba Bishuy in Wadi Natrun and then nominate a "committee of five" (*lajna al-khamsa*) to replace him, which included Matta al-Maskin. But the Holy Synod refused to recognize the committee, and Shenuda, unofficially, began personally managing church affairs from a distance, until he was officially restored to his office in 1985. Several political factors—at the international, regional, national, and sectarian level—converged, leading to open confrontation between Sadat and Shenuda.

At the beginning of the 1970s Shenuda and Sadat simultaneously reached the peak of their respective "nations." They each succeeded a charismatic figure (Cyril VI and Nasser), and each wished to initiate a change of direction. They had both had to impose themselves as the head of their communities and their peers. If he had not died suddenly, Nasser would have undoubtedly named someone else to the post of vice president. Sadat's nomination as vice president had not been taken seriously by Nasser's companions.[56] Yet 'Ali Sabri and his clan—strong figures in the Nasserist era—were expecting to use him for their desired political ends. Once he attained the presidency, Sadat removed Sabri and his allies (during the "corrective revolution"). To be sure, in the Coptic world Shenuda's name had been chosen by the drawing of lots. But Anba Samuel had previously received a greater vote than that of Shenuda. After the first phase of confrontation, triggered at Khanka in November 1972, Sadat and Shenuda saw several groups rise at their "right hands"—namely Islamists (of all trends) and Coptic activists abroad. In a way the Islamists' project overlapped Sadat's, just as the Coptic activists' project did Shenuda's, although they employed a more radical rhetoric. Yet, if these two trends could serve the leaders' objectives, they nevertheless espoused incompatible political agendas.

Indeed, the pope's international policies had aroused some emigrant Copts' interest in the situation of Christians in Egypt. Activists initiated protest actions in the United States to denounce the regime's attitude toward Christians. Certainly, Shenuda recognized the validity of Egyptian American activists' claims and understood the expatriates' anger. But he did not share all of their wishes and, a longtime Egyptian nationalist, he did not subscribe to a mode of dissent that would involve pressure from a third state or foreign institution to resolve national problems.[57] For his part Sadat did not oppose the (liberal) "Islamization" of Egyptian society, but would he sacrifice the realization of his own priorities (peace with Israel) for the project of the codification and application of shari'a? In fact, though he appeared in favor of the project (by forming a committee charged with drafting the code, discussing the text in high places, mediatizing the issue, etc.), he did not actually allow for its success. The issue was never submitted to a plenary session at the People's Assembly, and his successor closed the file.

The eventual codification of shari'a and the application of punishment for apostasy had, however, contributed to the second important conflict between the pope and the regime, and it drove the first protest actions of Coptic activists abroad. Sadat was willing to concede certain points to the Islamists, to avoid swelling opposition to his peace project with Israel.[58] However, there was no way he was going down in history, or to the White House, as an "executioner of Christians." He aspired to the role of champion of the Arab-Israeli peace and of Egypt's economic and political liberalization. So he was exasperated when, in August 1977, Christian activists demonstrated in the United States against the project of the codification of shari'a law. Rightly or wrongly, he held Shenuda responsible for their actions.[59] Through intermediaries, by threatening to annul the presidential decree endorsing Shenuda's nomination to the See of Saint Mark, Sadat convinced the pope to write to the activists, encouraging them to remain calm. On September 10, 1977, Shenuda wrote to the American activists, advising them to offer the president a warm welcome. Outside of this request Shenuda's role in the demonstrations remains a matter of discussion. To be sure, by strengthening the bonds between the church and the exiled Copts, he had fostered the rise of Coptic activism abroad. Furthermore, he had personally expressed his disagreement with Sadat's politics. There is no concrete evidence, however, of a collaborative project between the pope and the activists. Opinions diverge, especially on how quickly the pope had shut down their activity and the degree of ambiguity in the letter. Independently of his opinion on the demands of activists in the United States and the means used to achieve them, Shenuda was certainly reluctant to intervene without knowing whether this flock raised in a pluralist context, and outside of the Egyptian community, would willingly back him.[60] Rather, he mobilized the community in Egypt. He declared a three-day fast as a sign of protest in September 1977 and met with bishops, members of the Majlis al-Milli, and other representatives of the "Coptic people" at the conference in Alexandria several months later. Never before had the church organized an assembly of such import, comparable only to the Assiut Conference, which had been called for by laymen—a significant difference. The participants published a memorandum from the conference that outlined the different problems facing the community, particularly how to oppose the project of the application of shari'a. They addressed it to the "President of the Republic," other official bodies, embassies, and press agencies.

Most especially, Shenuda refused to support the peace initiative between Egypt and Israel, and he maintained the ban on pilgrimages to holy sites in Palestine as long as it remained under occupation.[61] For Sadat the inflexibility of the patriarchal position on this question was an unforgivable offense and violated the tacit understanding that state religious institutions were subordinate to the political government.

More than thirty years after the Khanka events, the Wafa' Qustantin incident marked the return of the "Coptic issue" to the center of political debates and tactics and the renewal of Coptic activism in Egypt and abroad. The shared elements of the two affairs are as striking as their divergences. At Khanka it was the monks, priests, and bishops that the pope called to dissent, providing transportation to the sites of the conflict. After 2001 the youth took the lead, railing against a journalist of the weekly *al-Naba'* that had revealed the sexual prowess of a defrocked priest. In 2004 they demanded Wafa' Qustantin's return, and then, in 2005, they retaliated when faced with attacks following the distribution of a CD-ROM containing a dramatic pamphlet hostile to Islam.[62] In 1972 the pope called clerics to prayer and sacrifice, drawing on the importance of the figure of the martyr in Coptic orthodox imagery.[63] In 2004 demonstrators brutally assailed public personalities and welcomed the forces of order by hurling stones.

The clergy and the patriarch, however, encouraged and framed the uprising. Indeed, several clergymen had instigated it when they spread the story of Wafa' Qustantin's kidnapping and forced conversion or when they failed to deny the rumor. Other clerics served to keep spirits up. Anba Yu'annis excelled in this function, and the pope had often turned to him when it was necessary to hold discussions with the youth.[64] Local clergy played a decisive role in other cases of mobilization—for example, at Dir Abu Hinnis in 2009. For his part Anba Matiyas Nasr Manqariyus founded an organization, Copts for Egypt (*aqbāṭ min ajl miṣr*), which has called for protests on several occasions since 2005.[65] Clergymen have played a crucial role in twenty-first century mobilizations in one other way: by taking on a fundamentalist stance, they had been the agents of twentieth-century change in the Coptic Church and, thus, of the formation of a closed communitarian space. Coptic youth have been born and raised in this space, never having known a time without sectarian violence, the memory of which their elders clung to.

Apparently, Shenuda led the battle in December 2004 and decided to change the scale of mobilization in favor of Wafa' Qustantin's return. A master in the art of anger and sadness, and able to draw on the symbolic register of religious rituals, the pope turned each tear into a political act. The patriarchal recourse to the religious repertoire as a mode of political dissent has been studied extensively, as has his call for the community to mobilize.[66] The retreat to Wadi Natroun, the suppression of the weekly sermon in 2004, and the three-day fast announced after government tanks crushed demonstrators at Maspero in October 2011 immediately called to mind similar gestures of the 1970s and early 1980s. But these spectacular acts are generally coupled with discussions behind the scenes, if not public threats. When, in December 2004, the pope announced that he would not preach and would retire to Wadi Natroun, he explicitly (albeit tacitly) signaled to the authorities that they could expect to do battle with thousands of furious youth, whose anger would increase tenfold after his departure, and not with clerics who were still novices in the art of public protest.

In this latter period young people have been equally important in the mobilization of the Coptic Orthodox Church's symbolic and material resources. In what was a rare occurrence before 2000, they display Christian symbols outside of the religious sphere. The church—as a place and an institution, with the structural and organizational resources that either provides—is no longer the sole space of dissent. The youth now invest the public space. After a first attempt to enter the streets of ʿAbasiyya was pushed back by security forces in 2004, protestors marched in Alexandria in 2005 while displaying the sign of the cross.[67] With this gesture they unambiguously placed Christian and sectarian values and norms in the public space, side by side with and equal to, or above, Islamic values and norms. Throughout the following years Copts have taken to the streets several times. In Cairo in February 2010, Copts for Egypt called a gathering in Tahrir Square as a sign of protest and mourning after the murder of six Copts in the Upper Egyptian village of Nagʿ Hammadi on Christmas Day. Carrying streamers, bearing large crosses, and waving Egyptian flags, the demonstrators chanted slogans that expressed their anger over the bloodshed. They called for the president's intervention, demanding justice and underscoring Coptic roots in the Egyptian soil ("*iḥna aṣl miṣr*," literally: we are the origin of Egypt). The public expression of Coptic anger sometimes took over villages, and the crowd that demonstrated in Dir Abu Hinnis, in the Minya Province, in June 2009 threatened to follow up the action in the capital. Women and children joined the men in Cairo and Dir Abu Hinnis, as well as in other demonstrations that followed at a rapid rate.

Having abandoned his rebellious attitude, why did the pope enter into a confrontation with the regime after the disappearance of Wafa' Qustantin in 2004, after the verdict pronounced in May 2010, and after the *al-Naba'* case in 2001? Was he truly taking on the confrontational stance that marked the Sadat era, an analogy often made by observers? On the problem of the relations between the church and the state, Mariz Tadros's work differs from mine, for several reasons. In her 2009 article she places great importance on the episodes of tension between the church and the regime—the confrontations with Sadat, the Wafa' Qustantin affair, and finally the 2006 coronation of Maximos (Max Michel, a dissident who had declared himself patriarch of a rival church)[68] and the pope's corresponding refusal to support the NDP in the Shura Council elections. By doing so, Tadros undoubtedly overestimates the disruptive force of these events. As I see it, she does not take a long enough overview of the structuring factors: the church's dependence on the state while the renegotiations of each of their prerogatives do not break the biased pact between the church and the regime party. I will clarify: in the 2000s Shenuda was not opposed to Mubarak's policies, in that they differed from those of Sadat on two essential points. For one, the patriarchal position on Israel no longer troubled the regime as it had during Sadat's presidency. For the other, the political elites surrounding the Mubarak clan were, on the whole, hostile toward the Brothers. This attitude evidently did not exclude their shared values, norms, and practices in a ruling elite and society saturated with Islamic codes. And, certainly, the ideological struggle of the NDP against the Brotherhood discourse unfolded in large part in the moral realm and by one-upmanship on the Brothers' opinions. But the alliance between the regime and the pope in the 2000s and the support that the latter granted the NDP during elections have not been fundamentally questioned. In fact, the church under Shenuda revealed several times that this support was not unconditional but depended on the regime's capacity to protect Copts and to accord the pope a certain autonomy in respect of Coptic norms and rules. Such was the tacit pact that founded the alliance between the church and the regime.

At the time of the *al-Naba'* issue the violation of the first "clause" of the pact increased the inflexibility of the patriarchal position. The paper revealed the sexual activities of a defrocked monk shortly after the bloodiest episodes that had been seen since 1981 (Zawayia al-Hamra), the second wave of violence in the village of al-Kushih, where twenty-one Christians were killed with impunity. Similarly, the increased attacks against Copts from 2006 to 2007 incited several bishops to launch a brief campaign against the possible candidacy of Gamal Mubarak in the presidential elections. And, for the first time, the pope refused to support NDP candidates in the Shura Council elections in 2006—which were admittedly less important than the People's Assembly elections.[69] But if the church had its own ways of pressuring the government, the pope had learned that their efficacy was minimal compared to what the regime could mobilize against the church. Shenuda knew that he could exert more influence over government decisions by being closer to the ruling circles. In other words one-time opposition to a state decision was not as effective in achieving the pope's objectives (enacting what he believed to be a satisfactory unified personal status law, for instance) as was a fundamental alliance and the respect of a pact, even a biased one, that would link him to the party in power. But the focus of international institutions on religious freedom and minority rights sometimes allowed the pope to negotiate a higher price for the church's active support, without appearing to comply with these institutions' demands. Hence, Shenuda always refused to receive delegates from the U.S. Department of State charged with investigating religious freedom in Egypt.

The regime and the pope also agreed on the second "clause" of this biased pact, the legislative autonomy of the church in matters of personal status, despite the recurrence of conflicts about the setting of precise boundaries to this autonomy. In the Wafa' Qustantin affair the church and the state merely violated the law and Wafa' Qustantin's rights. Although this mobilization has sometimes been interpreted to mean the return of confrontation between representatives of the church and the state, no norm was jeopardized, no political alliance broken. The church, the state, and society are fundamentally in agreement on the requirement that individuals maintain the "status quo" and not leave their religions. Wafa' was required to return, and order was restored without the difficult episode having affected the collusion between the leadership and the pope nor having disturbed the church's allegiance to the regime. At the most, some took it on themselves to "tease" the pope a little for a lack of moderation and for giving hubris free rein in his attempts to extend his authority outside of the religious realm: several observers read the 2005 CD episode in Alexandria and the Coronation of Maximos as a retaliation by State Security agents in attempts to embarrass the pope. But the principle of separated personal-status laws rarely arose at the time of this crisis. Far from showing the strength of the church—a "state within a state"[70]—that alone could make the regime submit to its desires, the incident revealed what everyone already knew: the patriarch's power and that of the Egyptian state representative were not built on the same foundations. The patriarch was endowed with authority. The power of the Egyptian regime was unfounded, illegitimate. The authoritarian regime was without authority. The arbitrary, alone, prevailed. This fact was one of the instruments of its power—it could punish or reward whenever, wherever, and whoever it saw fit—but it was also one of its sources of fragility.

These events equally reveal the existence of criticism within the church. By defending Coptic personal status law, the pope did not so much seek to establish his power on the national scene as to situate his authority in the community *in the first place*. We should devote as much attention to the internal power struggles of the church as to its more visible confrontations with state power, or between the pope and the regime. Internal dissension and increasing criticism of patriarchal power were essential factors in shaping dissenting action. In fact, internal tension determined Shenuda's choice each time that he led or supported a demonstration against the government. In 1972, for example, the episode at Khanka took place at a crucial moment for Shenuda, as a young pope attempting to prove himself on the Coptic and national scene. At that time the Coptic Church was experiencing "an open intra-ecclesiastical conflict for the first time."[71] In 1972 the pope was the principal leader of the mobilizations. After 2004, particularly with the Wafa' Qustantin affair, Coptic youth were at the forefront of the opposition. In an equally virulent manner they also denounced the church representatives' submission to the regime, which, indeed, is seen as a lesser evil, though still an accomplice, whether actively or passively, in the Islamization of collective space and of political language, anti-Coptic abuse, and the massive distribution of literature hostile to Christianity. In 2010 Coptic demonstrators entered into direct confrontation and violence against the security forces on several occasions, for example after the attack on the Two Saints Church in Alexandria from December 31 to January 1, 2011, when they criticized both the government's attitude and the pope's unwavering support for the regime. The patriarchal position on the Wafa' Qustantin affair only partially attained its objective, which was to assemble the community behind its leader. Faced with the deluge of criticism that it inspired, the majority of Copts were careful not to add to it. Those who admitted, privately, to disagreeing with this patriarchal interference on individual freedoms, did so only after the crisis had passed.

THE MARRIAGE OF CONVENIENCE BETWEEN THE CHURCH AND THE REGIME

Shenuda never called his alliance with political and economic elites into question. He remained loyal to the general line taken by the Coptic Orthodox Church, although there had been numerous revolts against the decisions of the temporal powers throughout its long history.[72] But neither Christian teachings nor the "statute" of being a minority accounted for the support that the patriarch and the majority of Copts showed for three successive rulers.[73] In a context of permanent tension and recurrent violence the Coptic Church, itself a state organ, remained dependent on the actions of the agents of other state institutions. Despite the autonomy that the church enjoyed, the state was still needed for any legislative modification, or to construct churches, and so on. The pope's official discourse, the close bonds between the high clergy and the economic and political elites (including the State Security and Intelligence services), and the church's position with regard to elections represented the three modes of allegiance to the ruling party and its henchmen, which endured until February 2011.

Shenuda III generally maintained a discourse marked by temperance; he showed his anger and disapproval by silence and actions. He always took care to remind his interlocutors that he spoke as a man of religion, and he was particularly careful to do so when discussing political issues. For the most part Shenuda would manage to give opinions in line with his own political agenda, to set forth a point of view in line with Egypt's political elite, to formulate the desires and grievances of his community, and to avoid angering either the activists abroad or the Muslim Brotherhood. To achieve such a feat required a certain lack of precision with language, but the pope's political actions proved that this ambiguity indicated neither confusion in his ideas nor a fault in his diplomatic intuition. A paragon of equivocation, Shenuda was one of the subtlest speakers on the Egyptian political scene.

His position on the Israeli-Egyptian peace had enraged Sadat. It harked back to the political line during Mubarak's reign: the regime would let slip its verbal support for the Palestinian people at opportune moments and would publicly oppose any normalization of relations with Israel, meanwhile still pursuing policies that were often favorable to Israel and carrying on de facto normalization in several economic sectors. Also, the patriarchal ban on travel to Jerusalem—first formulated by Cyril VI and reiterated by Shenuda III—created the illusion of Arab solidarity that, in the eyes of Egyptian opinion, bolstered the country's image more than tarnished it. Frequently invoked as proof of the pope's Egyptian and Arab nationalism, his position on the Israeli-Palestinian conflict seemed all the more remarkable in that, in its radicalism, it strengthened the government's official position and ran counter to a Coptic position that was inclined to reject Arabism.

An Egyptian nationalist, Shenuda did not conceive of the ethnicization of a community identity that, from his perspective, rested on religious foundations. The Copts' negation of Arabism did not align with the patriarchal vision of Coptic and Egyptian identity. Though certain bishops sometimes expressed a point of view that Shenuda would not want to be made public, Anba Tuma probably did not have the pope's tacit approval for his 2008 Hudson Institute speech. Nevertheless, by supporting the transformation and extension of the ecclesiastical space, Shenuda enhanced the emergence of the ethnicist narrative, which also drew on the international rhetoric around the rights and protection of ethnic minorities.

Shenuda III did not officially raise an objection to the maintenance of Article 2 in the Egyptian Constitution. The five-day fast announced in 1977 and the other signs of opposition to the codification of the shari'a were aimed at a legislative project to apply punishment for apostasy at a time of resurgent attacks against Copts. In his public pronouncements on the subject of the constitutional article, Shenuda would sometimes ask:

> What is shari'a? Is it what extreme radicals (*al-mutaṭarrifīn al-mutashaddidīn*) invoke? Is it what we read in the sura "al-Baqara": "no coercion in religion?" Or that of "Yūnus": "Had your Lord wished that all those on earth would believe, you would force them until they become faithful?" Is it shari'a when some interpret it to mean opposition to peaceful coexistence and mutual tolerance between Christians and Muslims? The interpretation of shari'a requires clarification so that no-one, not only Copts, but many categories of people, fears."[74]

Shenuda raised these questions in April 2007 after the president had submitted the proposal to amend thirty-six constitutional articles, not including Article 2, to referendum. The presidential decision presented an occasion to debate not only this article but major constitutional reform, which opposition activists in organizational networks deemed indispensable. The press campaign around the possible creation of a Brotherhood Party partially determined the content of these debates. As a harbinger, in 2005 Yuhanna Qulta, a Catholic, caused an uproar when he called for the removal of the article. Mahdi 'Akif, then the Supreme Guide of the Muslim Brothers, responded by saying that such a demand constituted "a red line not to be crossed." Copts expressed diverging opinions on Article 2. Some shared the patriarchal point of view. Others argued that the potential multiplicity of interpretations of Islamic texts should incite the Constituent to remove the references to shari'a, or to any religion as it were, from the Constitution. Several persons (bishops in particular) proposed revisiting the formulation of the pre-1980 amendment: shari'a is "a" source and not "the" source of legislation. Some suggested explicitly mentioning other sources: the Universal Declaration of Human Rights, international covenants ratified by Egypt, even principles of the Christian religion. The degree to which the Copts were amenable to accepting mention of Islam in the Constitution greatly depended, however, on the political context and manner in which the Constitution was enacted. Aptly, Samir Murqus remarked on this fact, although his analysis proposed a questionable vision, idealizing the so-called liberal period in general, as well as the committee in charge of drafting the 1923 Constitution in particular.[75] Shenuda protested against a project of shari'a's codification that would involve the application of discriminatory laws and oppose Christian principles in a context of exacerbated violence. Nonetheless, he presented no objection in principle to shari'a as long as its mention in the Constitution did not lead to the erosion of Christians' rights or undermine the foundations of Christian standards and values within the community. This position indicated that Shenuda's theological-political outlook was more easily integrated into a state governed in reference to Islamic religious principles, as long as state institutions recognized the church's legislative authority on Christians' personal-status matters, than into a secularized state that would not allow any legislative autonomy to clerical institutions. Unlike many Coptic activists, Shenuda was always opposed to using the term *minority* to qualify the political status of Copts. He also did not encourage the eventual creation of a Coptic party,[76] nor did he support the recurring demand for a system of affirmative action and proportional representation of Christians in the elected assemblies. Calling on Copts to engage in political life as citizens, independent of their religious affiliation, he enunciated a discourse that conformed to the one churned out by Egyptian leaders. This same discourse was repeated in chorus by most political figures who, holding that Christians and Muslims enjoyed equal rights, posited that distinguishing between them would endanger national unity.

The revival of Coptic activism in Egypt and in the diaspora, the attention that international bodies give to the freedom of belief and the respect for the rights of religious minorities, as well as the dwindling number of politically active Christians, all contributed to curbing the patriarchal discourse on Copts' political participation and representation. When asked about the quota system in 2007, Shenuda responded:

> The principal objective lies in opening the public space to citizens of all religions so that all may participate in the political life of their country. As for the means to achieve this and what we call it, that's another thing. What's important is that all religions in society are represented, independently of the proportion of that representation. It is necessary to give priority to the presiding spirit of political life, and not the letter of the law, and to pay attention to what experiences and circumstances tell us. The problem is not one of text, but effective solutions to come to a result that is acceptable for all.[77]

In this way the pope admitted the need for the political representation of religious communites. He took care, however, not to restrict the topic solely to Christians and to cut short the controversy around the number of Copts by specifying "independently of the proportion." This shift did not signal any change in patriarchal politics or the adoption of any new syntax. In his prudent and ambiguous response the pope managed not to completely exclude the quota solution, in this way addressing the diaspora activists, the majority of whom advocated for its establishment. He reaffirmed that concrete measures, more than new laws, would encourage Copts to engage in politics, this time addressing the leadership and the portion of Copts that were hostile to the idea of quotas. The style of patriarchal intervention in the Egyptian elections clearly showed how Shenuda based his tactics on "experiences and circumstances." Relying on the audible critique to his political plan, it would seem that neither the results nor the pragmatic solution were "acceptable for all."

Shenuda's official discourse and his public positions in favor of the regime and the NDP were but the most visible aspects of the system of alliances and allegiances among the clergy, the economic and political elites, and government representatives. These hierarchical networks of interests and influence were established according to rules common to all Egyptians and were based on family and professional relationships, local solidarities (*baladiyyāt*), skills, goods, and services that each could offer. At the apex the patriarch and the president could directly engage with one another. Diverse intermediaries sometimes took the role of spokespersons, like Zakaria al-ʿIzmi and Mustafa al-Fiqi, whom the president frequently gave the responsibility of carrying out discussions with Shenuda. The issue of the 2010 legislative elections was left to party representative, businessman, and MP Ahmad ʿIzz,[78] who was close to Gamal Mubarak and was charged with corruption after Mubarak's fall. Equally, Shenuda employed his contacts in State Security and Intelligence, as well as several members of the high clergy. Following transformations in the Egyptian political class, Coptic businessmen filled the ranks of the pope's entourage, multiplying the bonds between the high clergy and the Mubaraks' various political and business circles.[79] Like their Muslim counterparts, Coptic businessmen looked to play a role on the electoral and media scene. Tharwat Basili was a success story in both domains, a member of the Shura Council, the Pharmacists' Union, Majlis al-Milli, and founder and owner of the pharmaceutical company Amoun, and he helped to found a Coptic TV channel.[80] The election to the Majlis al-Milli often represents the first step on the path to national political notability. But both depend on the pope, who selects the names of winning candidates for the council and whom the NDP would consult to determine which Copts would be included on their lists for the assemblies. Moreover, a candidate's chances were almost nil if he were to seek an elected seat without the active support of the pope or, at least, of the local clergy.

Like the Islamic institutions, the Coptic Church always supported the sole candidate in the plebiscite elections for president without significant reaction from Copts (or Egyptians in general). Before 2005 it was also rare that any voice would be raised against the fact that the pope politically represented the Copts to the government authorities. Few Copts publicly protested against the elite leadership's consultation with the patriarch on the matter of whom he wished to see nominated to the People's Assembly.[81] By contrast, in the new context of presidential elections with several candidates, the organization of which raised hopes and loosened tongues, the patriarchal injunction to vote for the incumbent (formulated just after al-ʿIzmi's visit to Shenuda) drew significant criticism from both Muslims and Copts.[82] The critiques were more pronounced because of the timing, less than a year after the Wafaʾ Qustantin affair, when the pope had already overstepped his prerogatives. Denouncing politicians' propensity to make the Copts a quasi-political (or at least electoral) entity, the analyst Samih Fawzi consented that the church as an institution took a candidate's side but did not do so in the name of all those it represented in the religious realm.[83] Patriarchal intervention did not consist of a simple declaration but a full-scale campaign that included organizing transportation to polling stations. The Holy Synod addressed a letter of support to the president. The high clergy gave directives to all dioceses so that bishops and preachers would encourage their congregations to head to the polls. Anba Salib Matta Sawiris (bishop of the churches of Mar Jirjis, Shubra, and Cairo) and Murqus 'Aziz (bishop of the suspended church in Old Cairo)[84] defended the patriarch by referring to biblical teachings that advocated the church's submission to temporal powers, evoking the pope's right—his duty, even—"to orient the community on the right path and to distance them from the wrong one"; they denied the binding nature of his "advice."[85] Several bishops (including Anba Bishuy, the bishop of the Damietta diocese and secretary general of the Holy Synod) dedicated time to preaching in favor of Mubarak. Employing the biblical expression "blessed people" (*sha'b mubārak*), Anba Kirillus (bishop of Nag' Hammadi in Sohag) went as far as to say that voting for Mubarak was a divine injunction and that "the Church was the NDP."[86] Moreover, the church criticized, or even condemned, the regime's opposition. The pope declared that "the Church has nothing to do with George Ishaq [who is active in the Kifaya movement], who is not a son of the Church."[87] The priest of the Church of the Virgin Mary in Tawabiq, in Giza, Filubatir 'Aziz, was suspended from his function for his affiliation with the al-Ghad Party, which was led by presidential candidate Ayman Nour,[88] and because he had published political texts in the party paper.[89]

Shenuda III supported the regime and the NDP during the revolutionary days, after which the army "strongly recommended" that Mubarak step down on February 11, 2011. Two days later, certain that the president's departure was definitive, according to several observers, Shenuda praised "Egypt's courageous army" and the "honest youth of January 25 who had led a powerful revolution" and had "offered its blood." He pronounced himself in favor of a "civil [*madanī*] and democratic state" and "free elections." Questioning the criteria for creating parties from the outset, Shenuda had expressed the Coptic fear of the Brothers' accession to power in cloaked language. In the absence of a ruling party candidate in the 2011 legislative elections, the church recommended voting in favor of the Egyptian Bloc, an electoral coalition that included the Liberal Party, established by Coptic businessman Naguib Sawiris after the revolution. Faced with an Islamist electoral victory, Shenuda offered a gesture of reconciliation to the newly elected sovereign: in vain he invited the Muslim Brotherhood and Salafist parties to celebrate Christmas and expressed his support for the military, which had lost legitimacy in the months of repression that followed the revolutionary moment. After the year of fright during Mursi's presidency, the church and the majority of Copts have sided with 'Abd al-Fattah al-Sisi, who took care to renew the alliance with Tawadros, the pope crowned in 2012. Al-Sisi has increased attentive gestures toward the community—for example, attending the Coptic Christmas mass in January 2015 and again in 2016.

The reconfigurations of the Egyptian political scene did not lead to recreating the state apparatus nor to a redefinition of the relations between state institutions and leaders; the structural reasons for the church's bond to the regime, whatever its political orientation may be, have remained unchanged.

• • •

Changes in the Coptic Church under Cyril VI and then Shenuda III turned the community sphere into a space marked by ambiguity: it did not correspond to the ideal of *ecclesia* reimagined by the revivalists, who advocated a "return" to the original church in the sense derived from the ancient meaning of an "assembly of citizens"—that is to say, the "assembly of believers." Having become a world in itself, it was defined, by opposition to the exterior world, as a sacred space governed by religious rules. Yet the growth of the ecclesiastical space produced profane areas within this sacred space. Following the same logic, the attempts to sanctify the patriarchal authority, coupled with the expanding sphere of Shenuda's authority outside the religious realm, exposed the pope's theological and political positions to the relativity and diversity that define the secular world.[90] By "descending into the world," the pope had himself opened the door to criticism and renewed questioning of the principles that governed his own decisions.

Shenuda's theological-political project met with relative failure because of external factors, as well as contradictions revealed in its very execution. His expansionist aims weakened the centralizing project; all empire builders are confronted with this dilemma. Despite the control that the central bodies exerted over local bishops, the centers of religious and political authority multiplied, in part because of the establishment of bonds forged with other churches and overseas Christian organizations. Critics raised their voices in great number, challenging patriarchal positions in national politics and Shenuda's unwavering support for the Egyptian regime. Initially quiet and expressed, for example, in the unformulated refusal to follow the pope's electoral suggestions, critics—the Coptic laity, public personalities, dissident priests, and the youth—raised the volume of their voices. They saw their apogee in the revolutionary moment. Then, during the Christmas sermon in January 2012, the audience interrupted the pope in the middle of his address to the Egyptian army, shouting "Down with military rule!"[91]

The pope's totalizing project did not hamper the community's (particularly the youth element's) straying from the paths traced by the orthodoxy, and sometimes outside of the Coptic world altogether. Undoubtedly, he instead stimulated their search, just as his inflexibility on divorce had encouraged circumvention of confessional laws. The attitude of reconverts and young women appears in many ways equivocal, often falling under acritical subversion. Certainly, several reconverts fought for the adoption of a secular personal status law or demanded that existing Coptic orthodox law be amended to extend the number of cases eligible for divorce. Some formulated this demand publicly, in the press or through demonstrations. Many, however, used conversion as a subterfuge to avoid confrontation with the clerical hierarchy. More often than not, they simultaneously expressed an attachment to the current laws, which often goes hand in hand with a deep contempt for the "other's" law and religion. In a more radical manner, but without critiquing the patriarchal family structure that Shenuda promoted, young women converting to Islam opted for a brutal and total rupture from the family and the community. Yet this departure from a Coptic religious affiliation did not signify a rejection of the communitarian order.

4 INTRACOMMUNITARIAN DYNAMICS AND TENSIONS

Members of other Christian denominations, as well as Coptic lay elites, had long criticized the pope's policies and the authoritarian, even dictatorial, style in which he directed the community's affairs. Increasing cause for discontent, transformations in the Egyptian media, the impending prospect of the pope's succession, and the relative liberation of public speech from 2005 to 2007 enhanced the sometimes outrageous media coverage of internal church disputes and interclerical rivalries. Opposition to the pope's theological-political project did not express itself only through different points of view and internal conflicts. It also took shape through religious practices that, though they were the product of Shenuda's sectarian order, represented subversions or modes of resistance to the religious, political, and social orthodoxy that his project forged.

POLITICAL ACTIVISM IN THE LAITY: FROM THE UMMA QIBTIYYA TO THE PRESENT DAY

The experience of the Umma Qibtiyya (1952–54) was one of the last attempts at reform led by laypersons up to the present day, and the attempt remains something of a landmark. "God is our king, Egypt our country, the Gospel our law, the cross our emblem, Egyptian our language, and martyrdom for Christ our utmost desire." (*Allah maliknā, miṣr bilādnā, al-injīl shari'atnā, al-ṣalīb rāyatnā, al-miṣriyya lughatnā wa-l-shahāda li sāliḥ al-masīḥ ghāya al-rajā'.*)

The Umma Qibtiyya is best known for its exploit on the night of July 23, 1954. The event made the cover of *al-Ahram* and appeared in the foreign press.[1] In reality the episode speaks for itself, as it testifies to a salient and rarely mentioned feature of the Nasserist era: its "Ubuesque" dimension, in the words of

Aclimandos.[2] That night, armed men entered the patriarchal chamber, which was located at that time on Clot Bey Street in the Cairene neighborhood of Faggala, and demanded that Pope Yusab II renounce the See of Saint-Mark in favor of Anba Sawiris, the bishop of Minya. Dazed, Yusab II stammered in his astonishment: "But why? Why? Why?" Succumbing to their "arguments," as they dragged him, still in his nightclothes, to the Mar Jirjis monastery in Old Cairo, he signed the document of abdication to be submitted for approval by the Holy Synod.

Ibrahim Hilal, the group's leader, called General Muhammad Naguib, president of the Republic until November 1954, to inform him of the developments. Naguib exclaimed "*Ya Ibrahim*! As long as there is no blood and you don't implicate the régime, you are free to do as you wish."[3] In reinstating Yusab to the patriarchal seat, the state came up against the Holy Synod's refusal to recognize him and finally had to endorse his decision to abdicate. The kidnappers were arrested, but this was not the main charge brought against them at the court martial. As Kamal Zakhir and Muhammad 'Afifi have noted, the chief accusation concerning the pope's abduction was not mentioned until the very end of a list of charges. It was their prior program and actions that the regime considered a more serious harm than this operation, which touched only on the internal affairs of the church.[4] In fact, the organization had already been dissolved in April 1954, even before this armed feat.

Founded on Coptic New Year, September 11, 1952, by Ibrahim Fahmi Hilal, an eighteen-year-old law student, the Umma Qibtiyya obtained official status as an organization from the Ministry of Social Affairs. According to Hilal, the group was dissolved on April 23, 1954, because of a memorandum he had sent to the Constituent Assembly. The dissolution occurred at the moment when the regime had begun to limit any political or religious expression and to worry about the political consequences of an organization created in explicit opposition to the Muslim Brotherhood. It experienced a brief revival in 1955 during Nasser's judicial reform, but then its founder was forgotten, exiled in France, where he taught law. The organization's platform had two components. It wished to contribute to national construction while promoting Coptic culture rooted in a Pharaonic heritage, and it demanded a legislative and jurisdictional autonomy for the "Coptic nation"—the *umma qibṭiyya*.

"We were dreaming of constructing a new society, in collaboration with the new state," Hilal declared. With this in mind the organization addressed a memorandum to the Constituent Assembly, led by the doctor 'Abd al-Rizaq al-Sanhuri, who later praised Hilal's memory. In this memo Hilal noted that the promises of the 1919 revolution had not been upheld and that religious discrimination persisted in Egyptian society. He tried to convince the authors to draft a text that would establish a clear distinction between religion and state and that, consequently, would not mention Islam as the state's religion. He argued that Article 149 of the 1923 Constitution, which attributed a religious identity to the state, implied a denial of the Coptic presence in Egypt. According to Hilal, this article provided a pretext, or even a foundation, for the multiple discriminations that Copts faced in the professional and judicial domains. He also deemed it essential to recognize the right for individuals to convert to Christianity so that judges and administrative services could not refuse requests for conversion by referring to this article. Finally, Hilal called on the necessity to grant Copts the right to publicly and officially conduct religious ceremonies and disseminate news, a demand that was reiterated in a more detailed manner in the second component of the group's program, related to religious life.

Hilal presented the Umma Qibtiyya's program by stating three objectives: the church's prosperity, the application of the teachings of the Gospel to the people of the Gospel, and the practice of the Coptic language. He also announced several means to achieve these objectives: establishing an official radio station located in the center of Cairo, where there was a high density of Copts (Shubra, Faggala, etc.); publishing daily, weekly, and monthly papers that would act as a mouthpiece for the organization and Coptic opinion; scientific and modern instruction of the Coptic language; the creation of sports associations; and action taken with respect to the patriarchal seat.[5] On September 1 Hilal addressed his proposals to the Constituent Assembly, and on September 11, 1953, on the first anniversary of its creation, the Umma Qibtiyya printed and distributed half a million copies of its program. Nasser would have exclaimed: "This group wants to create a state within a state!"

This episode was long ignored by an Egyptian historiography that said very little about Coptic affairs in general and would rarely be disposed to remember the brief existence of a group whose mention called to mind the idea of Coptic separatism or, at least, a Coptic political movement. Several historians, like Yunan Labib Rizk, denied it any significance, arguing that the organization had no support in the Coptic population and suggesting that the abduction of the pope was more a schoolyard prank than a political action.[6] Other observers attributed their actions to a crisis in the church and limited the focus of their actions to that arena. Still others read this current of dissatisfaction as a response to diverse discriminations against Coptic youth,[7] and others, like Yusif Abu Sayf and Rafiq Habib, interpreted the emergence of the movement as a fundamentalist response to corruption in political life and the failure of the Coptic bourgeoisie to integrate into national politics.[8] Ghali Shukri, one of the first to remind his fellow citizens of this event, insisted on these two aspects. He saw in the group's formation a conservative religious movement and a simultaneous expression of political discontent within a social category, the Coptic bourgeoisie, disappointed with their exclusion from politics and treatment as a minority. The Umma Qibtiyya's action was not simply about the clerical hierarchy but, as Shukri insists, about the state itself. It denounced the absence of democracy and expressed its anxiety over the rising influence of the Muslim Brotherhood in social and political life.[9]

Setting aside those readings that minimize the magnitude and significance of the movement—the relevance of which lies mainly in that it calls into question the figure of ninety-two thousand members that Hilal claimed—the other points of view, far from being incompatible, reveal different facets of the movement. The Umma Qibtiyya constituted an emblematic phenomenon and marked a turning point precisely because it carried all these dimensions, as expressed in the memo to the Constituent Assembly. Protesting against these discriminations, the Umma Qibtiyya, indeed, was founded following the anger of Coptic youth over the church burning and murder of several Christians in Suez in January 1952. The event confirmed, moreover, the incompetence of the old guard in the Wafd, who had no knowledge of, or contact with, the younger generations. When members of the Umma Qibtiyya met Ibrahim Farag, the only Coptic cabinet member, in the hope that the government would intervene, he asked them, "Who are you working for?" and reproached them for threatening national unity.[10] In the eyes of Copts, Makram Ebeid's departure and the decline of the Wafd, which was placed in power by the force of British guns in 1942, contributed to breaking national unity and distanced them from the Egyptian political scene. At the very least, certain Copts were no longer disposed to make what they considered concessions in the name of national unity. There were many among them who, as Dina El-Khawaga has noted, spoke of the "price paid for inclusion" in political life and in the Wafd.[11] This reversal, tangible in the 1940s but perceptible as early as the 1930s, is evidenced in the example—eloquent though still marginal—of the changing outlook of Sergius, who, in 1919, preached in al-Azhar. His name is generally invoked to personify the Islamic-Christian symbiosis throughout the 1919 revolution. But during the crisis of the missions in 1933, Sergius formulated the hypothesis that the Copts would bitterly regret the departure of the British.[12] Other initiatives to create political platforms to make Coptic voices heard indicate Coptic elites' disappointment with an Egyptian political life marked not only by corruption but also by the rise of Islamist currents and fascist groups. In the 1940s the lawyer Ramsis Gabrawi, who was close to Hilal, created a Coptic party, the Christian Democratic Party (*ḥizb al-dīmuqrāṭī al-masīḥī*). In an attempt to gain support from the new regime after 1952, it adopted a name more appropriate to the nationalist rhetoric, the National Democratic Party (*ḥizb al-dīmuqrāṭī al-qawmī*), before being dissolved by the Nasserist regime, along with other political parties and groups.[13] Hilal denied having a political project, a simple rhetorical precaution, as it explicitly claims parallelism with the Muslim Brotherhood, as has been established by most authors: "Yes, we wanted to create an organization active in the religious and social landscape, an organization that focuses on the fate and well-being of Copts, against all currents of Arab and Muslim nationalism that view them as a negligible party."[14]

Finally, the critical situation within the church had motivated the initiative to abduct the pope. Yusab was living under the influence of his secretary, Malak, who attached less importance to the proper management of religious affairs than to his own personal benefit, among other matters. Inquietude took over the Holy Synod and the idea of removing Yusab became embedded in the minds of several members of the clergy and the lay elite. The youth of the Umma Qibtiyya thus benefited from the tacit support of members in the high clergy in carrying out their operation. Several observers (Muhammad 'Afifi, Muhammad al-Baz) thought that Hilal had obtained the approval of some individual(s) in the Revolutionary Command Council. Indeed, it would be surprising if such an action unfolded without the immediate intervention of the police or army, even if the officers were celebrating the anniversary of their seizure of power that night. Despite the circumstantial support, the Umma Qibtiyya irked every political group. The Islamic currents vehemently opposed any Christian political formation, which they considered a product of efforts to divide the Middle East on sectarian bases. "After the creation of Israel, a Christian state?" became a leitmotif at this time. The Nasserist regime wanted to reduce any religious expression outside the cadre of an Arab/Muslim nationalist discourse. At worst, they saw the organization as a Coptic separatist movement, at best, a current of Egyptian nationalist fundamentalism. Its position in the church was not much more comfortable. At first it benefited from the patriarch's support; he financed a part of the cost to publish its program, and in a March 25, 1954, speech he encouraged Egyptian churches to cooperate with the movement. Relations with the pope disintegrated after the movement's disbanding, although the pope consistently denied having signed the decision on its dissolution. In all likelihood Malak, the secretary, had once more employed his use of the pope's signature. Yusab did not undertake any initiative without the agreement of his secretary, any more than he tried to convince him to reconsider the act of dissolving the organization. The Umma Qibtiyya found allies in a clergy alarmed by the crumbling of the pope's authority, but this collaboration was limited only to securing his abdication; the clergy never viewed the emergence of a secular power sympathetically. The Sunday school organizers, for their part, wanted to establish their power over the clergy and would not tolerate any rivalry.

The experience of the Umma Qibtiyya was emblematic in that it marked an effective change in the history of relations between the church and the state and in the history of the church's internal workings. The last lay attempt to initiate social and religious reform after the loss of the Majlis al-Milli's prestige, the Umma Qibtiyya's action indicated, negatively, the emergence of the clerics and, thus, the end of the laity's role as intermediary between Copts and the country's political leadership. Moreover, its leader was the instigator of the first Coptic mass mobilization against a governmental decision. Finally, at the point of most extreme tension the Umma Qibtiyya crystallized two antagonistic and complementary tendencies that have animated the Coptic elite since the mid-nineteenth century: the Egyptian nationalist leaning, centripetal, oriented toward the construction of the nation versus the sectarian tendency, centrifugal, fostering a retreat, both forced and desired. In subsequent decades the rift between the national and community *Weltanschauungs* was produced alongside a transformation of the ecclesiastical space into a communitarian space under the growing influence of the clergy and, in particular, the religious and political projects that Shenuda instigated.

From the end of the 1970s until the recent past this episode became the object of renewed curiosity on the part of historians and the Egyptian media. It particularly aroused the interest of several Coptic lay personalities. Judging that the moment had come to overturn the trend and bolster the role of the laity once again, they considered taking some lessons from Hilal to feed their current reflections on the project of reforming clerical institutions.[15]

The "Lay Movement"

In 2006 members of the "laity" launched a public offensive.[16] Since the end of the 1980s, several personalities from across the political spectrum had been active on the Coptic stage and had started thinking about church reform, whereas, at the beginning of the new century, they presented their project in the national media and explicitly linked church and state reform. They organized their first heavily publicized conference in 2006, in an attempt to convince the pope to reform the clerical institution, beginning with the rules governing patriarchal election.

Relegating the patriarch's role to the spiritual and religious direction of the community, they opposed his interventions on the national political scene. Besides invoking biblical texts to support this view, they argued that by engaging in politics, men of religion enter into the world of relative truths and debate, lies and compromises. This, they believed, would undermine the foundations of spiritual authority and distort the political process by encouraging political exploitation of religion and the use of religious rhetoric in politics.[17]

Papers presented throughout this first conference focused primarily on administrative reform in the clerical institutions and the role of the laity. The problems diagnosed and the solutions proposed thus concerned the personal status of Christians. They advocated in favor of the law put forward by the Majlis al-Milli in 1938 and the adoption of a unified personal status law for Christians that would, among other amendments, expand the number of cases eligible for divorce to equal those in Protestant law. Moreover, they hoped to reassign administrative responsibility for personal status to the Majlis al-Milli. They bitterly noted that the current council had been deprived of its prerogatives to such a point that a change of name, at least, was necessary, and at worst its entire existence was called into question. One council member, opposed to the movement but finding it hard to defend the institution's immediate utility, reacted by saying, "It's up to the Majlis to search for other functions and a new role! Which should be dedicated to national unity, defending citizenship, and resolving the Copts' own problems."[18] Such questions, it seemed, were of no concern to those who made decisions or oversaw their implementation.

Complaining about the presence of clerics in the Majlis al-Milli, they also challenged the fact that all elected members originated from "Baba's list" (*qāʿimat al-bābā*), which was composed of names that had been selected or accepted by Shenuda. One supporter of the status quo argued in favor of this approach: "The votes for 'Baba's lists' are a popular plebiscite, a mark of support for his policies, the renewal of confidence. This is why people vote for the representatives he chooses, to whom he has given his blessing."[19] The reformers did not want to simply redefine the Majlis al-Milli's jurisdiction but to amend the laws and practices that governed the election of council members, in order to put an end to the supremacy of the *ahl al-thiqa* (people of confidence) and include in the Council the *ahl al-kafā'* (people of competence) and the *ahl al-khibra* (people of experience). They outlined several formulas aiming to broaden the electoral base and allow better provincial representation: taking the model of the People's Assembly, in which, at the time, all but ten members were chosen by universal suffrage; or taking the model of the Shura Council, in which only one-tenth were nominated by the president.

They were concerned with the lack of transparency in the church's accounting. For example, no information on revenue from the diaspora and monasteries was revealed or available; a significant portion of funds were disposed of without passing through a central body, as numerous emigrants donated directly to churches or monasteries in their home provinces. And, cleaning up the church's accounts was all the more urgent given the Egyptian press's propensity for scandals denouncing corruption in men of religion, not even sparing the pope's entourage. What's more, tabloid publications gladly ridiculed clergymen's economic affairs, assigning nicknames according to their level of corruption, like "villa-bishops" or "Mercedes-bishops." Hence, reform proposals advocated assigning the administration of church property to the Majlis al-Milli, along with affairs relating to personal status and religious schools.

The reformers considered it essential to publish the rules and procedures governing the clerical courts in charge of punishing violations committed by the clergy. Consisting of members of the Holy Synod, these courts operated in the greatest secrecy, following the orders of the pope or Anba Bishuy, who had the upper hand in this domain. Injustices multiplied after the 1990s, undermining the confidence of the laity and a number of clerics in the institution. The lay movement spokespersons claimed that their project benefited from the support of several influential clerics whose names were withheld. Without guessing the identities of those likely to be sympathetic to their project, it is probable that some lower clergymen, whose status was ill-defined and whose fate lay in the hands of the pope, would have supported the project behind-the-scenes.[20]

Finally, priority was accorded to amending the laws governing the pope's election, dating from 1957, so that they would be up to date with the church's expansion, social changes, and contemporary political needs.[21] Some suggested doing away with the final drawing of lots and to grant all community members the right to elect the pope. Many insisted on the necessity of revising not only the ways in which the electoral college was formed but the conditions of patriarchal eligibility—for example, that the seat is reserved only for those with fifteen years of monastic life. After the death of Shenuda III on March 17, 2012, Kamal Zakhir, along with the majority of Copts active on the religious scene, and supportive of the project to amend regulations, reluctantly agreed that it was no longer desirable to undertake this urgent reform before the patriarchal election: enacting new legislation would require the approval of a People's Assembly, where Muslim Brothers and Salafis prevailed. And the Copts feared that the text would only arouse opposition or would be viewed as unimportant and tabled indefinitely, postponing the organization of the patriarchal elections. Moreover, increasing tensions and the overall instability of the national situation were pressuring the community to select a new leader without delay. Thus, they decided to content themselves with several minor modifications that would not require the text to be reviewed before the People's Assembly, simply bringing the 1957 law up to date. For example, the electoral college would include representatives of the nongeographical bishoprics and of the dioceses abroad, which had been created after the 1957 law.

Activity in the laity diminished between 2007 and 2012, partly owing to internal disputes. Still divided, this "lobby [was] without influence in the ecclesiastic realm,"[22] wrote Hani Labib, a temporary member of this movement and the author of a contemporary history of the Coptic Church.[23] The pope never responded to their critiques—except for one. Its author had hit a nerve of the patriarchal edifice: the church's theology and religious culture.

From the first conference of the laity, the theologian George Habib Bibawi had analyzed "the reasons for the impasse of the Coptic Church's cultural-religious movement." According to Bibawi, the revival depended on the momentum of the Sunday schools' founder, Habib Guirguis, but had not survived him. Under the influence of Protestant missions, "the 'Sunday Schools' born of the Revival at the time of Habib Guirguis (1876–1951) had built their program solely on the study of the Holy Scripture; and this orientation was still pursued during the reign of Shenuda. Consequently, religious culture was cut off from liturgy and Patrology, the study of which had not only been ignored, but was simply nonexistent."[24] Recovering the Coptic heritage, especially the Alexandrine tradition, implied therefore the rehabilitation of Matta al-Maskin and his disciples, who were well-versed in the study of the texts of the Fathers of the Church.

George Habib Bibawi was not content with presenting his point of view on the necessary educational and theological church reforms but dared to utter the name of Matta al-Maskin, who was reviled by the pope. One year after the conference, Bibawi wrote an article published in *Ruz al-Yusuf*, in which he accused Shenuda of adhering to the Nestorian heresy (which holds that there are two separate natures of Christ, the human and the divine) and called the "bishops and priests to break ecclesiastic communion with the pope, by omitting his name from official liturgies."[25] The pope reacted immediately, excommunicating Bibawi from the Coptic Orthodox Church.[26]

The dispute concerned the theology centered on the divinization of Man, developed by Matta al-Maskin from a reading of the First Fathers of the Church (notably Saint Athanasius, then his successor, Cyril of Alexandria). In a series of articles published in *al-Kiraza* throughout 2003 and 2004, without naming al-Maskin, Shenuda had rejected this doctrine, which he viewed as "the heresy of the twentieth century." But in formulating such a judgment, "Pope Shenuda unfortunately showed his own ignorance not only of all the patristics of the early centuries, but moreover of his own Alexandrine tradition."[27] Jacques Masson outlines this theological quarrel. To summarize: Bibawi defended al-Maskin's mystical theology, according to which Christ, by incarnating, and by uniting with humanity, transforms it, reestablishes it in its original dignity, and divinizes it.

After the first conference of the "lay movement," Kamal Zakhir and other prominent Coptic writers published articles about Matta al-Maskin in the Egyptian press, in particular in the weekly *Ruz al-Yusuf*, and in the daily of the same name.[28] They turned the figure of "Matthew the Poor" into the countermodel of Shenuda on both the theological and the political plane. For intellectuals and laypersons who, by their own admission, did not fully grasp the subtleties of the divinization of Man any better than the ordinary person-in-the-street, the theological controversy was of little import. The political significance of the dispute, however—to bar access to the Patriarchal See for the followers of Matta al-Maskin, the monks of the Anba Maqar monastery—was obvious. According to Bibawi, Matta al-Maskin had cured his more than one hundred disciples of "the defects of Sunday Schools, the most important being narrow-mindedness, fanaticism, and a deification of their superiors."[29] In the 1950s al-Maskin had opened a center in Heliopolis dedicated to the study of original Coptic patrimony, which became the Patristic Center, founded with his disciple the deacon Nushi al-Shahid. Registered with the Ministry of Social

Solidarity as a nongovernmental organization in order to retain independence vis-à-vis the patriarchal theological seminary, the center still welcomes specialists, clerics, and laypersons and continues to publish translations.

After Shenuda III's death important lay figures, such as Kamal Zakhir, hoped that a monk could win the support to appear on the list of candidates and might become the head of the Coptic Orthodox Church. Zakhir expressed this point of view to the kaimakam. The election of a monk, he pleaded, represented the only solution to escape from the rivalries between corrupt bishops who had placed the institution in harm's way. Otherwise, he joked, they would be in the streets calling, "*Yasqut ḥukm al-usquf*" (Down with the regime of bishops).[30] Others argued that a monk elected to pope, ignorant of the communitarian power relations and without the support of the state apparatus, would be ill-equipped to guide an institution of international stature or to undertake the necessary reforms.

Interclerical Rivalries

The international development of the church during Shenuda's reign had enabled the pope to extend his reach into the corridors of power of the most important states on the planet, while international bodies paid close attention to the rights of minorities and respect for religious liberties. For its part the Egyptian regime wanted to ensure the support of a Coptic patriarch who knew how to tend his flock. Yet, even though he had proven his talent as a "tightrope-walker" by managing to satisfy the diverse needs of the "domestic Copts" without neglecting the demands of activists abroad, Shenuda himself had encountered mounting difficulties in moderating dissent and in drumming up votes for the NDP. Still, despite the criticism and rancor his patriarchal politics engendered, most Copts recognized him as a great statesman who managed the church's affairs during a particularly difficult time for the community. No personality of such high standing appeared among the potential candidates to succeed him.

But the expansion of the Coptic Church was not accompanied by the institutionalization that such an organization requires. Few clear rules defined the relations between the new administrative organs or the modalities of nomination and revocation of a large part of the clergy and personnel active in the church. All had remained under the supervision of a single man whose will had the force of law. In the absence of sufficient institutionalization to ensure the continuity of the clerical organization's functioning during a power vacuum, Shenuda's death plunged the church into a chaotic transitional phase. Moreover, the personalization of patriarchal power and the strengthening of links to businessmen close to the NDP had bred corruption and rivalries in the clergy. While the final draw is theoretically impossible to influence,[31] the preceding steps of the selection process had become a theater of tough negotiations between different groups wishing to place men of their choosing among the candidates and members of the electoral college, sometimes at the cost of bending the rules.[32] These factions were engaged in bitter fighting after Shenuda's death, but clerical rivalries had already begun to show in the Egyptian media as early as 2006.

An indication of the interclerical fractures, a demonstration at the cathedral in 'Abasiyya, had gathered several hundred Copts, who had come from the distant province of Suhag to protest the Holy Synod's decision that Bishop Kirillus of Nag' Hammadi be relieved of his functions. Unlike the protests organized in response to attacks against the community, this public and widely covered mobilization expressed, for the first time, the massive and explicit refusal of a patriarchal verdict. Admittedly, the dissent was aimed at Anba Bishuy, bishop of the Diocese of Damietta and Kafr al-Shaykh and secretary of the Holy Synod, the most powerful man in the church after the pope, and the protesters demanded that Shenuda see that justice was done, where Bishuy had not. Some, without a doubt, hoped to open Shenuda's eyes to the actions of his secretary, rightly or wrongly believing that he did not see them. But the pope endorsed the verdict, and his intransigence was the object of severe criticism. This unforeseen action did not simply confirm the steep decline in Shenuda's popularity throughout the 2000s. It signals that submission to a local religious authority could outrank the pope's authority. In other words recognition and hierarchization of religious authority depend on shifting landscapes of powers.

Publicly revealing the disputes between a group of bishops in Upper Egypt and the secretary of the Holy Synod, this incident made the fight for succession to the See of Saint Mark visible. In a rare occurrence Shenuda returned the decision to the Holy Synod, which ultimately ruled in Kirillus's favor, despite Anba Bishuy's furious fight against such a verdict. In July 2007, during Shenuda's hospitalization in the United States, anxiety increased among the bishops in Upper Egypt that Anba Bishuy would succeed Shenuda. This was all the more troubling because the secretary of the Holy Synod had again issued a verdict that they deemed unjust when he decided to defrock a monk in Suhag, called Bula Fu'ad. The bishops, led by Anba Wissa, reiterated their rejection of this decision from the Holy Synod. And the "Bishops of the *Sa'id* Front" was then created in opposition to the Committee of Ecclesiastical Courts, where Anba Bishuy and Yu'annis were seated.

Denying the existence of any dissension, members of the clergy suggested that ill-intentioned individuals had taken advantage of a disagreement about the court's decision to conclude that there was a division in the Holy Synod. Nabil 'Abd al-Fattah assessed that the creation of the front was a formal confirmation of the Holy Synod's split into two clans—that of Anba Bishuy and that of the *Sa'id*—and it made the struggle public.[33] The front did not assemble all the bishops of Upper Egypt; it drew suspicion and criticism from the bishops orbiting Anba Tuma of the al-Qusiyya diocese in Assiut, who considered members of this group corrupt and driven by their own project for church reform, distinct from that of the lay movement.[34]

NEW RELIGIOSITIES AND SUBVERSION

Transdenominational Pilgrimages and Charismatic Revival

The expression of Coptic fervor outside of the official places of worship is not a new phenomenon. The church had encouraged an array of "popular" religious practices, such as the *mulids*,[35] the miracles, and saint-worship under the Patriarchate of Cyril VI, whereas Shenuda had attempted to regulate and control them.[36] Contemporary religious practices are indicators of the shifting relations between the individual and the group. Affecting the Muslims as much as the Christians in Egypt, these new religiosities appear at the intersection of several interdependent processes: an individualization of religious practices combined with the growing sectarianization of public space; the widening gap between religious, communal, or national senses of belonging; the increased reference to community values; and the growing impact of transnational standards on the redefinition of religious and community practices.[37] The renewed appeal of the Protestant churches and the emergence of charismatic Coptic Orthodox priests bear witness to this network of social and religious changes. But these new religious practices do not simply reveal the contemporary aspirations of the faithful. They signal alternative ways of challenging the church's hegemony over religious and social practices.

Over the course of the past twenty years Egypt has not escaped upheavals in the Christian world. Given the government's tight control over non-Sunni religious activities, the penetration of unrecognized religious groups in Egypt has remained limited. Those foolhardy individuals who recently dared to evangelize on Egyptian soil generally belonged to groups with previously established bonds in Egypt, most often from the beginning of the twentieth century. Sometimes referenced in the Egyptian press, the Mormons were active in Upper Egypt. The presence of Adventists was mentioned from the beginning of the twentieth century. Pentecostal and Baptist missionaries, as well as Jehovah's Witnesses, had embarked for Egypt's shores in the 1930s.[38] Muzzled after the coup in July 1952, these groups reappeared, discreetly and in small numbers, during the 1970s. Since 1989, the Holy Synod of the Coptic Church has denied that Jehovah's Witnesses and Adventists are Christians and has refused to recognize the translations of the Bible that they use. Present in numerous "informal" neighborhoods, their activities gained visibility in the 1990s, which prompted Shenuda to refute their doctrines (in 1994 and then again in 2002 and 2003) and to warn against "the deleterious activity of a banned religious group with no relation to Christian denominations."[39] Other Egyptian churches also refused to recognize the two groups, criticizing the lack of discretion in their initiatives to rally followers, so their influence remains quantitatively negligible in Egypt.

Instead, the charismatic movements and the televangelists recently set off new trends in world and Egyptian Christianity, especially in the Egyptian Presbyterian Church,[40] which was more receptive to charismatic input. The Protestant churches once again attracted Orthodox Copts, inspiring clerical resentment for these rivals, from whom the Coptic Church had borrowed to modernize its teachings. The fear of losing adherents has regularly gripped the Coptic Orthodox clergy. Since the massive penetration of missions at the end of the nineteenth century,[41] and even since the first arrival of missionaries in the seventeenth century, this fear had fostered the will to reform and incited the Coptic popes to undertake pastoral visits from the north to the south of the country.[42] The Protestant churches recognized by the Egyptian state had regularly welcomed Orthodox Copts into their churches or associations, generally without the faithful needing to formally renounce their Orthodox affiliation. But the revival in the twentieth century had enabled the Coptic Church to mobilize the community, and the institution appeared more attractive in the eyes of a community less inclined to seek spiritual nourishment outside of the Coptic world. But by the end of the 1960s, the Coptic clergy felt renewed concern over dwindling communities. In the context of this rivalry the apparition of the Virgin Mary at Zaytun in 1968 provided the church with the occasion to affirm its superiority over other Christian denominations.

Over the course of the last two decades several pastors have observed a significant increase in Coptic attendance of Protestant churches and activities.[43]

Pentecostal churches, in particular, like the Assemblies of God, a Protestant denomination in Egypt since the 1930s, continue to attract a growing number of Orthodox Copts. Sympathizers of the Protestant churches cover many different cases. Although they generally do not question belonging to the Coptic Orthodox community, their attitude amounts to a critique of the patriarchal hegemony exercised over religious practices. In most cases they are able to explain the reasons for their choices and their criticism of the patriarchal orthodoxy and the clerical class: the length of rituals; the shackles of a strong, hierarchical structure that weighs on relations between the laity and clerics; the lack of emotion in orthodox religious ceremonies; and the absence of flexibility and liberty.[44]

These religious pilgrimages partly unfold in continuity with Orthodox Copts' practices. Many search for answers to their personal questions and their religious aspirations by blending the complementary teachings of preachers who are distinguished from one another by their personal styles, their specialization, and their primary interests. Yet contemporary religious practices have diversified as the religious market has expanded, offering an array of new products. Insofar as such spiritual "goods" are disseminated on the Internet, they are accessible to a larger audience, even to the most remote villages of Upper Egypt.

Abuna Sam'an and Muqattam: The Axiality of the Margin?

Several Coptic Orthodox priests, like Sam'an, Makari Yunan, and Zakarya Butrus,[45] have integrated elements of the discourse and practices that were brought in by the charismatic movements and televangelists.

Muqattam Hill rises beyond the ring road that separates the eastern part of Cairo from the City of the Dead, swarming with rats and feral dogs, pigs, waste, and illiterate citizens forgotten by church and state. Mostly natives of Upper Egypt, the Christian inhabitants of this eccentric hill on the desert's edge often survive by recycling garbage or, until 2009, raising pigs. Policy makers do not take this area into account, unless under pressure to maintain national security and thus hold back a possible deleterious swelling of the periphery. After the earthquake in 1992, the Muslim Brothers were the first to assist the local population, displaying a kind of benevolence toward their Christian compatriots. During the flu outbreak in 2009, State Security agents entered the neighborhood to ensure that the president's decision to massacre the pig population was carried out. Then, in March 2011, the army brutally repressed Copts and Salafis when clashes increased in response to Salafist demonstrations demanding the liberation of women converts to Islam and the attacks on Christian churches in the Cairene suburbs, then later in Aswan. Under the direction of Anba Samuel, at the end of the 1970s, the Bishopric of Social Services had dealt with the most urgent cases in the neighborhood without putting any mechanisms in place for social assistance or educational development. The first to tackle this task was Sister Emmanuelle, who raised a school with the help of religious Egyptian women.[46] Better educated, a number of the inhabitants integrated their recycling activities into more complex production chains. Several NGOs subsequently took notice of this neighborhood.

Abuna Sam'an, for his part, wanted to save souls. But this spiritual enterprise still required the deployment of political, media, and narrative strategies and was embedded in the transnational dynamics of changing religious practices. Previously a place of neither faith nor law, Muqattam became the center of renewed Coptic fervor and heterodox practices in the eyes of the clerical hierarchy. Churches arose, literally, from beneath the rocks, and neighborhood residents (re)discovered the path of a regenerated church. Into this marginal space, the top of which can only be reached on foot, Christians—and some Muslims—were funneled right to Abuna Sam'an. They would arrive from central, or even wealthy suburban, areas to assist him in exorcisms and sermons. Thanks to satellite channels, Sam'an was even able to broadcast his charisma to an audience abroad, as well as to the farthest reaches of the country.

Born in a delta village near Mansura, the son of small landowners, Sam'an discovered Muqattam in 1974. According to the hagiographic account of his biography and one of his press interviews, he went to the *zabalin* (garbagemen) neighborhood after a holy call had told him to accept the repeated invitations from garbagemen who worked in Shubra, where Sam'an was living then with his wife.[47] He returned there regularly to preach and save the souls of this marginalized zone's inhabitants, which had no waste management or educational infrastructure. In the early 1980s Sam'an finally moved to Muqattam.

He built his local reputation on his capacities in playing the role of intermediary between Egyptian and foreign NGOs—which had begun working in the neighborhood—the residents and the local clans, as well as in raising funds from various sources, including even the pope, in order to build his church.[48] A remarkable diplomat, Sam'an established close contacts with Catholic and Protestant elites, with local political authorities, and with well-placed individuals in the media (he had worked at the newspaper *al-Jumhuriyya*). He drew his religious legitimacy from the authority conferred on him by tradition and from his power as a redeemer. Sam'an had forged the narrative of his own redemption following the model of the local saint, Sam'an, whose name he adopted, who had supposedly converted Calif al-Mu'izz.[49] Yet the narrative also brings forward the experience of revelation and sudden change: a divine voice had called him to leave his life of sin. Sam'an thus borrowed from the contemporary register of born-again Christians, as well as the Coptic Orthodox tradition. Digging up the story of this saint's life (little-known up to that point, though mentioned in the *History of the Patriarchs* and the *Synaxarium*), the Church of Muqattam published his hagiography in 1987. This narrative also circulated orally and was well-known and often recounted by all the residents, who would also readily tell any visitors their own personal stories of redemption following an encounter with Christ and their subsequent return to the church.

Like Makari Yunan, who was also inspired by Zakarya Butrus, Sam'an had developed a televangelist style and rhetoric. And just like Makari Yunan, Sam'an practiced miraculous healings, exorcisms, and conversions. The figure of the healing Orthodox priest attracting Muslims is an ancient one, but healings and exorcisms now became embedded in a new symbolical *dispositif*. The exorcist used to officiate only when an individual "possessed by a demon" came to him to ask for *baraka*. Now, Sam'an and Makari practice exorcism following a weekly timetable. The hour and the place of the exorcism are established like the schedule of a show; and this show is broadcast online. Furthermore, never had a personage combined the function of baptizing a Muslim convert with the power of healing or exorcizing—which could, admittedly, lead to conversion. Certainly, the lives of saints have often linked conversion and miracle—exorcism and healing. A revelation of the power of religion, the miracle reveals truth to those who witness it or benefit from it and sometimes inspires conversion—such as, for example, the case of Saint Sam'an's story. More rarely, a holy healer will also claim a baptism. Abraham's hagiographies in the 1960s insist on a dimension of saintly action previously ignored, his struggle in the field of conversions, and relate the baptism of a Protestant woman's child: after having several times lost a newborn, she had made a vow. If another infant was born, she would bring it to the saint to baptize. But this was not a conversion, let alone the conversion of a Muslim. *A contrario*, in the more recent hagiographies Abraham intervenes to punish or stop a conversion to Islam: "After having tried in vain to reason with the candidate for conversion, the saint chases her from the bishopric, telling her, '*idhabī, Allah ya'rif shughalu fikī*!' (Go on, God knows what to do with you!) But the saint, after having prayed by the water, makes the sign of the cross on her face; the young woman comes to her senses and immediately begins to praise God."[50]

With Sam'an and Makari Yunan, conversion, healing, and exorcism form a new symbolic configuration centered on purification. Coming from Muqattam to deliver residents from sin and deviant practice, Sam'an exorcises in public and at fixed hours. The sessions are filmed and uploaded on YouTube. Similarly, Makari broadcasts his purifying actions on the Internet as well. In one of these videos the "possessed" person collapses, screaming, his face contorted, drooling (in all likelihood a case of epilepsy). The priest officiates, pronounces several words, blesses him, and the man finally calms. The power to heal confirms the strength of the Christian religion and even gives it the power to vanquish the religion of the other. Incidentally, Muslims explain the power of these priests by virtue of their secret conversion to Islam. If Sam'an does not comment publicly on Islam, Makari Yunan and Zakarya Butrus resolutely attack Islamic teachings and call on Muslims to convert. Makari, like Sam'an, baptizes. In this new configuration healing, exorcism, and conversion combine and form the three phases in the purification of evil.

5 SECTARIANISM, AUTHORITARIANISM, AND THE DYNAMICS OF FEAR

The "Coptic issue" is located at the juncture of contemporary transformation of social norms—which involves a new delineation of the boundaries between the visible and the taboo—and of current changes in the authoritarian situation, which imply new rules of differentiation between informal and institutional practices. The Coptic issue emerges as highly symbolic of political demands to establish the rule of law and citizenship, while it remains an instrument in politicians' struggle for power, and the motive to exacerbate antagonisms. Combining a long view of the twentieth century with a sharper focus on the last thirty years, an analysis of the Egyptian political scene enables us to highlight the ruptures and the continuities in the authoritarian regimes of veridiction and legitimation.

The question of Coptic participation in the political game is a recurring theme, which, since the beginning of the twentieth century, always comes to the forefront after a political crisis. Furthermore, every crisis in Egypt is formulated in terms of identity. Over the past thirty years, the rivalry between the National Democratic Party (NDP) and the Brotherhood, as well as the demand for political language that conforms to international standards, has turned the Copts into an empty signifier that is used by both sides to different ends. In this regard I propose a historical account of the Brotherhood's policies through the lens of the sectarian question. The ideological and organizational characteristics of the Egyptian state greatly determined both the Brotherhood's attitudes and the changing features of sectarianism. Discussing ideology, however, does not simply mean analyzing discourses and ideas.[1] It requires considering what the Brotherhood actually does, says, and supposedly believes, as elements forming a system of meaning embedded in a national—even transnational—context. Thus, I combine the study of the evolving political landscape with an analysis on the implications of the reference to Islam, not only on the national stage but even within the Muslim Brotherhood. Indeed, in Chapter 3 I insisted on the internal dynamics of the Coptic community to carry out the analysis of the church's politics and of social communitarization in Egypt. Similarly, one should pay greater attention to the power relations within the Society of Muslim Brothers, and to their objectives, in order to fully understand their posture—their tactics, as well as their opinions—and, thus, their failure in 2013. This is not to suggest that transformations on the national political scene should be neglected as an explanatory variable; one certainly needs to take into account "the environment in which the Muslim Brothers operate"[2] since the power relations existing on a national and transnational level play a decisive role in defining their postures and alleged doctrinal shifts. It is important, however, to accurately assess their impact on the organization.

REPRESENTING THE COPTS

"Why Do Copts Do So Badly in Parliamentary Elections?" was the title of an article published in November 2005 in the weekly *Ruz al-Yusuf*. The journalist stated, with some surprise, that all parties used communitarian tactics. He pointed out with indignation the fact that Copts in electoral contests are commonly considered church candidates (*bitāʿ al-kanīsa*) or designated by the title "independent Copt." "The use of this category, which is not found in any political dictionary, merely explains why the Copts fail in elections: they campaign on a religious basis."[3] His finding needs to be qualified: many analysts have a short memory and will dwell on this subject, refusing to see the truth until they are forced to admit it. In the present case the journalist himself discriminates by presenting sectarianism as a purely Christian practice. But religion is always brought up, by all parties, in Egyptian elections. And what is remarkable is that this would suddenly seem intolerable in the eyes of any observer—all the more so, perhaps, from the point of view of the cited journalist, because the Copts would now also exhibit the Christian label. Or, at least they attach themselves to the labels they are assigned. During the past fifteen years, news reports in Egypt had been listing the candidates in the following manner: "Nine Watani; Two Tajammuʿ; One Copt; Two women," without mention of the Copts' (or the women's) party affiliation. Coptic and women candidates take on the role of community or gender representatives, while the very idea of proportional representation for Copts encountered a massive opposition in public and political opinion.

Since the beginning of the twentieth century, the problem of Coptic integration into social life and politics was formulated in terms of "representation," raising the question of a possible proportional representation in the People's Assembly and the Shura Council—or other state institutions. The issue has been debated from time to time over the course of the past hundred years. Similar arguments were, each time, advanced for or against such a system and concerning the precise mode of its execution.[4] At the 1911 Assiut conference the participants agreed on the necessity to end the tacit discrimination in state and other governmental institutions but opposed establishing quotas. Tawfiq Dus, a member of the Liberal Constitutional Party, argued in favor of quotas in 1923. In 1911, however, he had stated that only competence should dictate the choice of those elected to the assemblies and those carrying out the high functions of state institutions. For his part Murqus Hannah (minister of public works from 1923 to 1924) proposed to take into consideration wealth, previous positions, and education in the selection process of possible parliamentarians, but he expressed his clear rejection of minority representation as such.

Several years later, the negotiations between the Christian elite and Sa'ad Zaghlul provided a concrete response to the question of Coptic representation in nascent political formations. Al-Bishri relates the episode of integrating several Christians into the elite of the future Wafd Party. This text appears even more remarkable insofar as it reveals, despite the intention of the author, the sectarian hiatus and the effort to deny it. Several months before the 1919 revolution, having found no Christian name on the list of delegates to meet the British representatives in 1918, a few Coptic notables decided to mention this problem in front of Sa'ad Zaghlul. Several among them—including Fakhri 'Abd al-Nour, who related this episode—held discussions with Sa'ad Zaghlul, who "welcomed their idea and spoke with them about the choice of a Coptic notable who would become a member of the delegation. . . . George Khayat asked Sa'ad: 'What is the Copts' place? And what will be their fate after their representatives are integrated into the delegation?' Sa'ad answered him: 'Rest assured, Copts will have the same rights and duties as us, in all equality [*li-l-aqbāṭ mā lanā min al-ḥuqūq wa 'alīhum mā 'alīnā min al-wājibāt 'ala qadam al-musāwā*].'"[5] Al-Bishri interprets this integration as additional evidence of the successful union between Copts and Muslims, brought together by the project of national construction.

In Zaghlul's words, however, the use of "we" confers an irreducible otherness on the Copts that separates them from Muslims. And the posture of the two protagonists in the dialogue even further signifies the subordination of the one to the other. Khayat's question itself presupposes that the fate of the Copts rests on the decision of the other, the "we," the Muslims.

With British demands increasing pressure, in 1922 the issue presented itself to the Constituent Assembly. The debate on a system of representation that would favor the Copts' integration into political life still took a backseat to the urgent need to define a constitutional strategy to limit British interference. Indeed, while the British authorities had, in the declaration of February 28, 1922, announced Egypt's formal independence, they nonetheless had four reservations. One of these stipulated the possibility of British intervention to protect minorities. In the name of union against the occupying British, the majority of the Constituent Assembly, whether Coptic or Muslim, judged it preferable not to establish a system of quotas but, instead, to inscribe in the Constitution the equality of civil and political rights for all citizens without distinction of race, religion, or gender, as well as the freedom of worship. In so doing, they intended to affirm that the Egyptian state itself would guarantee minority rights and freedoms.

Al-Bishri, who meticulously relates the Constituent Assembly's propositions and the press exchanges through which the Wafd participated in the debate,[6] focuses on the question of minority representation but only briefly evokes the inscription of Islam as the state's religion in Article 149 of the 1923 Constitution. Yet, while the Copts refused to establish a quota system, a number among them, as well as several Muslims, disapproved of the introduction of this constitutional article. In the eyes of Tawfiq Dus and the writer Mahmud 'Izmi, mentioning religion in the constitutional text would justify advocating in favor of proportional representation for Copts:

> The representation of minorities is necessary as long as the Constitution has not revoked the antiquated social principles that widen the gulf between Christians and Muslims. We would not speak of majority and minority if unity rested on the principle of civil (*madanī*) legislation. But until this principle is established, we must recognize facts. Woe to whoever does not take this into consideration. . . . The situation in Egypt is such that even the greatest thinkers in the country have not dared counteract the proposal to add an official state religion to the text, even though they have no confidence at all in such a proposal.[7]

And in 2005 Samer Soliman commented:

> Despite their absolute commitment to establishing a secular state, 'Izmi and Dus ended up pleading the case of religious-based representation. . . . 'Izmi's clairvoyance encourages us to listen when he assures us that it is not possible to accept the Islamic identity of the Egyptian state if no representation is granted to minorities. Whether we drink down to the dregs the bitter cup of sectarianism; whether we establish, from A to Z, a secular state, which draws its legitimacy from the assent of the people. 'Izmi chose to drink down to the dregs the cup of sectarianism, because he had lost all faith in the Egyptian élite.[8]

Throughout the so-called liberal period, religion and confessional identity already represented one normative pole and the instrument of political tactics. But the presence of a common enemy motivated the elaboration of a project of national emancipation in whose name sectarian frontiers appeared porous, all things being otherwise equal. The memory of the Islamo-Christian symbiosis in the 1919 revolution seemed to excuse playing down the importance of the repeated attacks against the Wafd as a "party of Christians" and to consider the campaign against Christians in general as against foreign Christians, the missionaries. At last, the Copts' elite could participate in political life. Their desire for integration was so great that they stopped being the liaison for the Copts' demands altogether. Coptic grievances were often submitted to the Palace by the parties directly concerned, in the laity or clergy: men or women from diverse regions and socioprofessional categories.[9] And, for example, Coptic parliamentarians kept a low profile during any discussions on state finances for religious schools.[10]

The persistence of discrimination against Christians, the closure of the political sphere under the July regime (1952–70), the development of the Coptic Church, and the attacks against Coptic candidates and the electorate in the 1980s and 1990s contributed to the Copts' retreat from political life. The pluralization of the political opposition during the 1990s and 2000s, as well as the demand for social justice and respect for citizenship rights, placed the Coptic issue at the heart of demands for political reforms. In this new configuration the solution of proportional representation and the installation of a quota system were discussed from time to time. Broadly, three arguments were used then, as now, to justify the antagonists' positions. First, the rejection of a quota was founded on the theoretical argument that adherence to a religion neither determined political affiliation nor implied the existence of any specific political demands. Sociological arguments supported this reasoning: the Copts did not form a homogenous social or economic group, their orientation and political interests differed, and their political representation *en bloc* therefore seemed meaningless. The political argument fell within a secular conception of power and political action that was sometimes grafted onto this kind of discourse: demands specific to Christians could—and, from this perspective, should—be examined and treated "on the basis of citizenship and not through a sectarian logic."[11] Following a second line of argument, reasserting national unity would justify the rejection of quotas: to establish quotas would reinforce sectarianism. Also, in 2009, as the People's Assembly voted for a quota system in favor of women, the debate drifted dangerously toward the question of Coptic representation. Gamal Mubarak declared that the Copts' problems "should be resolved by dialogue and not by quotas."[12] The analyst Majid 'Atiyya drew up a list in response, including those who "promptly affirmed with one single voice, as if the affair threatened their lives: "No, no quotas for Copts," and he scoffed:

> We hear everywhere that Copts are part of the national fabric, that quotas imply a religious categorization that would divide the country. . . . But what about women? Aren't they elements of the national fabric? Or peasants and workers? And if the Copts are indeed elements of the national fabric, why doesn't the NDP include them on their lists, either in 1990 or in 1995? Because, as al-Shazli, an NDP member of the "old guard" who was elected to Parliament several times, said to Salama Ahmad Salama, the editor-in-chief of *al-Ahram* for several decades, followed by *Shuruq*—and I have published this comment in *al-Musawwar*—"Egyptians don't vote for Copts or women, and we want a majority for the NDP. To include a woman or a Copt on the electoral list is to lose that constituency."[13]

Against this reasoning, 'Izmi and Dus—or their contemporary heirs—state that the very existence of sectarianism, as epitomized in Article 2 of the Constitution, and the enduring discrimination against Christians are a resonant argument in support of a quota system, whether temporary or permanent. For them a quota is necessary to remedy the shortcomings of the social and political system.

The three presidencies have nevertheless expressed concerns about representing the Copts, beginning with the embrace of the Coptic pope as the official representative of a community whose plurality was thus ignored. Appointments in the People's Assembly and Shura Council created a de facto system of limited representation, while Coptic representation became an electoral leitmotif, with two variations: supporting or stigmatizing the Copts.

MUSLIM BROTHERS, COPTS, NDP: ELECTIVE AFFINITIES

The Brothers and the Regime: Repression, Accommodation, and Co-optation

In the 1930s several intellectual and political currents take shape, in opposition to the continuously renegotiated consensus between the authoritarian pro-British monarchy, relying on a semireligious legitimacy, and the nationalist majority Wafd Party. Over the course of the following decade the Society of the Muslim Brothers emerged as the most powerful among these currents.

In 1928 Hassan al-Banna founded the Society of Muslim Brothers in Isma'ilia, as an act of resistance to the British occupation. Aiming to create an "Islamic society," the Muslim Brothers first attacked Christian missionaries, who were numerous in this canal city of strategic importance for the British, and who were accused of subverting Islamic principles, teachings, and values.[14] From the work of Rashid Rida, one of the key figures of Muslim reformism,[15] al-Banna retains the idea that Islam is the cornerstone of social and political regeneration in Muslim societies. He does not commit himself, however, to a reading of primary textual sources, which would have led to a redefinition of the relationship underlying religion, knowledge, and politics. Rather, the vague and encompassing project of the Muslim Brothers allows malleability, insofar as reference is made to poorly defined Islamic norms. Indeed, for al-Banna political action is the priority.

From its outset the organization appears as a flexible combination of political pragmatism and of a hard nucleus of credo and narrative themes. As early as 1942, during the negotiations with the Wafd Party,[16] the Brotherhood reached an agreement with the ruling forces, whereas it maintained an oppositional stance. The first tactical alliance between military officers and the Muslim Brotherhood formed in the underground struggle against the British presence. And it was discarded in 1954 as violently as the short-lived marriage of convenience between the Supreme Council of the Armed Forces (SCAF) and al-Banna's contemporary heirs. In a power grab the organization's founder sought to infiltrate the ranks of the army.[17]

In the early 1940s al-Banna met separately with several members of the Free Officers' Movement, including Sadat, al-Baghdadi, and Wagih Abaza. Though seduced by his personality, they were reticent to engage unconditionally with a group whose primary goal was to take power and Islamize society rather than to resist the British occupation.[18] They agreed, however, on the principle of collaboration. This was cemented when the Brothers recruited ʿAbd al-Monʿim ʿAbd al-Raʾuf, "who undertakes to 'convert' officers."[19] A former soldier, Mahmud Labib was in charge of the military cells affiliated with the Brotherhood but that still enjoyed a relative autonomy. This formula allowed the Brotherhood to integrate nationalist activists who did not adhere to the movement's beliefs and maintained a critical distance from its practices. In return the military activists expected to benefit, among other things, from the convening power of the organization in the struggle for national independence.

Throughout this "strange relationship," as Khalid Mohi al-Din has termed it, several incidents aroused mistrust with regard to Hassan al-Banna and his intentions.[20] Nasser and other officers found it difficult to understand exactly what the Brotherhood wanted from the military. A number of the officers expressed discomfort with the "fanaticism," or "sectarianism," in the Brotherhood's discourse. Finally, "the escalating confrontation between the rulers and the Brotherhood, culminating in the assassinations of Prime Minister Mahmud al-Noqrashi [by the Brotherhood] and Hassan al-Banna [by the royal police], shocked several officers, as do the Brothers' attacks and violence against Egyptians, at a moment when the country was at war, and internal security was of vital importance."[21] Some remained members of the Society, but others ended their collaboration at different moments and for different reasons. Nasser's defection and the creation of the Free Officers' Movement in 1949 marked an end to their cooperation.

After the Free Officers' coup d'état on July 23, 1952, the Brotherhood was still a powerful organization, having been spared from the decision to dissolve all political parties and organizations in 1953.[22] Then, when the Brotherhood attempted to assassinate Nasser in 1954, the floodgates were opened for the brutal repression of the organization. Jailed, tortured, or driven into hiding, the Brothers acted in the shadows and on the margins until the 1970s; many left to continue their fight outside the country. These constraints and the prison experience strengthened an organizational mode based on the rule of secrecy and blind obedience to the leadership, and fed the *Weltanschauung* of the Muslim Brothers, who considered the world divided by the antagonism between friend and enemy.

"How Gamal Brought the Whole Mubarak House Down"

An outgrowth of the Arab Socialist Union (*al-ittiḥād al-ishtarākī al-ʿarabī*) and extension of the regime, the National Democratic Party (*al-ḥizb al-waṭanī al-dīmuqrāṭī*) was born in 1978 by Sadat's decision.[23] In December 1962 President

Gamal Abdel Nasser had formed the Arab Socialist Union, as a unique political platform, a strict hierarchy that was tightly controlled by the Free Officers (*al-ẓubbāt al-aḥrār*), and aimed to mobilize the population to carry out Nasserist reform projects.[24]

Sadat tried to roll back the state control he inherited from Nasser to rehabilitate the private sectors and stimulate foreign investment. And the co-optation of the Muslim Brothers, whose cadres often came from landowner or business families, was thus carried out in the dynamics of *infitāḥ*, or "open door," policies. Despite the rise of a class of entrepreneurs and the enrichment of segments of the middle class during the late 1970s, the majority of revenues remained under state control and were held in the coffers of the national treasury, while state expenditure rose. At the end of the conflict with Israel in 1973, Egypt once again enjoyed financial benefits from the Suez Canal and Western financial assistance. This rentier income balanced the deficit from low taxes and, by the early 1980s, represented half of all public revenue.[25] On the political front, in 1975 the Arab Socialist Union comprised three forums that, a year later, transformed into political parties. The NDP emerged from the center forum, initially called the Egypt Arab Socialist Organization. The law of June 29, 1977, governed the return of party pluralism, and a fourth formation appeared on February 4, 1978: the new Wafd. This Wafd Party presented itself as the heir to the old Wafd, the liberal and nationalist party formed by Sa'ad Zaghlul in 1919.

Despite the democratic rhetoric of Sadat, and then Mubarak, and the enforced pluralization of the Egyptian electoral scene from 1978 to 2011, the NDP remained the dominant party, the pillar of the authoritarian regime, and the operator of co-optation of the political and economic elite. From the outset its organic relationship with the regime and the objective to serve the president's policies determined its structure and operating modes. As the cohesion of political elites constituted a key factor in the consolidation of authoritarian regimes, the NDP played the role of "essential operator of adjustment between engineering coalition, policies, and the regime," up to the moment when the meteoric rise of a new faction jammed the cogs of the regime.[26]

At the end of the 1990s the business community considered it necessary to restructure the Egyptian economy, putting emphasis on privatization. After having ascended to the presidency, Hosni Mubarak had limited the relative liberalization undertaken by his predecessor and implemented a five-year economic plan. The draconian drop in rentier revenue at the end of the decade, at the same time as a demographic boom, pressured the government to revise this policy and accept the conditions set forth by the IMF and the Central Bank in 1991. Nevertheless, Egypt's participation alongside the United States in the first Gulf War had been rewarded with substantial financial assistance, and half its debt was cancelled. The government was thus spared from making massive subsidy cuts for basic necessities like bread and gasoline. Even with these saving graces, however, debt continued to rise. Various devaluations and other attempts at more or less direct taxation alienated the regime from its supporters in the population.

Educated in North American or English universities, a new generation of businessmen wished to enter politics. The president's son, Gamal Mubarak, would be their intermediary. He would know how to convince his father to integrate them into the political scene and to foster a resolutely neoliberal political economy. In the mid-1990s the businessman, and member of the Presidential Council, Ibrahim Kamel traveled to London to share these views with Gamal Mubarak, who was working there as an executive at Bank of America. In the autumn of 1999 Gamal Mubarak became a member of the NDP's General Secretariat. Several months later, Ahmed 'Izz[27] and Yusuf Butrus Ghali (the finance minister from 2004 to 2011) joined him.

While several NDP leaders were accused of corruption, the NDP held its eighth congress from September 15 to 17, 2002, under the slogan "The New Thought" (*al-fikr al-jadīd*), a title that formulated the challenges of the meeting: reforming the party and integrating the youth generation. A new committee, the Policy Committee, directed by Gamal, was created and charged with elaborating the guidelines for the party's general directives and policies.[28] Despite internal rivalries and dissension, especially during the legislative elections in 2005,[29] Nazif's second government (December 2005) and the reconfiguration of the NDP secretariat in 2006 endorsed Gamal's rise to power, although they blurred the distinction between the old guard and the new reformers that had often dominated media debates on the NDP. Indeed, three figures from the old guard gained key positions in the party and would be part of the small circle of decision makers around the president during the first revolutionary situation in the winter of 2011.[30]

Even though they embraced reformist rhetoric, neither Gamal and his allies nor Hosni Mubarak undertook any major reforms. On the political, economic, and partisan levels they were content to oversee only the changes necessary to successfully hand power down from father to son, to quench the insatiable thirst for wealth in their coterie, and to tentatively encroach on the military's economic empire. After 2002 they endeavored to promote the growth rate. Nazif's government launched a wave of privatization intended to attract foreign investment and aid and thereby to stimulate the Egyptian economy. From 2006 to 2007 the growth rate reached 7 percent, but only a minute portion of the Egyptian population felt any benefit from it.[31] Rather, even the middle classes found it difficult to balance their family budgets, and a growing portion of the rural and urban population found itself in an impoverished and precarious position.[32] Yet there was no social policy aimed at a more equitable distribution of wealth, although the government had taken several emergency measures to attend to the most abject of the poor. Corrupt land and building deals abounded, orchestrated in the ministries by the Garana, Mansour, and Maghrabi families, respective ministers of tourism, transport, and housing, among others. Corruption had become blatant. More insolent than ever, the powerful revealed their contempt for the people.[33]

But the struggles between rival factions in the party and the interdiction that weighed on the military's private preserve set limits on the power of Gamal and his men. On the one hand, officers opposed to the succession scenario held the ministerial portfolios of defense (Mohamed Tantawi), civil aviation (Ahmed Shafiq), and military industry (Sayyid Mishaal), as well as the directorship of intelligence services (Omar Suliman) and a number of other posts in the state apparatus. On the other hand, Gamal Mubarak could rely on the police. In police circles Habib al-'Adli, interior minister from 1997 to 2011, was nicknamed the "CEO of hereditary transmission."[34] On the national and partisan levels of the political scene reformist rhetoric did not inspire much enthusiasm. Its objective was clear in the eyes of many political figures: nobody could "deny that [the NDP] was anything more than an instrument of succession," NDP member and academic Hala Mustafa stated outright to the *New York Times*.[35]

Instead of reform, Gamal's *inqilāb* (coup) modified the engineering of partisan and government functions. The degree of proximity to the heir increasingly became the decisive criteria of co-option and promotion, creating new dissension in the party and fostering numerous defections. Especially at the time of the legislative elections in 2010, Gamal and his allies committed several errors that accelerated the disintegration of the NDP's clientelist system: they underestimated the weight of provincial notables, misunderstood the dynamics of local politics, and neglected an opposition that could easily have been tamed with a few seats in Parliament. These elections were a turning point in the eyes of many Egyptians. In particular, they were a turning point for the majority of the electorate and political actors that had supported the NDP, even if only tacitly, in various ways up to that moment; this was the crucial difference that affected the subsequent course of events.

With respect to this decay in the party, the presidential clan had committed the error of too exclusively depending on the small circle of businessmen and on a despised police force. As the years passed, Hosni Mubarak found himself more and more isolated, while developing an attitude of flattery that was not present in the first two decades of his presidency. Since the installation of the Nazif cabinet in 2004 and, especially, during the elections in 2005, all the political actors started to take their marks in anticipation of an imminent succession. The military assured that it would recognize the legitimacy of an election, all the while affirming that it would intervene to uphold public order. It expected that the vote needed to secure the "democratic" transition of power from father to son in 2011 could not fail to incite trouble in the country.[36] Before such a vote was even announced, Gamal and his clan's ascension clashed with the military's disciplinary culture and threatened its economic and political power. The military was ready to engage in action on the day of the transition, whenever it fell, foreseen or otherwise and whether precipitated by the elder Mubarak's assassination or by electoral means.[37]

Exhibiting and Stigmatizing the Copts

With regard to Coptic candidates the ideological orientation of the political parties did not dictate a specific course of action to be followed in all circumstances and in all constituencies. In general the objective was to first win the election; therefore, local power relations defined possible alliances. Every candidate running for election had to mobilize a vast client base that would bring Egyptians to the polls and then, in the case of victory, return favors and hand out benefits—preferably jobs, and if possible, jobs in the public sector. Since the 2000s, vote-buying is no longer sufficient to ensure victory against a candidate who could deliver on the potential benefits and promises.[38] The capacity to provide the desired rewards, with the general exception of jobs in the public sector, explains in part the rise in power of businessmen in Parliament. Local configuration of power determined the tactics to be used in public and which maneuvers to execute behind the scenes. On the national and local stage a politician's skill consisted in judging the appropriate moment to stigmatize religious affiliation, and in front of which audience, as an incentive or obstacle to voting, when and where to enter into a public alliance with a Christian candidate, and on what occasion and in what manner to support or dismiss one, albeit more discreetly.

Only when it began to take part unofficially in electoral contests did the Brotherhood concern itself with adopting a position on Coptic involvement in politics and its relationship with Copts.[39] If they wanted their political activities to be tolerated, Brotherhood members had to distance themselves from the radical Islamist movements that the regime was severely repressing at that time. Hence, during the 1980s the Brotherhood used a variety of tactics with Copts, in all the different areas where it intended to affirm its presence, such as the professional Trade Unions and the electoral processes. In the 1984 elections the Brotherhood shared a ticket with the New Wafd, a nationalist and liberal party, and in the 1987 elections it formed an alliance with the Liberal Party (*ḥizb al-aḥrār*) and Ibrahim Shukri and ʿAdil Husayn's Socialist Labor Party (*ḥizb al-ʿamal al-ishtarākī*), which was influenced by the writings of Tariq al-Bishri (b. 1933) and Salim al-ʿAwwa (b. 1942). Both times, the Brothers shared the ticket with some of the few Copts that were on the Wafd Party or the Alliance lists.

By 1987, this turned out to be problematic: the Socialist Labor Party chose a Copt, Gamal Asʿad, to be number one on their list for the Assiut electoral district. Until the preparatory phase of elections the Socialist Labor Party had been dominated by socialists, with Ibrahim Shukri as president and Hilmi Murad as secretary general. When ʿAdil Husayn became a member of the party's executive committee, he advocated for an alliance with the Brotherhood and the Liberal Party and supported the rise of Islamist elements in the party apparatus. What at first should have been an electoral strategy to unify opposition forces—one that would have included the Nasserist Party and the Tajammuʿ Party—was transformed into an alliance in which the Brotherhood, the Socialist Labor Party, and the Liberals designed a joint program that excluded the other parties. The Brothers fought to chair the Alliance lists and managed to oust the Socialist Labor Party personalities that had been elected to Parliament in the previous elections. Labor Party officials would not change their minds: they needed the Coptic vote and, therefore, needed Gamal Asʿad to be head of the list for the Assiut electoral district. As Asʿad was very active in his hometown, al-Qusiya, and had achieved a high number of votes as a candidate of the leftist Tajammuʿ Party in the 1984 parliamentary elections,[40] they knew that he had good chances of winning the seat once again. But the Brotherhood insisted that Muhammad Habib take the number one position. In vain, discussions lasted for ten days, running late into the night. Among other arguments, Ibrahim Shukri argued that their registration on a list led by a Copt constituted a strong political sign from which they could profit. The party leaders then turned to an Assiut shaykh affiliated with the Liberal Party, hoping that he would accept being second on a list led by As'ad. But when As'ad presented this idea, the shaykh exclaimed, "Gamal As'ad 'Abd al-Malak the Nazarene would be first, and I'd be second!" Consequently, Muhammad Habib ended up running for the individual seat, while As'ad became head of a list stripped of any candidates from the Alliance.[41] At first taken aback by the developments that caused the Socialist Labor Party to join in a durable alliance with the Brotherhood, As'ad solicited Shenuda's opinion. The pope supported As'ad's candidacy as long as the members did not campaign under the slogan "Islam is the solution." The NDP members exploited this situation. They attracted Wafdist candidates to their list, including one Copt. They fought against their rival from the Alliance by spreading doubts over As'ad's religious beliefs in order to discredit him in the eyes of his fellow Copts. Local NDP candidates claimed that the Alliance was directed against Copts, that Gamal As'ad was nothing but a traitor and an apostate, and that any votes cast in his favor would only benefit the Muslim Brotherhood. Both were elected in spite of this "dirty tricks" campaign by the NDP.

Encouraged by the pope, the Copts timidly returned to the electoral competition in 1995; however, the use of sectarian slogans was becoming more and more frequent. All the Christian candidates found themselves confronted with some sort of stigmatization at one moment or another of their campaign. Both the Brotherhood and the NDP occasionally supported Coptic candidates: for example, in the parliamentary elections of the year 2000 the Wafdist Mounir Fakhri 'Abd al-Nour—heir to a prominent Coptic family long involved in Egyptian politics—won his seat thanks to the Brotherhood's public support after the NDP candidate organized an anti-Christian campaign against him. Both groups also frequently used anti-Christian slogans, depending on the position of the rival and on the composition of the constituency at stake.

The NDP limited the number of Copts on the lists, while at the same time attempting to demonstrate the opposite. After the presidential elections in September 2005, the Egyptian press relayed the feelings of disappointment a number of Copts felt when they learned that only Yusif Butrus Ghali (the minister of finance) had taken a seat in the cabinet under the NDP banner. Meanwhile, the church had campaigned in favor of Mubarak. Several members of the high clergy denied the existence of a formal alliance between the patriarchate and the NDP, which would have urged the ruling party to include Coptic candidates in exchange for the church's support in presidential elections. Being recently fond of Coptic affairs, the press systematically covered the meetings, and the critiques they inspired, between NDP representatives and the church before the elections: "Who chooses the Coptic candidates for the People's Assembly? Baba [the pope] or Gamal Mubarak?"[42] Likewise, in May 2010 Ahmad 'Izz paid a visit to the patriarch, and the steel magnate affirmed to Shenuda that "the NDP held that the lists of party candidates for the 2010 Shura Council elections include Copts. Part of our strategy is to ensure the principle of citizenship is implemented and to encourage Copts to actively participate in political life."[43] At the last moment two Coptic candidates disappeared from the definitive party lists, along with other potential candidates.[44] But in the weeks leading up to elections, journalists strove to predict the number of Copts that would run in the elections under the banner of the NDP, which would neither confirm nor deny the predictions. Critics were usually, unsurprisingly, focused on the pope's interference in national politics. Inevitably, there ended up being few or no Copts on the lists put forward. The media attention did create one paradoxical phenomenon: in reality there weren't any Copts on the NDP lists, but there was nonetheless discussion about the question, which produced an effect of reality on the media debate and, thus, in the public imagination. Meanwhile, quite the opposite was happening far from the eyes of the media: the party was crowding out potential Coptic candidates, a tactic rendered easier because, since 2002, the NDP cadres had centralized the party "political decision-making process."[45]

Once reformed, the party should have enabled Gamal to win by way of the ballot box and to thus circumvent the majority of military officers who opposed him, while at the same time satisfying the requirements for democratization. To this end it was necessary to develop an ideological line that could rival the only competing political discourse—that of the Islamists—and "to transform this régime antechamber into a political formation with a partisan identity: this would primarily strengthen the organization's cohesion against the Muslim Brotherhood, who were the principal, and only, true adversary for the presidential party in the electoral context. This battle held a central place in the Party's strategy, as illustrated by one interviewee (who wishes to remain anonymous), who tied his sidelining for the post of Secretary of Political Education and Training to his Christian faith."[46]

When, in December 2005, the Brotherhood won 88 of the 444 parliamentary seats, many individuals expressed fears about the Brotherhood's surge on the political scene, pushing the Society to clarify its conception of the state and citizenship, as well as to consider the possibility of establishing a proper political party. Consequently, the Brotherhood adopted a reassuring form of behavior. Mahmud ʿIzzat, then member of the Guidance Bureau and one of the organization's strongest personalities (and who became the Supreme Guide after the arrest of Muhammad Badiʿ in 2013), announced that the Brotherhood was planning to publish a document stating its political ideas and its conception of the status of Copts and women in a Brotherhood-led state.[47] Continuing its rare and sporadic attempts to open communication with Coptic figures, the Brotherhood organized several dialogues. In 2005 these amounted to performances for the international audience and Egyptian intellectuals and political figures. To give one example: under the initiative of the Guidance Bureau a meeting took place in the headquarters of the Coptic weekly *Watani* in November 2005, bringing together, among others, *Watani*'s editor in chief, Yusif Sidhum, and the journalist Muhammad ʿAbd al-Quddus, who was part of the Brotherhood network and son of the famous writer Ihsan ʿAbd al-Quddus. The Brotherhood argued that it was necessary to restrict the subjects open to discussion in order to focus on topics unifying the participants and leading to active steps in their common interest, such as the development of cultural activities for youth, the fight against sectarianism and violence, and so on. Among the taboo issues were the role of the Brotherhood members in the attempt to assassinate President Nasser in 1954 and, more broadly, their activities before they renounced violence; the contradictions between secret and public assertions; their opinions concerning the poll tax and the access to the supreme functions of the state. Such a "dialogue" never led to an implementation of common projects, nor did it allow any real dialogue between the participants.

In December 2005 Rafiq Habib contacted Samir Murqus to organize another meeting in the Brotherhood-linked NGO Sawasiyya Center; the center would publish the speeches given by the guests.[48] As a Coptic scholar who had long been involved in promoting citizenship and interreligious dialogue, Murqus accepted, only on the condition that he write an introductory text to engage the debate on core issues. The day of the meeting, the Brotherhood had invited the press and TV without forewarning most participants, drastically altering the terms of the discussion. Media coverage temporarily conjured up two nonexistent realities: first, that of a dialogue between Copts and the Brotherhood; second, that of the existence of two monolithic and unified groups—"The Brotherhood" and "The Copts." In effect the Copts, considered as a monolithic bloc, often served as a foil, allowing the Brothers to appear as the only representatives of Islam.[49] Before these debates Samir Murqus had insisted that the organizers mention the diversity of the Copts' political orientations and their social heterogeneity. Also, in the introduction Rafiq Habib's reasoning traveled a tortured path to include all the Muslim players and to present a sort of Brotherhood unity against . . . Coptic diversity.[50]

• • •

Only by taking into account the social and political plurality of the Brothers can we understand the crucial role these internal dynamics played in determining the attitude of the Brotherhood, and its failure in 2013, as well as the reference to Islam as a principle of cohesion. At that time the Brotherhood did indeed attempt to clarify its doctrinal positions on Coptic citizenship.[51] But the Brothers were not the first to reflect on the "Coptic issue," as the "independent Islamists" had preceded them. Throughout the 1980s Tariq al-Bishri and Salim al-'Awwa, for example, had elaborated a theory of the state that reconciled the religious prescriptions of Islam and granted the same rights to Muslims and non-Muslims.[52] From the end of the 1970s Coptic personalities like Samir Murqus and William Suliman Qilada organized interfaith dialogues, in which Salim al-'Awwa took part, and published the texts of these discussions, notably those that touched on the theme of citizenship.[53] An exhaustive study of Brotherhood members' opinions would require an analysis of five types of documents: texts published in the name of the organization; writings by authors linked to the Brotherhood;[54] statements made to the press (these three first mainly addressing political figures, Christian citizens, and the international audience); secret documents, since made public; and literature intended for its grassroots members. Though the content of these last two types of document would undoubtedly contradict some of the principles outlined in the first three, reviewing the contradictions would require a specific study and is not necessary to reveal the full diversity of the antagonistic positions adopted by Brotherhood members. To understand the frame of reference in which the Brotherhood operates, I will therefore base my argument primarily on its public statements and on a number of writings published under the name of the organization.

Over the course of the 1987–2000 legislatures a number of sessions were held in Parliament on the subject of shari'a, with Brotherhood MPs calling for its codification and enforcement. After remaining silent for a while, Gamal As'ad decided to go forward and question members of the Brotherhood over the rulings of shari'a concerning Christians, their place in society, and their rights. Quoting the relevant yet contradictory verses from the Qur'an, he asked them which interpretation they recommended and what their conclusions were concerning the status of Egyptian Copts. He did not get an immediate answer. Maybe a meeting to discuss the subject was in order before a Brotherhood parliamentarian, Muhammad Habib, expressed an opinion over the matter before the People's Assembly: "We believe that our Christian brothers have the same rights and duties as we do (*lahum mā lanā wa 'alīhum mā 'alīnā*) and benefit from all the rights guaranteed by citizenship. What is more, a non-Muslim ruler that is just is of better worth than an unjust Muslim one."[55] Thereafter, the Brotherhood has oft repeated the saying "*lahum mā lanā wa 'alīhum mā 'alīnā*." Although its origins remain unknown, this slogan had previously been used by nationalist leader Sa'ad Zaghlul (1859–1927).[56] Needless to say, its meaning remains obscure and could lead to several contradictory interpretations.

In the first text published under the name of the organization, *Document on Consultation and the Multiparty System* (*Wathīqa al-shūra wa ta'addud al-aḥzāb*, 1994), and in the subsequent *Statement to the People* (*Bayān li-l-nās*, 1995), the Brotherhood amended several points of Hassan al-Banna's dogmatic views. It accepted the principle of partisan and multiparty politics, as well of the transfer of power through elections by a general vote. It also recognized, albeit still ambiguously, that the Copts had the same rights and obligations as Muslims (*lahum mā lanā wa 'alīhum mā 'alīnā min al-ḥuqūq wa-l-wājibāt*).

As for the *jizya*, in theory, most of the organization's members have accepted the fact that such a tax is not appropriate to current political and social organization. Blunders have frequently occurred, however. In 1997, for example, the English language newspaper *al-Ahram Weekly* quoted Mustafa Mashhur, then chairman of the Brotherhood, saying that Christians and Jews should pay the long-abandoned *jizya*. Claiming that a translation error had distorted his statement, Mashhur even took the trouble to write a letter to Pope Shenuda to clarify "the principles adopted by the Brotherhood, as prescribed by the Book and the sunna . . . which are confirmed by the good and close relations between the Brotherhood and their Egyptian Christian brothers."[57] Ten years later, Deputy Chairman Muhammad Habib made a similar assertion.

Ambiguity also frames the Brotherhood's positions on building new places of worship, which under Ottoman rule required the ruler's authorization: while churches still need to request a presidential permit, the main obstacles to church construction lie at the level of local and neighborhood administrations. In 1980 the mufti of the Brotherhood issued a fatwa in the Brotherhood journal stipulating that no church should be renovated or built.[58] At best, those already existing could be tolerated in certain areas. The Brotherhood never officially disavowed this declaration although some members argued that it did not express the organization's views. In spite of this confusing attitude the Brotherhood seems to agree, in theory, on the promulgation of a unique law regulating the construction of places of worship, be they Muslim or Christian. It sometimes continued by specifying that new construction would be restricted to cases of need, depending on the number of inhabitants, without ever giving details about how the need for a place of worship would be calculated on a per inhabitant ratio. It also remained unclear which authority would codify and enforce such regulations. Even though the drafts of Brotherhood party platforms published in 2004 and 2007 are significantly more detailed, this kind of information was often put off until a more convenient time or submitted to a committee of specialists.

In 2004 *The Reform Initiative* (*mubādara al-iṣlāḥ*), drawn up at the instigation of Mahdi 'Akif, the new Supreme Guide, outlined the Brotherhood's contemporary views on citizenship, state, and the role of religion. The Brotherhood, while rejecting the concept of a religious state, recommended applying Islamic prescriptions through the framework of a modern civil (*madanī*) state in compliance with constitutional institutions and democracy. Concerning the *wilāya al-'āmma*, the functions of authority and of leadership, its position on the status of women and Copts remained the same as in 1994 and 1995: non-Muslims and women are still barred from senior positions in the state, especially from presidential office. In February 2005, however, Hosni Mubarak's announcement of multicandidate presidential elections unleashed hopes that also spread to the Brotherhood's ranks. For the first time a few voices, especially among the organization's youth, publicly questioned its leadership and the tight hierarchy based on blind obedience to the leader.[59] They went on to criticize the organization's ideology, primarily its positions concerning the *wilāya al-'āmma*, the functions of authority, and a leadership that, according to several currents of political Islam, includes religious duties. At that time, and once again during the discussions related to Article 2 of the Egyptian Constitution in 2007, the differences among senior Brotherhood members 'Abd al-Mun'im Abu al-Futuh, Mahmud 'Izzat, and Muhammad Habib's visions of Islam and the modern state became public.

Political scientist Husam Tammam, who was once close to the Brotherhood before becoming ever more critical of it, hoped that the creation of a new balance of power, both within the Brotherhood and nationwide, could persuade the organization to reform its theoretical and organizational framework. He noted the existence of a democratic trend represented by the generation now known as "intermediate," including, among others, Abu al-'Ila' Ma'adi, the founding member of the al-Wasat Party, and 'Isam al-'Iriyan, who helped the Brotherhood reintegrate into the Egyptian political scene, especially through its success in winning over several professional trade unions in the 1980s. Tammam wondered what obstacles hindered the "progression of the democratic current within the Brotherhood?"[60] Political scientist Khalil al-Anani echoed his views, asking what was hindering the "conceptual shifting"[61] that would have allowed the full integration of Copts and other non-Muslims into the Brotherhood's Islamic conception of state and society?

They do not belong solely to the theoretical domain, argued Tammam, as 'Abd al-Mun'im Abu al-Futuh, the only member who truly constructed a reformed conception of the state, dared to take the leap. Following Tariq al-Bishri's reasoning, 'Abd al-Mun'im Abu al-Futuh insisted that in a modern and democratic state, in which individuals only have a representative function irrespective of their religious affiliation, Christians and Muslims should share the right to hold the highest offices of state, including that of president. The al-Wasat Party incorporated this clause into its platform. Certainly, the repression it had endured for decades, and the Salafist competition after 2006 had reinforced the predominant Qutbist wing in the leadership and further marginalized the reformist trend, represented by Abu al-Futuh, by the cadres of the so-called intermediate generation, and by some elements of the younger Brotherhood. Competing with the Brotherhood to be heard on satellite TV and to control mosques and charities, the Salafis played a part in strengthening the positions of Qutbist hard-liners in the Brotherhood apparatus. Hence, 'Abd al-Mun'im Abu al-Futuh remained a lone warrior who never held any decision-making position in the organization, from which he was expelled after the January 25 revolution. In contrast, Mahmud 'Izzat, a major figure of the hard-line majority current, was one of the Brotherhood's strongest men. On January 22, 2007, the Arabist-Nasserist and Islamist-inclined weekly, *al-Karama*, published an interview with this so-far little-known leader. In the interview 'Izzat reiterated that no Christian should ever win the presidency because the highest office of state has a religious dimension. According to his argument, ruling Egypt would be "a terrible transgression for a Christian, because I would demand him to do things he does not believe in, for example calling the believers to prayer, to the point where my brother, the Christian, would himself refuse to hold such an office."[62]

The final draft of the party platform of 2007 revealed that the remodeling of the Brotherhood's theoretical framework never happened.[63] Compared to several declarations made by Brotherhood members such as Abu al-Futuh and al-'Iriyan in the wake of their electoral success in 2005, this final draft expressed the strengthening of the hard-liners and the Brotherhood's growing preoccupation with prohibiting the Salafis' predominance in the Islamist field. While the Brotherhood spoke increasingly of an Islamic frame of reference (*marja'iyya*) and less of the codification and implementation of shari'a, non-Muslims and women were still barred from senior positions in the state, especially from the office of president. An overwhelming majority of Brotherhood members agreed on this matter, and, notwithstanding Abu al-Futuh's opinions, differences mostly revolved around defining which offices would be barred to non-Muslims. Furthermore, the respective roles of the Brotherhood and its political wing remained undefined, as long as the Brotherhood did not clarify the distinction between preaching (*da'wa*, literally: to call) and politics.[64] Finally, the document recommended creating a council of religious scholars whose word would be binding and not merely advisory, where shari'a rule was considered definitive and not to be altered by changing social and historical circumstances.

Husam Tammam provided a trenchant analysis of the historical and structural obstacles opposing the advancement of the minority voices who favor a reform of the Brotherhood's theoretical and organizational foundations: the lack of a democratic "culture" in Egyptian politics and in the organization itself; the fact that the Brotherhood's key positions, as well as the lion's share of its second and third circle of cadres, are occupied by "Qutbist" hard-liners such as Mahmud 'Izzat, Khayrat al-Shatir and Muhammad Badi' (who was elected Supreme Guide in January 2010), or by members sympathetic to Salafi trends; and the diverse range of profiles that led to a bewildering number of points of view that hinder the formulation of a unified political platform. These obstacles constituted barriers to creating a real political party. This endeavor would require rethinking the modes of organization and recruitment, as well as financing, and determining a political orientation. "The specificity of the leader's role in the Egyptian association, with respect to the Brotherhood in other countries,"[65] was also at odds with its transformation into a party, which would imply a restriction of his action at the national scale. Finally, and most especially, the creation of a party supposed that the Brotherhood renounced its all-encompassing pretentions to be "a Sufi way, a political organization, a sports club, a scientific and cultural organization, an economic enterprise, a social concept . . . " according to the celebrated formulation of founder Hassan al-Banna, which was derided by Tariq al-Bishri, who often described the Brotherhood doctrine as "*ghumūḍ*" or obscure and confusing. And, once again, al-Bishri emphasized that they must distinguish between preaching (*da'wa*) and politics.

If, over the course of the last years, the organization had allowed its differences to appear in public, it also knew when and how to close ranks and present a united front each time it sensed danger. The contradictory discourses, the opposition between act and speech, between secret and public, did not simply express the Brotherhood's inability to elaborate a pertinent theory. Rather, they express the diverging stances on the very definition of a political project and the means to realize it. The Brotherhood certainly did not need a theoretical framework or a program. On the contrary, from its creation to the election of Mursi in June 2012 and his fall in June 2013, blurred doctrine reinforced its organizational effectiveness, while the rigidity of the organization and the absence of any reflection on its principles prevented its adaptation to contemporary Egyptian society.

THE BROTHERHOOD'S FAILURE IN THE NASCENT PLURALISTIC SYSTEM

The January 25 Revolution and the Explosion of the Political Islamist Scene

The January 25 revolution confronted the Muslim Brotherhood with the rise of several rivals on the Islamic political stage. In these unprecedented circumstances the Brotherhood gave up its reluctance to create a political party and, in March 2011, announced the foundation of the Freedom and Justice Party. Supreme Guide Muhammad Badi', along with other Brotherhood cadres, insisted that the party did not replace the Brotherhood but represented an independent entity. The January 25 revolution also revealed to an international audience the Salafist roots in several parts of Egyptian society. One of the prominent features of the transformations brought about by this upheaval lies in the advent—or the legalization—of different political formations with an "Islamic reference."

Although the al-Wasat Party was finally legalized in 2011 after Mubarak's departure, it was not the main force with which to reckon. Meanwhile, the Salafis, which up until then had been working on the ground, had to quickly revise their conception on the participation in political life. Their newfound visibility shed light on the diversity of trends labeled by the "Salafi" designation, as well as on internal differences, especially the generational gap. Salafist parties began to proliferate: the al-Nahda Party was created, and the al-Nur Party organized its first press conference in July 2011, in Alexandria.[66] The most important among these, the al-Nur Party, benefited from the financial and ideological resources, the organizational framework, and the social anchorage of the Salafist Call. In 1977 Alexandrine shaykhs who were moving in the sphere of the *Jamaʿa al-Islamiyya* at the Faculty of Medicine had created this school, the Salafi Call, to combat the growing influence of the Society of Muslim Brothers in the *Jamaʿa* and to distinguish themselves from the oldest Salafist organization, *Ansar al-Sunna*, established in Cairo in 1926.[67] State Security services had, from the beginning of the 1990s, hampered the shaykhs' movements and limited the organization's influence to Alexandria. Though it has regularly cracked down on the most virulent Salafist currents, the Mubarak regime showed itself to be largely indulgent with regard to the Salafist Call, which was able to continue its activities and maintain a network in the majority of the national territory and also to benefit from the rise of satellite channels after the year 2000. From its birth al-Nur had forty branches in the city of Alexandria alone, thirty in the province of Damietta, twenty in Giza, and at least one in each of the other provinces. Al-Nur made a much-noticed breakthrough in Egyptian politics and scored an electoral success at 2012 parliamentary polls.

Yet the same game started all over again. Some protagonists had momentarily disappeared (the NDP), while others made their entrance (the Salafis), trying to fit into the ongoing story and influence its course. Once more, the status of Copts became the benchmark issue by which to gauge political participants' capacity to handle rhetoric on democracy and national unity. Preaching love or hate, discourses related to the Copts allowed the Salafist and Brotherhood figures to position themselves with, or to distance themselves from, the others. Such a competitive interplay also includes the state institution al-Azhar, which was supposed to represent "moderate" Islam, and was in the process of redefining its role, although internal divisions hampered the development of a genuine reform project.[68] Before the 2012 presidential elections the Brotherhood continued to offer ever-increasing signs of friendship toward Christians, especially during the Christmas celebration, inviting them to join the party and proposing dialogues with the "Coptic youth" and with members of the clergy. Simultaneously, the Brotherhood reiterated its view concerning the possibility of Copts or women becoming president. Furthermore, it turned the March 2011 referendum into a vote for or against Islam[69] and did not refrain from shouting slogans against Christians during the 2012 parliamentary elections in districts where such tactics seemed expedient.

Although Salafist leaders might not have always controlled violent grassroots initiatives against Copts, they frequently spread anti-Christian views on TV channels. Meanwhile, their newfound visibility forced Salafist actors to conform to the rules of speech and action in the political and public space.[70] For example, after the different episodes of violence targeting Copts in midwinter 2011, instigated by individuals from the Salafist milieu, Shaykh Muhammad Hassan participated in a "reconciliation session" in the Atfih neighborhood of Helwan. The shaykh himself, however, affirmed that "Islam forbids Muslims from smiling at infidels." He reiterated the old narrative that denounces the Copts as fifth columnists, seeking foreign intervention to protect themselves, and supporting the old regime through their vote in favor of the candidate Ahmed Shafiq, who had campaigned among Christians and gained their support. At the same time, citing either Islamic beliefs or respect for the state, Shaykh Hassan would nevertheless court the love of his Christian brothers, who should enjoy equal rights with Muslims.

While at first the Brotherhood had to demarcate themselves from radical groups by expressing "moderate" Islamic views, they soon had to compete with fundamentalist trends threatening their monopoly in the field of political Islam. Hence, if they wished to keep a firm grip on their fiefdom and still pretend to be the sole representatives of Islam, they also had to fit into the fundamentalist perspective. Or, conversely, while in Parliament or in the Constituent Assembly in 2012, they could rely on Salafist MPs to express the conservative views and thus appear "more democratic" or "more progressive." In the "fast delivery Constitution"[71] promulgated in December 2012, the articles related to shari'a were the result of a compromise among secularist politicians, the Brotherhood, and the Salafist members of the Constituent Assembly. Article 219, especially, set out to clarify the meaning of Article 2. Jurist Nathalie Bernard-Maugiron explains:

> This article (219) sets out very technical notions of theology and traditional Islamic law, the exact meaning of which can be understood only by a small number of initiates. It defines the principles of Islamic shari'a as the scriptural sources, that is, the Qur'an and the sunna; the principles of *usul* and *fiqh* (*al-qawā'id al-uṣūliyya wa-l-fiqhiyya*), that is, the great principles to be drawn from the works

of the specialists of the science of the sources of *fiqh* (jurisprudence); and by the rulings of the jurisconsults, as "the sources recognized by the people of the tradition and the community" (*al-maṣādir al-mu'tabara fī madhāhib ahl al-sunna wa-l-jamā'a*). While the exact reach of such a provision is difficult to assess, it is clear that it aims at countering the modernist interpretation of Article 2 adopted by the Constitutional Court.[72]

Furthermore, drawing on the 2007 draft program of the Brotherhood, the Constituent Assembly decided that al-Azhar's Council of great *'Ulama* should give an advisory opinion on matters related to shari'a and Article 2. The institutions involved, however—essentially the Parliament and the Constitutional Court—would be free to either follow such an opinion or ignore it. "The Salafis would have liked to take away the contentious jurisdiction of Article 2 from the High Constitutional Court to entrust it to al-Azhar, but this proposal was not adopted, and the shaykh of al-Azhar himself was opposed to such an extension of his competences and the excessive politicization of his institution."[73]

The Dynamics of Fear

How can the rapid about-turns of most protagonists in 2013 be understood?[74] Indeed, several trends and individuals had initially shown a grudging willingness to cooperate with Mursi, despite the differences or even animosity that marred the relationships between both revolutionary and counterrevolutionary protagonists and the Brotherhood.

To be sure, even before Mursi rose to power, the results of parliamentary and presidential elections proved that Egyptians did not overwhelmingly support the Brotherhood. Although it was the only well-organized political force that had access to extensive funding and enjoyed a large clientele network in all of Egypt's provinces, the Brotherhood could not secure a majority of seats in Parliament, obtaining low scores at both parliamentary and presidential elections in Alexandria and in Cairo. During the second round of the presidential elections, the Brotherhood also benefited from the fact that members of the Supreme Council of the Armed Forces (SCAF) did not all support Ahmad Shafiq,[75] and finally made a deal with the Brotherhood. Even so, the majority of Egyptians, from all political tendencies, wanted to forget the oddities that had tarnished the voting and to give the first elected civilian president a chance.

The size of the task, notably on the economic and security fronts, ruled out any hope of a quick improvement in the situation. The Brothers' inexperience and the systematic sabotaging of their actions do not provide the keys to sufficiently analyze the appalling results of that year in power. The alacrity with which "the street" and the army turned against the president cannot simply be attributed to the political performance of the head of state. At the time of the 2012 election the Brotherhood had many assets at hand. On the international scene the United States, Qatar, Turkey, and the European Union were ready to cooperate with the new power, and new alliances could have been forged with Japan and China, among other nations. The Brotherhood had allies in business and with provincial notables, as well as members in many professional and trade unions. It could count on a portion of the armed forces, who were convinced of the need to transfer power to a civilian, and even had established connections in the police services, the Brotherhood's historic enemy.[76] Yet the Brotherhood progressively alienated itself from its immediate or potential allies, from a portion of its electorate, and from the groups in which it did have supporters or contacts—particularly in the professional, middle-class unions of doctors, engineers, teachers, pharmacists, lawyers, journalists, and especially students, whereas the Brotherhood never had much clout among the workers. In most sectors the Brotherhood's initiatives were perceived as clumsy, brutal, or dogmatic. From the head of state to the local level, the Brothers in power showed their allegiance to the Brotherhood more than to the institutions they were meant to serve.

The Brothers, like the armed forces, had interpreted the revolution as a movement of the youth that it would quell by force or appease with several "carrots." Having poorly evaluated the import of the revolutionary situation, and simply taking into consideration the lack of unity in opposition currents, the Brothers chose an alliance with counterrevolutionary forces: the military, the police force, the Salafist milieu, and the former NDP network. Yet the Brotherhood had long held relationships with each of these groups that were, albeit punctuated by sporadic pacts, characterized by distrust or rivalry, at best, and outright animosity or even hatred, at worst. For the security apparatus, cooperation made sense insofar as the Brotherhood enjoyed popular support and electoral legitimacy that allowed it to halt the revolutionary dynamic. Similarly, the Salafist movements consented to support their rivals while waiting for a redistribution of privilege and a sharing of power. They were to be disappointed.

Once in power, the Brotherhood did not even listen to the two main revolutionary demands: Bread and Liberty. Mursi's presidential declaration on November 22, 2012, in which he granted himself extraconstitutional powers and forbade the dissolution of the Constituent Assembly, provoked a wave of protest across the country. It marked the "point of no return."[77] The Brothers called their rank and file to support the president in front of the Ittihadiya Palace, where those opposing the constitutional declaration had rallied. The confrontations there on December 5, 2012, divided the nation,[78] fostering a momentary union against the president, while reinforcing the Brotherhood's cohesion, up until its isolation. But in losing "the street" they had so neglected, the Brotherhood removed any remaining motivation for the counterrevolutionary forces, first and foremost the military, to further tarnish their image by supporting them.

As much as its decisions, the Brotherhood's methods and rhetoric set a portion of the country against it, alienating the organization not only from refractory allies but also parts of the pious Muslim electorate, who were weary of receiving lessons in matters of Islam. The Society did not break with a violent and sectarian rhetoric. Violence carried out against Christians intensified and became even crueler after the fall of Hosni Mubarak. But under Mursi's presidency the head of state abandoned any conciliatory appearances. By its symbolic weight the attack on Saint Mark's Cathedral in April 2013 traumatized the Copts. Even before the investigation into the events was concluded, the president, who had not met with the pope since he took office, accused young Copts of having printed the sign of the cross on the wall of the al-Azhar building in Khusus. The incident was at the origin of confrontations in that locality and then provoked the neighbors in the area around the cathedral, in 'Abasiyya.[79] The sectarian rhetoric, embedded in a matrix of war, was not confined to Christians alone. Pressures and successive decrees sought to muzzle intellectuals, human rights organizations, and private media that were more and more critical of the government. The prosecutor general harassed journalists and intellectuals, activists and opposition figures, all the while turning a blind eye to the recurring acts of violence committed by Brotherhood militias. The intellectuals and media positioned themselves early on against the new power and played a crucial role in the media "lynching" of the president. Initiated by private media, resistance to the Brothers' policies extended to national television channels, where several personalities protested the government's attempts to curtail freedom of expression. During the Mubarak years intellectuals and artists had been relatively well-treated. They opposed the regime merely when questions of promotion or prestige were at stake. Under the Mursi presidency they believed that their very existence was under threat, as the testimonies of a number of Egyptian scholars and artists have attested.

For their part the Brothers felt attacked from all sides. The former Brotherhood member ʿAbdallah al-Nafissi remarked that they had always had trouble identifying pertinent information and then analyzing it to form any plan of action. They indulged in imaginary conspiracy theories with no foundation in reality, and they missed many genuine threats. Society members expected what they thought was just recompense for decades of suffering: lucrative posts in the state administration. Some Brothers argued that Mursi had made too many concessions and should have used his power more radically, pointing to the fact that, even after the ministerial reshuffles in May the Brothers held only a third of the ministerial portfolios. Indeed, the Brothers had attempted to co-opt individuals in all professional and state sectors and sought to reassure the inner circles of the state by integrating technocrats and former pillars of the regime into the government. But, they did not often take their opinions into account or purely and simply did not bother to ask them. And the composition of the government signaled the Brotherhood's desire to retain control of the presidency. Choosing Mursi as a presidential candidate over Khayrat al-Shatir already clearly indicated that the party, and the presidency, would remain under the Brotherhood's control. A member of the Guidance Bureau, Mursi was, par excellence, a man of the apparatus, bound and disciplined, who climbed the ranks by his obedience and loyalty to his superiors, who had never criticized a Guidance Bureau choice, and who remained loyal to the most powerful man in the Society, Khayrat al-Shatir. The Brothers placed several former Guidance Bureau members in the presidential team. They also took pains to ensure that the presidency did not make close alliances with other groups or lead an autonomous life that would risk producing a rift in the organization. If defection among members of the younger generation garnered media attention, it is likely that the direction of the Brotherhood placed more importance on preserving the cohesion between the members responsible for preaching and those in political roles, particularly at the national level. Ambiguity surrounded the respective roles in the Society and the party, so as not to make distinctions that could be perceived as a source of the group's weakness.

Hence, it is difficult to ask, "Why did [the Brotherhood's] behavior change so erratically during the post-Mubarak years rather than remaining cautiously conservative?"[80] It appears, on the contrary, that structural and long-standing characteristics of the Brotherhood's behavior prevailed and that this is precisely the main reason explaining its failure. First, the Brothers have never been interested in thinking about the social question from a political point of view, and they did not begin to do so, even though revolutionary and leftist trends at first massively supported Mursi.[81] Moreover, they have continued working as an autocratic organization, making decisions secretly and imposing them on others: "While this well-knit structure safeguarded the Brotherhood from Mubarak's brutal repression and preserved its cohesion, it became a hurdle after the uprising. The Brotherhood continued to operate as a secretive and underground movement without any attempt to modernize its code of values."[82] Thus, they epitomized the identitarian dynamics that govern not only the prevailing divide between Christians and Muslims but the rift between the Brotherhood and *all* other groups or individuals, who are henceforth considered enemies. In March 2013 several youth launched a signature campaign to withdraw confidence in the president and provoke early elections.[83] The Tamarrod (rebellion) movement was conducted under security surveillance and, little by little, gained the support of all political forces, including the police and the military. At the end of June 2013 tens of millions of Egyptians mobilized to demand the president's resignation, while the Brothers and their supporters amassed at Raba'a al-Adawiya Square. Far from breaking with the logic of Brotherhood discourse, the new government equally adopted a rhetoric embedded in a matrix of war. On July 3 the army deployed in the streets. In the evening General 'Abd al-Fattah al-Sisi announced Mursi's replacement by 'Adli Mansur, the president of the High Constitutional Court; the dissolution of the 2012 Constitution; and the promise of legislative and presidential elections. Most of the Brotherhood's leadership was arrested. Brotherhood members, supporters, and militants occupied Raba'a. The army assured popular approval in the request for a mandate "to put an end to terrorism" and called for demonstrations on July 26. Then, on August 15, police violently cleared Raba'a Square, and another encampment at al-Nahda Square, killing over a thousand men, women, and children at the sit-ins. The Brotherhood was steamrolled, traumatized. Could a different environment have led to structural changes in the Brotherhood's attitudes and organization? How repression will affect the Muslim Brothers remains an open question for the time being.

Whether as an enemy or a co-opted ally of the regime, the Brotherhood has served as a collective operator of authoritarian order. As a product of this order, it carried out its structural identitarian dynamics. Triggering this dynamic, it was locked in a suicidal stance and sacrificed as a scapegoat.

6 CONTESTING SECTARIANISM

The controlled pluralization of political life was carried out in conjunction with the transformation of the Egyptian and international media landscape. Hence, it is embedded in the broader context of a change in the *regime of visibility*, which involves a reconfiguration of the interconnection between the informal and the institutional, the conventional and the taboo, and so on. In an attempt to adjust to, and to capitalize on, this new "*partage du sensible*,"[1] the regime strove to circumscribe the spaces and modes of the visible. It deployed different tactics to control political activism, while presenting itself as the sole mouthpiece and guarantor of rights, upon which, however, it never ceased to trample. Similarly, after January 25 each government claimed to be fulfilling the objectives of the revolution.

EGYPTIAN ACTIVISM BETWEEN CITIZENSHIP AND COMMUNITARIANISM

"Copts at Home," "Copts Abroad"

Shawki Karas, the "father" of Coptic activism outside Egypt, founded the American Coptic Association in 1974, while his compatriot Salim Naguib created the Canadian Coptic Association.[2] They shared an outlook that revolved around the theme of the millenary persecution of Copts by an Islam that was fundamentally and inevitably hostile to Christians and Jews. The most radical argument applied "genocide," as a legal category for the situation of Christians in the East. To support their argument, they attempted to show how this genocide had been planned for the longest time, even for all eternity; they furnished "proof" of complicity between the Egyptian state and the Nazis. Whether they went along with this reasoning or not, the majority of activists in the diaspora shared the view that the Egyptian government intended to eliminate Christians and Jews and that this plan was inherent in Islamic teachings.

The statutory organization of these first Coptic associations was poorly defined and their size relatively small. The founder was often the main representative, while four or five administrative staff ensured the effective functioning of the association.[3] Searching to make sense of the Copts' situation to people outside Egypt, they often resorted to "scandalization."[4] Following a second line of attack, they addressed themselves to the Egyptian regime by practicing a "form of interbranch lobbying" (for example, U.S. senator Frank Wolf wrote to the Egyptian head of state) or resorting to "accountability,"[5] setting public interpellation procedures such as targeting the Egyptian president by petitions, demonstrations, and flyers. These actions required finances but no mass recruitment effort, which they would not have had the capacity to carry out. In fact, often coming from well-off social milieux, or holding liberal professions, and situated to the right of the political spectrum, the activists in the diaspora principally attracted the sympathies of transnational Christian associations and members of the American (neo)conservative, Islamophobic, and sometimes Zionist, right.

These activists, however, represented but a tiny minority of emigrant Egyptian Christians. The mother church in Egypt and the churches abroad dissociated their statements and actions from those of activists who were trying to resolve the "Coptic issue" through foreign pressure on the Egyptian government. The churches judged it more opportune to publicly disavow the activists' rhetoric and activities, particularly as the Egyptian president had tarred the church and the activists abroad with the same brush and had cracked down by dismissing Pope Shenuda in 1981. The clergy, who had raised their voices at the end of Sadat's presidency, demanding Shenuda's return to the See of Saint Mark, then adopted a conciliatory attitude toward the government of Hosni Mubarak. But the diaspora activists saw no reason to be so submissive, and they did not fail to (privately) evoke the priests' cowardice. They mocked the clerical conception of the suffering martyr as a mode of political protest that they believed was inappropriate for the modern world. In addition to the pope, Coptic politicians, like Gamal As'ad, usually did not appreciate the public denunciation of the representative of the Egyptian state and advocated a resolution of Egyptian problems "from the interior." Some did not hesitate to discredit the diaspora activists, thus serving the political line of the regime, as well as their electoral interests. This public consensus, which came out in one way or another every time the question of external intervention emerged, was wedded, however, to ambivalent and equivocal positions with regard to the foreign and diaspora activists. The pope benefited from their activities during periods of negotiations with the regime, their simple existence weighing on unfolding discussions. The attitude of the Copts in Egypt was no longer devoid of ambiguity. A number of Egyptian Copts provided the activists with information relative to violence and discrimination, nourishing antagonistic fears and hopes: hoping that justice would be done, they mentioned at times their desire for foreign intervention, given that relying on the Egyptian state appeared a lost cause. And yet, persuaded that the North American and European states were concerned only with achieving their strategic and economic objectives, they also doubted the possibility and efficacy of such an intervention. Fearing the revival of the image of Christians as a fifth column of the subjective enemies (but objective allies), the United States and Israel, and attached to what was left of the national ideal, they rejected the idea of external interference.

Coptic organizations multiplied in North America. Christian Copts of California (CCC), the U.S. Copts Association (USCA), and the aforementioned American Coptic Association (ACA) were the three principal Coptic activist organizations at work in the United States during the 1980s and up to the 2000s.[6] They had won over the old continent the moment the project of the codification of shari'a was published in the Egyptian press, previewing the application of punishments for apostasy, before their removal under Shenuda in 1981. Disseminating its paper to Coptic churches in France, as well as in other Christian communities, the ACA stimulated the emergence of a dissenting viewpoint in Europe. Despite personal differences among their members, the organizations in North America became closer "at the end of the 1990s—in the International Coptic Federation (ICF), which also featured a Canadian, Australian, and French organization."[7] Before this date their founders had not taken any steps to federate the organizations, which did not maintain contact and only occasionally undertook actions together on the basis of personal relationships between certain members. Coptic organizations proliferated in Europe and Australia at the end of the 1990s.[8] Only Adil Abadir could coordinate, as best he could, the activists' actions via his organization, the Unified Copts (*al-aqbāṭ al-muttaḥidūn*), based in Zurich.[9] After Abadir's death in 2008, attempts at coordination occurred, though they still rarely managed to overcome individual or internecine rivalries. These efforts did result in a project to unify European Coptic organizations, the attempt to create a Coptic "Parliament" in 2009, and, finally, the creation of Coptic Solidarity, in June 2010.

Not content with simply quoting international treaties, diaspora activists sometimes attempted to contribute to their revisions. Michael Mounir (alias Michel Meunier), a friend of 'Adli Abadir and president of the USCA, though now more active in the ACA, intervened "around the hearings of the Human Rights subcommittee of the International Relations Committee in Congress, on the occasion of the legal project that would become the International Religious Freedom Act of 1998, a text that makes the defense of religious liberty abroad a priority of American foreign policy. Egypt, one of the largest recipients of American aid, was oft-cited as an example. Meunier also met with members of the U.S. Commission of International Religious Freedom (USCIRF)."[10]

Beginning in the 2000s, several factors contributed to the rapprochement between Coptic activists abroad and at home, despite the persistent differences of opinion over the courses of action needed to improve the Coptic situation. Changes in communications technology facilitated exchanges between activist networks in Egypt and abroad.[11] 'Adli Abadir gave four conferences between 2004 and 2006, which gathered emigrant activists in Egypt and members of the NDP, among others. Yet, in proposing to hold a conference on Egyptian soil in 2007, he crossed a red line and raised an outcry in the national press. Several activists in the diaspora then took their turn on the Egyptian scene, organizing less-important conferences in Cairo, and discreetly participating in NDP-organized demonstrations to promote the new democratic rhetoric in the reigning party. Better informed, some Christian activists living abroad nuanced their discourse, while the degradation of the daily lives of Christians and the growing discontent with patriarchal politics incited not only activists, but clergymen, to put forth less-guarded opinions on Coptic activity in the diaspora. For example, when the U.S. Department of State published its 2007 annual report on religious freedom, the American Coptic Union, which counted several members of Congress such as Senator Frank Wolf among its sympathizers, criticized Shenuda's political positions and demanded that the American government reduce or suppress economic aid to Egypt. Rather than join the choir of those who denounced the treason of these emigrants, the priest Murqus 'Aziz called the Egyptian regime itself into question but without going so far as calling for the adoption of economic sanctions.[12]

A specific trait of the last decade, the Copts' dissenting actions in Egypt frequently criticized the regime and patriarchal policies. Thus, Coptic youth expressed their opposition to the Mubarak regime, sometimes violently, by turning their backs on patriarchal authoritarianism, while the lay movement placed its proposals for clerical reform within the broader project of state reform.

Coptic Activism and the January 25 Revolution

Coptic activism reemerged on the national scene as part of a general resurgence of political activism. The electoral and partisan scene controlled by the ruling party was no longer an appropriate place of action to instigate political reform. Throughout the 1990s, political activists turned massively to civil society activism, in Egypt and in the wider Arab world.[13] In the new millennium dissent arose anew. Analyzing the genesis and limits of political activism in Egypt during the early 2000s requires placing local dynamics in the new regional configuration. Indeed, the Palestinian Intifada of the late 1980s and then the Iraq War encouraged many activists of the 1960s and 1970s generation to participate again in the political struggle, while fostering the political commitment of younger protagonists who have renewed the repertoire of contention of dissenting action.[14]

As early as the year 2000, anti-Mubarak protests had taken hold of the university campus.[15] Protests against the Israeli reprisals in 2001 and against the American intervention in Iraq in March 2003 drifted toward a public critique of the government's policy of alliance with Israel and the United States. Moreover, they led to a shift in the terms of the ongoing debate over the position to be taken regarding foreign institutions, primarily American.[16] Denouncing American policy in the Middle East should not hinder cooperation with foreign agencies altogether, insofar as this could enhance the prospects of the establishment of the rule of law in Egypt. Dissenting organizations began to form. University professors, journalists, and lawyers, who were former activists in the 1960s and 1970s, created *al-Hamla*, the popular campaign for change (*al-ḥamla al-sha'biyya li-l-taghyīr*), with a Marxist leaning. Equally driven by protagonists of the 1960s and 1970s generation, Kifaya, the Egyptian movement for change (*al-ḥaraka al-maṣriyya li-l-taghyīr*), first led by George Ishaq, brought together personalities from all strands of the political opposition, including Islamic movements. They planned to enter into action before the 2005 referendum on presidential election and the legislative poll, in order to challenge the transmission of power from Hosni Mubarak to his son. Hence, the rallying cry of the group—"*Kifaya*!" (Enough!)—expressed the rejection of both father and son. In the petition signed in September 2004, marking the organization's public birth, the demand to reform the modes of presidential investiture was added to the general demands formulated by the political opposition, such as an end to the state of emergency and the pluralization of the electoral scene. Three months later, on December 12, the group broke new ground again, this time taking its eminently political slogan into the public arena, pointing directly at the president: activists demonstrated in the streets in silence, their mouths sealed by yellow tape that bore in red letters Kifaya's slogan: "No to prolongation; no to the hereditary transmission of power." In the wake of this dissenting dynamic several professional organizations of lawyers, journalists, doctors, engineers, and artists, alongside young Egyptians, created their own movement, whose activities were carried out in coordination with Kifaya.[17]

The presidential decision to organize elections with several candidates invigorated political actors and groups, creating greater synergy among them, while at the same time intensifying competition and, thus, the radicalization of demands. This relaunched debate on the organization of the political scene—e.g., the attitude to adopt regarding the referendum on the constitutional amendment—then the presidential and legislative vote, and the rules of the election process. Even more remarkable, participants opened a debate on previously taboo subjects, such as the retention of Article 2 in the Egyptian Constitution. Nonetheless, in this unforeseen configuration the forces of opposition, divided and without social support, were not capable of organizing a front to rival the NDP in elections, even less because the conditions for candidacy posed difficult obstacles, undermining the Article 76 amendments that should have allowed for greater pluralism. The only opposition current with a solid financial base and an electoral clientele—the Brotherhood—took eighty-eight seats (20 percent) in the 2005 elections, which unfolded amid violence and massive electoral fraud.

These elections propelled reformist judges to the forefront of the opposition. The judges' supervision of elections since 2000 had changed the modes of politicizing a body long active on the political scene and whose decisions carried political weight, in particular those of the High Constitutional Court.[18] Following the parliamentary elections, reformist judges supported by Kifaya and other opposition groups had fought arduous struggles against the public powers in order to invalidate the electoral results in several constituencies and, by the same token, to defend the (controlled) independence of the profession. In 2009 Ahmad al-Zind's election to the presidency of the Egyptian Judge's Club signified the victory of the opposing camp, worried about preserving the integrity and interests of the profession without interfering in the political field or questioning the absence of accountability.[19]

The meager concessions wrestled from the regime did not hamper its electoral domination, and two years later, new amendments to the Constitution paved the way for the succession.[20] The regime hardened its tone. Al-Hamla disappeared from the political scene, and the Kifaya movement ran out of steam. Certainly, demonstrations and sit-ins had become a part of shared spaces. Critiques, demands, and derision were expressed in media, which was experiencing accelerated change with the rise of a nongovernmental and nonpartisan press and the emergence of social media. But the street remained under state control.[21] Police brigades generally marshalled the protesters, and police numbers often exceeded that of people attending the demonstrations. Tacit and explicit rules regulated the channels and the content of criticism and determined the limits of the spaces where it could be expressed.

Moreover, opposition groups in 2004 and 2005 did little to mobilize outside of activist and intellectual circles in the Egyptian capital. Kifaya leaders argued that the movement had lifted a taboo by attacking the person of the president directly. And several analysts submit that the movements had presented alternative structures of opportunity, thus explaining the multiplication of workers' actions after 2006.[22] By establishing a causal link between the anti-Mubarak actions in 2004 and 2005 and the expansion of social mobilization from 2005 to 2011, this reading ignores the specificity of the professional groupings dynamics and activist trajectories. It does not sufficiently take into account the existing gap in Egyptian society between the diverse socioprofessional categories and economic classes. The rare attempts to coordinate political activism from the educated middle or upper classes with the workers' struggles were failures. When, in 2008, the April 6 Youth Movement planned to organize a general strike in solidarity with factory workers from the Egyptian Spinning and Weaving Company in Mahalla al-Kubra, the initiative was aborted because of a mutual lack of understanding and diverging interests, in addition to the deterrent measures taken by the government.[23] The renewal of union activism in Egypt was embedded in a broader protest movement against the effects of neoliberal capitalist projects promoted and exported by the IMF and the World Bank.[24] Privatization or expropriation measures carried out by Ahmed Nazif's government affected sectors that had previously been relatively protected—the banking sector, for example. At a time when purchasing power was drastically reduced, a growing number of individuals in the NDP's electoral base found themselves vulnerable, particularly urban workers and those in rural areas.[25] This experience of vulnerability occurred at a time of change in the regime's attitude. In 2006 and 2007 activists were not repressed in the same brutal manner as from 1980 to 1990, opening the space for new structures of political opportunity. Thus, criticizing the tendency to view structures of political opportunity as an explicative hegemonic model, and ignoring other variables, Marie Duboc proposes integrating the notion of threat to the analysis of social mobilization from 2006 to 2011.[26] She points to the determinant role of fraud in the 2006 union elections as a catalyst in the process of mobilization. The unions' allegiance to the ruling party was perpetuated from the Nasserist era until the 2000s; in the 2006 union elections workers once again opted for regime candidates. Initially hostile to the idea of forming independent unions, the majority of leftist union members from UGESTE finally accepted them after massive fraud in these elections was revealed. Without organization at the national level, the workers' actions were better prepared at the local level, mobilizing "urban networks close to the factories."[27] This newfound requirement of autonomy went hand in hand with the development of a practice of dissenting critique. And the workers' mobilizations were in themselves a radical challenge of the government's neoliberal policies.[28]

During the winter preceding the insurrection, social mobilizations multiplied in the hospitality and port industries, in rail and road transportation, in particular in the Delta and in Suez, Isma'ilia, and Port Said. A weeklong truck drivers' strike caused serious budgetary losses for the government and several companies. Invigorated by the uprising of January 25, actions spread to most sectors of the economy, explicitly linking their demands to the "revolutionary" wave. Five days after the beginning of the revolutionary insurrection, on January 30, 2011, the creation of the Egyptian Federation of Independent Trade Unions (*al-ittiḥād al-maṣrī li-l-niqābāt al-mustaqīla*) was an important marker in the workers' and union movement that had been under way since the end of Nasser's presidency.[29] After January 25 these new organizational bases allowed workers to launch actions at the national level. Yet rivalries and differences of opinion between the union leaders contributed to blocking a permanent independent federation of unions after January 25.[30]

• • •

The majority of Copts feared the political rise of Islamist trends. But many Christians celebrated Mubarak's downfall, even if they had previously kept the insurgent movement at arm's length. By and large Copts were at first uneasy but then, like their fellow citizens, saw the horizon peel away and the future become possible once again. In the midst of the uprising, however, the majority of Copts remained in limbo. Some distrusted a movement that they believed had been infiltrated by the Brotherhood and the Salafis, evidenced as they saw it by the growing number of beards in Tahrir Square, so they refused to take part in the mobilization. Nonetheless, the number of Copts engaged in revolutionary action, far from negligible, caused the church to nuance its position, and a week after the uprisings began, it declared, through unofficial channels, that it was not opposed to Christians' participation in demonstrations that demanded the respect of their rights and freedoms as citizens "in the proper conditions."

The majority of Christians and other Egyptians that came into the streets on January 25 or the following days were not affiliated with any opposition party, advocacy group, or any other dissenting body. The actions of multiform and sectoral dissent that spanned the first years of the twenty-first century reawakened a critical sense even in those who had no thought of engaging in politics in an authoritarian situation. Although since the end of the 1940s the Copts had been progressively disinterested in a national political life from which they felt excluded, the new vitality of dissent in the national arena swept through the ranks of Christians and was stimulated by the diaspora activism. Representing just a small proportion of the workers, Copts barely participated in the wave of strikes in Egypt's factories. But those who did take part in these actions often contravened the church's directives. A Christian coordinated a long strike for property tax collectors in 2007, and another did so for the railways. Workers' mobilizations were an (almost) daily spectacle from 2006 onward, and sometimes these yielded positive results, while the politicization of demands had a decisive impact on the slow maturation of the revolutionary movement. They familiarized Egyptians with the idea that dissent was not only possible but sometimes garnered a certain measure of success.

Present in diverse formations on the left of the political chessboard, Copts also contributed to the recent rise of advocacy groups and Egyptian NGOs. Most often, young Copts passed to activism through communitarian networks. Coptic mobilizations multiplied from 2008 at the instigation of organizations like al-Katiba al-Tibiyya, which was supported by the church, or through mobilizations launched in response to an immediate event, especially in Upper Egypt, or in the trash-pickers neighborhood in Muqattam.[31] Mona Mina, the figurehead of Doctors Without Rights, an organization founded to defend the rights of doctors and to thus counterbalance the inaction of the official union, and George Ishaq, the best-known Christian leader in the opposition and cofounder of the Kifaya movement, found their place in Tahrir Square on January 25, 2011.

In contrast, at the beginning of February 2011, on the Coptic diaspora organizations' websites, time appeared suspended. Since the attack in Alexandria the previous month, nothing had been posted. Despite the vehement criticisms they levied at the regime and the pressure they attempted to exert on it, the diaspora activists, for the most part, were apprehensive about the fall of a government that represented for them the final bulwark against a complete Islamization of Egyptian society. On February 4, however, Coptic Solidarity published a communiqué demanding Mubarak's departure, the dissolution of the People's Assembly following a referendum, and the installation of a transition government within the legality of the Constitution. The Protestant churches, however, took part in the revolutionary movement from the very first days, first and foremost the famous Qasr al-Dubbara Church, located a stone's throw from Tahrir Square and nicknamed the "church of the revolution," as several Coptic Orthodox priests called it.

The military repression of a Coptic demonstration on Cairo's Maspero Bridge set off protests. On October 10, 2011, following aggression against Copts in Upper Egypt, several advocacy groups and political formations had engaged in a peaceful march. Indignant at the outbreak of violent acts against Christians, they demanded justice. The march started at Shubra, a neighborhood north of the Ramses Station, best known for the goodwill that reigned between Muslims and the important Christian community there.[32] The *baltagiyya* headed off the procession and began beating the marchers. Others threw projectiles from the bridge. Without fear of ridicule television stations broadcast the message: "Copts are attacking the Army. Egyptians must take to the streets to defend the army."[33] Military vehicles intervened. Mina Daniel, a young Christian activist, was killed during the assault and became one of the emblematic figures of the revolution, often coupled with another revolutionary "martyr," Shaykh 'Imad 'Ifat. The Maspero Youth Union brought together a number of young people who were active during the Coptic protests after the 2010 attack in Alexandria, as well as on other occasions during the revolutionary movement. They also united members of al-Katiba al-Tibiyya and a number of priests. The movement's positions, different depending on the political situation, were under more or less strict church control. But the movement was also characterized by the diversity of the activist profiles and individual backgrounds.[34]

A year after the president's departure, the majority of Copts active on the national political and activist scene recognized the legitimacy of the elected Parliament and planned to continue the struggle for the reconstruction of the state apparatus. But others, equally numerous, resigned and withdrew behind the supposed fatality of a Coptic destiny for martyrdom, paying more attention to Shenuda's successor than to national elections. Throughout the weeks that followed Mubarak's downfall, the rash of attacks against Copts and the intensive instrumentalization of religious slogans had two parallel effects: they nourished the tendency to retreat behind the walls of the all-embracing church, and they motivated the expression of demands around community values.

The sectarian fracture that poisoned political and social life also tainted Egyptian activism. Both abroad and inside Egypt, Coptic activism was characterized by the diversification of modes of action, the sectorization of demands, the growing number of actors, the increased communication between activist circles, and the predominant reference to human rights. And both abroad and within Egypt, Copts oscillated between citizenship and sectarian demands. Ambivalence, thus, characterizes Coptic activism, which attempts to breach sectarian boundaries but sometimes feeds sectarianization.

Miṣriyūn Against Religious Discrimination (MARED—Miṣriyūn Ḍidd al-Tamyīz al-Dīnī)

Revolted by an attack carried out against Christians in Alexandria in April 2006, secular Muslim activists created the group muslimūn ḍidd al-tamyīz (Muslims Against Religious Discrimination). On April 30, 2006, the group published its founding communiqué, initialed by two hundred people, expressing sadness in hearing of "those who are ignorant and radical, who stab and kill in the name of Islam." Citing verses from the sura "al-Baqara," which calls for fraternity with non-Muslims, the group rejected the propagation of "hysterical Salafist discourses" that stirred up hatred of Christians in mosque sermons, in sidewalk publications, and on the Internet. It denounced the conflation of attachment to nation and to religious belonging, which drove the idea that Christians were a "fifth column of foreign Crusaders." It also opposed the application of the *Humayuni* clauses concerning church-building, and the "religious discrimination in the appointment to various functions, as well as the state's intervention in limiting Christian presence in state institutions and to important functions like provincial governors, or ministers, as well as entry to the higher posts in the police, the army, and universities."[35]

In August of that year an inaugural text signed by three hundred people announced the creation of Miṣriyūn (Egyptians) Against Religious Discrimination (MARED—miṣriyūn ḍidd al-tamyīz al-dīnī). Its authors described their motivations, the goals of their initiative, and offered a plan of action. Convinced that religious segregation was threatening Egypt's future even more than the existing divisions between class and gender, they engaged in the struggle for respect of freedom of belief and worship and for the penalization of discriminatory acts. The text defined two types of activities, which were linked but nonetheless distinct. In the first plan of action, the group intended to carry out educational work and promote "the values of freedom of thought and belief, and a culture (*thaqāfa*) of citizen's rights" by means of communiqués, conferences, publications, and discussions. Each year, MARED organized several conferences, as well as a two-day seminar, and financed the publication of the participants' contributions. The first colloquium, "Egypt for All Egyptians" (*Miṣr li kull al-miṣriyūn*), covered various themes, while the following two concentrated on specific issues: discrimination in education in 2009, discrimination in law in 2010.[36]

In the second line of action, fueled by a project to reform state institutions, the authors of the communiqué described spheres of intervention, specific objectives, and the appropriate modes of action to achieve them. Combatting all forms of "discrimination in law, official documents, education, and the media," they called for mobilizations to demand the promulgation of a unified law on the construction of places of worship and the penalization of acts of religious discrimination, and they listed the suppression of the line for "religion" on official forms and work applications as a primary objective.

Often in coordination with other figures on Egypt's activist scene, MARED participated in numerous demonstrations or sit-ins and addressed petitions to state and governmental bodies regarding requests made after instances of discrimination. In particular, MARED engaged in mobilizations in favor of Christian and Bahai plaintiffs who had undertaken judicial actions against the Ministry of the Interior. Conducted simultaneously with the court proceedings, the occasionally successful activities contributed to reconsidering the terms of the debate around the problem of national identity and citizenship.[37]

This problem concerns the divergence between two conceptions of secularity that run through Egyptian—and Arab—intellectual history. Along with the majority of actors in the non-Islamist political scene and Egyptian thinkers, the majority of MARED activists were willing to consider the teachings of Islam among a number of normative principles that oriented their struggle against religious discrimination. For example, the group's founder, Munir Megahed, did not justify the legitimacy of reconverts' demands simply on the basis of the Constitution, substantive law, and the international treaties that Egypt has ratified; he also referred to the Qur'anic text.[38] Similarly, the authors of the EIPR's report on the case of Bahais and reconverts highlighted the verses that denounce coercion in religion.[39] Still, some members see it as necessary to limit reference only to international treaties and Egyptian legal and constitutional texts that stipulate freedom of belief and equality for all citizens regardless of religious distinction. In this sense they argue that recourse to Islamic texts opens the door to a multiplicity of interpretations and, therefore, to debate, the outcome of which is uncertain. Among those who support abandoning any Islamic reference, some, particularly Christians, objected as a matter of principle that rights and freedoms would be founded on Islamic religious teachings. Combined with the questioning of Egyptianness, the attempt to circumscribe secular spaces ran up against the ethnicized conception of Coptic identity, which is shared by several Coptic activists. And the difference of opinion has morphed into an insurmountable antagonism among some members of the group. Following Anba Tuma's August 2008 speech to the Hudson Institute, Magdi Khalil expressed his agreement with the bishop's point of view on Arabism.[40] The debate on Egypt's Arab identity polarized the MARED activists. In other words the particularistic logic reiterated by the voices of Coptic figures under the guise of a universalist discourse undermined the very discourse itself, as well as the effort to create universal values from an Islamic singularity.

Aside from these internal divisions, MARED suffered from its members' lack of regular involvement in its activities. And it failed to attract other activists. To broaden its audience and reach those, presumed to be numerous, who were not sensitive to the phenomenon of religious discrimination, but would not tolerate violence and murder, MARED formed the National Committee Against Sectarian Violence (*lajna waṭaniyya ḍidd al-ʿunf ṭāʾifī*). Members of the group originally had the idea of educating the public on the tenuous link between "physical" violence and "symbolic" violence that was exercised daily through multiple discriminations and, thus, between the committee's activities and those of MARED. The inaugural demonstration in January 2010 was a success: it gathered several hundred people, shocked by the murder of the six Christians in Nagʿ Hammadi that had happened a few days earlier. The committee, however, did not achieve its desired objective, in part for organizational reasons. MARED's active and regular workforce was reduced as a number of its activists dedicated their efforts to putting the new structure in place. But its creation failed to rally the unanimous support of members of the group or of other organizations, even those that shared the same concerns. Seeing the committee as superfluous, several organizations abstained from signing the letter calling for the government to take measures to put an end to sectarian violence by enacting a unified law on places of worship and penalizing criminals, which the activists handed over to the authorities after the protest march.

Moreover, they had to overcome tedious administrative red tape for more than three and a half years before the Ministry of Social Solidarity would agree to grant them legal status as a nongovernmental organization. Finally, State Security agents raised further obstacles to hamper MARED's activity: "We succeeded in organizing this [first, April 11–12, 2008] colloquium despite the resistance put forth by proponents of discrimination allied with State Security," reported the authors of a MARED booklet in 2009. After long negotiations with State Security agents, the group obtained authorization to hold a meeting at the Journalists' Syndicate, presided over by Makram Muhammad Ahmad, who was in favor of the project. On April 11, 2008, the entry to the Syndicate building was blocked, and large posters denounced the plotting of Zionists, Bahais, and diaspora Copts. Gamal 'Abd al-Rahim and his cronies, who had spent the night inside the locale in anticipation of the event, blocked the activists' entry and became aggressive, resistant to any effort of conciliation.[41] Makram Muhammad Ahmad refused to alert the security forces, in order to avoid the violence that would turn the illegal occupants into victims. Several testimonies lent credence to the idea that the Muslim Brothers—or some among them—supported Gamal 'Abd al-Rahim's efforts, perhaps even financially, and that this collusion was unfolding against a backdrop of internal rivalries within the Syndicate. One testimony suffices: several days after the incident, Muhsin Radi, a Brotherhood leader in the Delta region, called Makram Muhammad Ahmad and said, "We scored a great goal against you, don't you think?" 'Abd al-Rahim had apparently tried to gain the endorsement of an officer in the State Security's political office but was told not to "bother Makram." Could another agent have contravened this position despite Ahmad's longtime relations with senior officers in State Security? Maybe the officer's response was somewhat ambiguous? Although State Security—not without some grumbling—had granted the authorization to hold the conference, they had declined to intervene when it was being sabotaged on April 11, despite having been—in all likelihood—previously informed of the intention to do so. Makram's refusal to contact State Security reveals the limits of support he was accorded when he set foot in the minefield of religious discrimination.

NEUTRALIZING CRITIQUES: GOVERNMENTAL POLITICS AND SOCIETAL DYNAMICS

Several recurring processes reveal constants and logics of action in governmental policies that, with regard to the confessional issue and Coptic demands, are neither unified nor unanimous nor clearly enunciated. Here, two contradictory logics of action are intertwined. The majority of state and government actors constantly make use of the "religious issue," thus exacerbating tensions. But leaders want to avoid the worst situations and preserve order while maintaining the status quo. To this end they simply ensure that excessive violence is carefully managed. Following this wait-and-see approach, characteristic of the Mubarak era, they avoid an explosion but also avoid a potentially dangerous attempt at defusing the issue, with its uncertain outcome and seemingly greater risk than political reward.

Physical repression remains the means employed by the Mubarak regime's successors in calming all kinds of activists' ardor for reform, as well as for hindering electoral procedures. It consists of arbitrary arrests under the guise of the "state of emergency" and is generally followed by torture, imprisonment after a military trial or before a supposedly impartial court, as well as the use of force during protests or elections, whether by uniformed security officers or *baltagiyya*.[42] Using lethal force or extended imprisonment to neutralize Coptic and advocacy activists was generally even less necessary as they do not enjoy the support of a large social base, mobilize very rarely, and do not plan violent action against the government. And the regime may count on social regulation mechanisms to limit the impact of demands that, touching the heart of the normative order, call into question not only governmental policies but also the social norms reiterated by individuals.

Discrediting and Co-opting

Hosni Mubarak's government excelled at orchestrating campaigns to discredit critics in the eyes of a supposed majority opinion. Direct governmental interventions to suggest emigrant Copts' entanglement in a foreign plot have proven superfluous. Policy makers know that someone else will invariably take the first step and that the ballet of denunciation of a foreign enemy will continue until all the dancers have left the stage. Yet they sometimes choose who will lead the dance, preferring a personality who enjoys notability and has the required credit to this end. In the Higazi affair, for example, they did not let Yusif al-Badri occupy the field alone. Al-Badri had, for decades, been listing insults against Islam day and night, and had instigated dozens of judicial actions against those who committed such crimes. The governmental press entered the dance, shaming one Coptic organization in particular and proselytism in general. The accused organization, MECA, and its members who were arrested and harassed, represented the target of a smear campaign, at the same time as being an element of discourse within other conflicting situations. Indeed, the repression against MECA also targeted emigrant Christian activists in general, as they were suspected of inciting the U.S. Congress, which lent an attentive ear to their discourse, to grant a portion of annual U.S. aid to the Copts. The press campaign followed the publication of an annual report on religious freedoms around the world by the U.S. Department of State. The report's authors treated Egypt severely, placing it among the seven countries where religious freedom was found to be the worst. Through the arrest of the MECA members the governmental press reaffirmed the sovereignty of the Egyptian regime on national soil. And, following the usual tactics, the regime thus competed with the Muslim Brothers on their own field by setting itself up to be the guardian of morality and religion. Finally, the government addressed itself, primarily, to the Coptic Church. After attacks against Copts occurred a few months earlier, several clergymen had carried out a brief campaign against Gamal Mubarak, thereby signifying that their support for the regime depended on its capacity to guarantee the Copts' security and to take the necessary steps to this end, first and foremost to submit a unified law on the construction of places of worship to the People's Assembly. Moreover, the church had taken a position against state institutions in the trials of reconverts. Even though the Coptic Church has always distanced itself from proselytism, accusations levied against foreign institutions directly target the church since everyone almost automatically links the church and foreign Christians and, more exactly, foreign funding.

The government press rarely launched campaigns of this magnitude, accompanied by repressive action, against proselytizing, whereas the Egyptian independent press regularly ran stories about the arrests of evangelists, the seizure of Bibles and counterfeit copies of the Qur'an, and, for the most part, were passing on information provided by intelligence agents. Drawing on the register of scandal, other articles published in the independent press evoked the revelation of a secret, or a conspiracy, and warned the credulous populations about the activities of groups employing the most perverse subterfuge in order to convert Muslim men and women. One journalist, for example, described three particularly dangerous individuals, hanging about in specific downtown locations, and listed the deceptions they used to trap Egyptians in their nets.

These themes can be instrumentalized since they involve societal norms in the process of their redefinition. The Higazi, Wafa' Qustantin, and *al-Naba'* affairs take shape at the juncture of media mutation in the 2000s and the liberation of speech in mid-2005, and especially the temporary removal of the Coptic taboo. Indeed, beyond the emergence of audiovisual and Internet media, the written press has diversified in the 2000s, and an independent, nonpartisan, and nongovernmental press developed, for better or worse. This journalistic literature was avid for scandals, which do not afflict liberal democracies alone, as Andrei S. Markovitz and Mark Silverstein would argue, assuming that this phenomenon requires the existence of a public space, guaranteed respect for freedom of expression, and regime accountability.[43] Neither is it confined to authoritarian regimes where it could be interpreted as an "alternative mode, or most effective instrument to cross certain red lines and (re)activate political accountability."[44] Scandal is often defined as a "public event fed by public condemnation of the transgression of norms."[45] Rather, the Higazi and Qustantin affairs reflect a more complex situation: they make the confrontation between several normative orders visible and, by throwing them into relief, indicate that the transgression is tolerated. Only accepted transgression raises scandal. But scandal reveals the redefinition of the transgression's rules of visibility. In the Higazi case the publicity surrounding the conversion, and not the conversion itself, appeared scandalous. More precisely, the provocative theater of conversion broadcast in the news heightened the scandal.

Though it unfolds within the dynamics of an ongoing normative recomposition, the cognitive force of scandal is not powerful enough to trigger a process of symbolization of emotion, as it happened at the beginning of the revolutionary process. The premeditated torture and murder of Khalid Sa'id might have remained confined to a small news item. But *il a fait événement*. One further injustice crystallized political desires, despair, and anger. It matters little why, but how? This imponderable has catalyzed a process of symbolization of transindividual emotion, whereas scandal falls within a social dynamic that neutralizes the subversive element. The one-upmanship by scandal, visible as a sort of excess, effectively produces blindness and thus neutralizes the subversive potential of the critical element. Scandal is the apparition of paradox. Scandal makes visible a break in the normative order, while reasserting the norm and the order, and, as such, it consists in a mode of social self-regulation.

The government press frequently attacked Coptic activists abroad, under the presidencies of Sadat and Mubarak alike. The most common maneuver consisted of letting a Christian personality lead the assault to discredit undesirables:

> Egyptian civil society is not wanting for personalities, or Christian personalities, ready to speak out in the interest of preserving national unity. . . . On November 5, 1998, Rami [Raymond] Lakah, a rich Christian businessman, bought an entire page in *The International Herald Tribune* and in the *Washington Post*. The inset, entitled "A Message from Egypt's Christians," denounced "obscure forces outside Egypt" that "deformed the image of the Egyptian people and government in the international community." . . . If for Lakah it was an opportunistic act, [it is unlikely] that the other signatories were up to speed on the governmental origins of the initiative. As a matter of fact, numerous Coptic personalities do denounce the nefarious influence of Coptic activism in the diaspora.[46]

After 2005 the excessive media coverage of the "Coptic issue" and the revival of interconnected Coptic activism abroad, and in Egypt, propelled the emigrant activist to the forefront of the Egyptian media landscape. The designation "the leader of the Copts in diaspora" (*qiyāda al-aqbāṭ fī al-mahjar*), as 'Adli Abadir, the organizer of a conference in Washington during the 2005 legislative elections, was called, appeared regularly in the government and independent press. It suggested the existence of an organized, powerful, and menacing political group. The activists' initiatives to act on Egyptian soil inevitably aroused fierce resistance. In November 2007, for example, when Magdi Khalil organized a conference called "Where Is Egypt Going?" in Cairo, the independent weekly *al-Usbu'* entered the ring. Adroitly, it did not denounce his Islamophobic rhetoric, which Magdi Khalil did not employ inside the national territory, nor did it mention his collusion with the "Zionist enemy." It "revealed" his acquaintance with the Egyptian regime, with the objective of discrediting him among his allies. State agents produced similar effects by deploying emissaries charged with—literally—buying or co-opting activists. For example, agents of Egyptian State Security have manipulated Michael Munir. Anxious to play a role in the national political scene, he was eager to visit Egypt at the invitation of the Security State agents. But when the media then exhibited this "alliance" between Munir and the regime, numerous activists vilified him as a "sellout."

Yet attempts at rapprochement at the instigation of government agents often remained secret. And the NDP's Policy Committee was prone to pose as the new interlocutor for Copts, both abroad and in Egypt.

The co-option by the regime—that is to say the formal or informal integration of individuals into the NDP network—constituted just one among many methods of institutionalizing and, thereby, neutralizing, dissent and criticism.

Institutionalization and Informality

In line with the logic governing the electoral game, the regime dedicated itself to neutralizing criticism while reaping the benefits of a new visibility. Not only did it partially institutionalize the key protagonists, but it strove to incorporate the very concepts and rhetoric of critical discourse.

Thus, in reaction to the public voicing of demands for rule of law that guarantees civil, political, and religious liberties for all citizens, the regime attempted to pose as the sole guardian of the rule of law. Hence, citizenship as the founding principle of the Egyptian political system was inscribed in the first article of the Constitution in the amendment that was approved in a March 2007 referendum. In so doing, the regime integrated one concept of the critique at the same time as it responded to the requirement for conformity with the transnational democratic rhetoric. Yet the regime restricted the "where" and the "when" for the expression of this rhetoric and created organizations dedicated to the promotion of citizenship or religious freedom, like the National Council for Human Rights (NCHR), founded in 2003: "Its members first assembled in February 2004 and published a report in April 2005 that was surprising in its relatively critical character. One of the Council's prerogatives was to investigate complaints submitted to it concerning human rights violations. Although not explicit, discrimination against Copts was considered to be part of the mandate from the first discreet discussions that had preceded the Council's creation."[47] Following the 2005 constitutional amendment, the NCHR organized a conference on Citizenship in a five-star hotel on the Nile Corniche. The regime indulged in giving the floor to the Copts, naming Butrus Butrus Ghali as the NCHR president and exhibiting several "Copts of the court," like Nabil Luqa Bibawi. The author of several works on the Coptic issue, Bibawi expressed the government's views and "spontaneously" advocated for the regime. In this guise he asserted that in the Wafa' Qustantin affair both the state and the church had respected Egyptian law and Islamic principles since, according to these laws and principles, the conversion of Wafa' was ruled null and void. By appropriating the concepts of critique, the regime produced a discourse that duplicates critical discourse. But a gap remains between the original and its copy.

The regime tolerated the activity of advocacy organizations whose protagonists were often working in the institutional realm, in cooperation with governmental and institutional agents. The regime generally provided them with some kind of legal recognition, while it created spaces of informality within the institutional machine and most often kept these organizations in this gray zone. Rarely did they obtain the requested status. For example, the Minister of Social Solidarity did not authorize any association founded by Coptic lawyers to function as an advocacy association. The EIPR had applied for NGO status, but it had to function as a society of lawyers. Thus, at any moment security services could argue the illegality of their activities to engage in an action against their members. Such a situation encouraged activists to exercise caution, or, as Husam Bahgat and several other activists have remarked, to practice "self-censorship."[48] Similarly, while no law forbade proselytism as such, the regime de facto tolerated evangelization in tacitly but precisely delineated spaces, which nevertheless remained under the constant menace of possible repression, under the guise of emergency laws. For example, the security services did not bother one protestant church committed to the conversion of Muslims, as long as its activities did not extend beyond church precincts and insofar as converts did not publicly or officially claim their new religion or forge false identity documents.

Samer Soliman reads this informality as a "loophole," a "strategy to address the limitations of a system" or to "escape an irreconcilable conflict," a strategy that the regime puts to work in all political, economic, and social domains: "The informal is the loophole of Mubarak's political régime. . . . Thus, the informal type of solution proposed for the problem of conversions is not exceptional. It is part of the Mubarak régime's political pattern."[49] By employing the term *pattern*, Soliman signals that the informal did not simply constitute an anomaly but served as a structural operator of Egyptian authoritarian logic. In this singularly perverse configuration, informality produces the figure of exception, and its three variants that sometimes overlap: the law of exception turned into rule, the exceptional satisfaction of a demand, and the exceptional enforcement of law.

The exception becoming the rule—such as a state of emergency that is maintained for forty-five years, minus a few months in 1980 and 1981—is "the state of exception," wrote Giorgio Agamben, who does not confine the analysis to the practices in so-called authoritarian regimes.[50] All things being equal, so-called democratic regimes have also resorted to exceptional measures, such as ruling by decrees. The margin of informality and the frequency of exceptional measures thus constitute one of the hallmarks of authoritarian situations. Two previously studied cases correspond to the second variant of exceptionality. The issuance of a permit to construct a church happens as a kind of presidential clemency. Similarly, in the Wafa' Qustantin case, satisfying the demand was in itself exceptional. The head of state responded favorably to the request of the Coptic demonstrators and the pope. This case is particularly problematic: the president transgressed national legislation to satisfy an illegitimate request, but he did so without questioning the laws and (unfair) practices that led to the conflict. A similar process is at play in the third variant, the exceptional application of the law: some reconverts could win their case owing to a lucky coincidence, a judge happening to sympathize with the cases brought to him. Others are still waiting until their request is examined, and their future remains uncertain. The repetition of these requests and, especially, the presentation of identical requests by Muslim-born plaintiffs (Higazi, then al-Guhari) have led to the suspension of Article 47 of law 143/1994 on civil status (*qānūn al-aḥwāl al-madaniyya*), as judge al-Husayni has demanded the High Constitutional Court examine the constitutionality of this article that authorizes changing information concerning religion on official documents.

The appearance of (re)converts in the institutional space of the courts gave them visibility, while subjecting them to the vagaries of another mode of informality, exceptionality, ruled by the random and arbitrary application of law. The struggle of advocacy groups aims precisely at reducing the gap between the law and arbitrary practices. Embedded in a normative framework at least partially distinct from the norms conveyed by the Egyptian legislative system, the practices of institutional agents have widened this moat between diverging normative orders. (Re)converts are relegated to an informal space that takes shape in this vacuum, at the juncture between diverging normative systems.

If its genealogy can be traced back to the historical formation of Egyptian legal and court systems,[51] such a genealogy does not fully explain it. Were we considering that the Egyptian legal and court systems are the product of a failed secularization, or of an imposed and imported modernization, and do not comply with alleged Islamic norms, we could then argue that the practices of institutional agents ensure the persistence of an authentic Islamic normative order; we might even view them as a kind of resistance to an imposed legal system. Instead, individual practices prove that Egyptians have learned to play with codes, rules, laws, and norms in order to satisfy their personal interests. Thus, the state is the main agent orienting the practice of institutional protagonists. They do not refer to an existing Islamic normative order; they create a new normative order, which, although referring to Islam as an empty signifier, simply concretizes the new security order relying on exclusion and segregation.

The institutionalization of concepts and procedures and, for example, the adoption of a rhetoric that features rights and democracy, the introduction of citizenship in the first article of the Constitution in 2007, the installation of multicandidate presidential elections in 2005, and so forth, which marked the end of Mubarak's presidency, could have remained formal and simply been ignored. Adopting rhetoric and procedural systems antagonistic to the political and social order is, however, a perilous exercise: people might try to bridge the gap between the rhetoric and the real. In fact, they have attempted to do so.

SUBVERSION AND THE RESTORATION OF IDENTITARIAN DYNAMICS

On January 25, 2011, Egyptians took to the streets, shouting "'Aysh, ḥuriyya, al-'adl al-ijtimā'iyya!" (Bread, liberty, and social justice!).[52] As early as January 28, the protagonists gave the name *thawra* (revolution/revolt) to this movement triggered by the Tunisian *thawra*. The use of the word *thawra* signals explicitly that what was at stake was not simply the overthrow of the presidential family. The revolutionary wave resulted not only from a crisis of the state and the ruling party but from much broader social mutations. The Arab revolutions opened a breach in the vicious circle of identitarian politics. From Sidi Bouzid to Tunis, from Cairo to Damascus, from Der'a to San'a', individuals and groups came together against the identitarian security state to demand the respect of inalienable rights, independent of class, gender, generation, or religion. The revolutionary moment opened a "horizon of expectation." Yet the January 25 revolution has not led to the elaboration of a new discourse to replace the old. The new attempts to express itself by taking over former symbols and narratives, but, failing to radically subvert them, it becomes lost. The more or less disappointing results of the democratic revolutions of 2011 are due, in part, to the incapacity of revolutionary currents to truly break "the identitarian articulation of meaning."[53] On the contrary, the revolutionary dynamic has reactivated an exclusionary nationalist rhetoric that had lost the power to mobilize over the course of the preceding years. Thus, the current success of counterrevolutionary trends also plays out on ideological and symbolic planes. And the victory of the counterrevolution implies the restoration of the identitarian logic, with a religious reference, which constitutes the structuring principle of the Egyptian state despite notable transformations having taken place in the state apparatus since the July regime (1952–70).

Revolution and Counterrevolution

To explain the mechanism of revolutionary change, the historian Charles Tilly "uses the image of the traffic jam that forms when different traffic flows, each with their own distinct causes, converge to create a huge gridlock. The revolutions were produced during several converging lines of 'normal' causalities (economic, demographic, constitutional, international)."[54] Revolutions are surprising not only because of their abruptness but because they reveal and hasten these processes. They accelerate time: the long, medium, and short terms swiftly telescope into one another.

A crisis of political legitimacy undermines the state-government *dispositif*, principally affecting the NDP and the security services. At the end of 2010, internal dissension in the NDP, exacerbated by the ascension of Gamal Mubarak and his allies, accelerated the rupture of a fragile political equilibrium governed by an informal system of co-opting opposition formations. This political failure and the delegitimation of the presidential clan were welded to the rivalry between a police force allied to Gamal Mubarak and his men and a military élite opposed to hereditary transition. After 2004, when the Nazif Cabinet was appointed, runaway liberalizing economic measures stimulated the extension and diversification of social and political dissent, particularly among workers. Furthermore, American and Israeli interventionist policies in the Arab world, along with the disintegration of the national political system and the formation of dissenting transnational political movements, rekindled political activism in Egypt throughout the early 2000s.

But the traffic jam would not have produced a revolution if it had not been overdetermined by impassioned dynamics. January 25 expressed the rejection of arbitrary policing with limitless power over lives and bodies. The revolt against torture unified Egyptians momentarily around a single specific objective—the fall of the president, the fall of the regime.[55] The revolt channeled passions and posed an imperative ethical order: the requirement for dignity (*karāma*). By catalyzing these dynamics and embodying them, the image of Khalid Sa'id, assassinated by the police, immediately echoing that of Tunisia's Muhammad Bu'azizi, precipitated the overlapping temporalities and causal chains.

In Egypt and in Tunisia the revolutions toppled heads of state without external interference: the pressure from the street accelerated a rupture at the highest levels of state and doubled as a palace revolution. Yet the state actors—the military in the Egyptian case, which aligned itself with the revolution—only consented to change, and usher Mubarak to the exit door, in order to better preserve the status quo. But the challenge of the revolution resides in the reconfiguration of the power and authority structure. Revolutionary action rages against authority in all sectors, or at least as it was most often known in Egypt, against the form of hierarchical authoritarian organizations. At the outset the rallying of the military to the revolutionary cause produced a situation in which revolutionary forces were dependent on counterrevolutionary ones.

The revolutionary event, however, (momentarily) posited the people's sovereignty as a principle of political legitimacy and guarantor of plurality. The occupation, first at Tahrir Square, not only broke the habitual rhythm of time; it installed a space of political experimentation that cemented, in the here and now, an alternative that is evidently possible, as it was actually being lived through. This ephemeral experience did not offer any rule of government that translated to the state level. It simply proved that other ways of "living together," notably between Christians and Muslims, are possible. And this experimental living together in Tahrir Square did not even provide a model. The space of emergence of the multitude took shape as a heterogeneous area, a space bursting with plurality and thus with conflict and antagonisms—a space of fraternity but also of rape, of solidarity but also of looting and killing. This space was defined by the appearance of singularities irreducible to a homogenous entity. The revolutionary action claimed to have invented, in the field and in the moment, another order: the rule of plurality and the civic spirit. A political desire and an ethical demand animated the participants: "I can't stand to see my country like this anymore"; "I can't stand what they've done to us anymore" (i.e., the regime corrupts the citizen); "I am never going to ask for bribes again"; and so forth. These sentiments affirmed the revolutionary protagonists, conscious that the reversal of the authoritarian arbitrary required a struggle against corruption, which is all the more vicious in that most individuals had endorsed it. The Egyptian revolution made the emergence of "the people" and the expression of an ethical demand possible. In this regard it generated *enthusiasm* in the sense that Kant gave to this notion as he witnessed the French Revolution.

But the ethical demand is often muted in a process of purification that gets carried away in violence. After the moment of rupture the time comes for a new Constitution and government—the representation of plurality. And, already, the logic of exclusion is in full swing. Slightly numb, it had never ceased to stoke revolutionary arguments. Sometimes merely throwing back the rhetoric of the official mouthpieces that treated the revolutionaries as agents of the West, the revolutionary discourse derided the regime as a foreign enemy, an instrument of American-Zionist interests, as was demonstrated by the portraits of Hosni Mubarak overlaid with the Israeli flag and its numerous variants brandished in Tahrir Square. Sectarian divisions quickly reestablish themselves. The divisions had never really disappeared, although during the first days of the uprisings they only showed their "reassuring face," as the "union of the two elements of the nation."

Broadly, the story of the five years after Mubarak's fall is one of confrontation between revolutionary and counterrevolutionary dynamics, albeit complicated by rivalry and then by the existential struggle between two principal counterrevolutionary groups: the security apparatus and the Muslim Brotherhood. The first (and perhaps last) episode of the revolutionary process, which took place between January 2011 and July 2013, ended with the victory of the counterrevolution dynamic; the revolution was put on hold.[56]

The first phase, from February 2011 to November 2012, was defined by the stormy alliance of counterrevolutionary groups. First working alongside each other despite themselves, the Brotherhood and the Armed Forces took control of the electoral process and presented it as a step on the roadmap to democratic transition, which they opposed with the revolutionary dynamic. The "revolutionary forces," for their part, were subject to the pressure of rival hegemonic projects of "conservative forces,"[57] but they drew their strength from their capacity to take the streets from the timely rallying of several categories of the population that were usually inclined toward the status quo. Scattered, they developed neither a program nor well-defined arguments to coordinate their efforts in the long term, respecting the plurality of voices and political orientations. In contrast, the "conservative forces"—the military and the Muslim Brother elites—despite their internal divisions and bitter struggles to ensure respective key positions in the state apparatus, worked together to hold on to the reins of power. To this end they benefited from symbolic, financial, and institutional resources at the local, national, and transnational levels. Talking about a revolutionary dynamic not only relates to revolutionary protagonists. Rather, the revolutionary event became a founding event to which reference should be made to define and legitimize forthcoming policies and politics. After January 25 all policy makers claimed to realize the objectives of the revolution. Thus, the roadmap to an alleged democratic transition was set forth by the hegemonic groups' claims to fulfill the aims of the January 25 revolution. But electoral procedures sidelined the revolutionary currents and barely addressed revolutionary demands, at the forefront of which were to bring to justice those responsible for protestors' deaths and any corrupt elements of the "old regime," as well as a complete reform of the security sector.

The second phase was marked by runaway counterrevolutionary measures and relaunching the revolutionary dynamic. At the end of autumn 2012 the government of the Muslim Brotherhood president Muhammad Mursi, who had been elected in June of that year, had alienated itself from the revolutionary camp, many of whom had voted for him, and thus deprived him of the support he enjoyed from the military. In July 2013 Mursi was overthrown by a strong popular uprising and a call from the security apparatus—this time including the police—and the majority of political parties and organizations. Now vested with counterrevolutionary forces and rhetoric, the revolutionary dynamic at its apogee turned into its opposite and triggered the counterrevolutionary dynamic.[58]

The third phase, which began in July 2013 and remains ongoing, started with the popular legitimization of the new ruler and the suspension of the revolutionary dynamic.

'Abd al-Fattah al-Sisi: The Restoration of Security

The new government presented itself as a "war government." As with the Brotherhood, 'Abd al-Fattah al-Sisi, elected in May 2014, moved the front lines, and redefined friends and foes, without derogating from the regulatory principles of the identitarian order. The president's religious policy at that time revealed how the president relaunched the identitarian dynamic, while making minor modifications. In a few statements the president defined enemies and prohibitions, orienting in this way the actions of state agents and drawing the limits of all possible debate.

The enemies are, on one side, Islamist radicals, and on the other, atheists and homosexuals. Before even having been elected, al-Sisi had set the tone. Interviewed by journalists Ibrahim 'Issa and Lamis al-Hadidi, al-Sisi discussed the neighborhood where he grew up, al-Gamaliyya in Cairo, and the religious pluralism that used to reign there. Deploring the diffusion of "radical and sectarian Islamist discourse," he concerned himself with "avoiding excesses similar to those that we are currently confronting: people who kill, vandalize, and destroy in the name of religion. This causes immense harm to Islam and to Muslims." He continued, "I have read a lot so I can understand how we got to this point in the religious realm: religious discourse, throughout the Islamic world, has deprived Islam of its humanity."[59]

Several months later, the president gave an address to the *'ulama'* at al-Azhar:

> We spoke earlier about the importance of religious discourse, and I repeat it. We did not commit ourselves to the true religious discourse. The problem has never been with our faith. The problem lies in ideology, an ideology that we have sanctified.
>
> I am calling for a religious discourse that is in keeping with its times.
>
> I am addressing religious scholars and clerics. We must take a long, hard look at the current situation. I have spoken about this several times in the past. We must take a long, hard look at the situation we are in. It is inconceivable that the ideology we sanctify should make our entire nation a source of concern, danger, killing, and destruction all over the world. It is inconceivable that this ideology—and I am referring not to "religion" but to "ideology," to the body of ideas and texts that we have sanctified over the course of centuries to such a point that challenging them has become very difficult—-it is inconceivable that this ideology has become hostile to the entire world. Is it conceivable that 1.6 billion Muslims would kill the world's population of seven billion, so that they could live by themselves? This is inconceivable.
>
> I say these things here, at Al-Azhar, before religious clerics and scholars. May Allah bear witness on Judgment Day to the truth of your intentions, regarding what I say to you today.
>
> You cannot see things clearly when you are locked [in this ideology]. You must emerge from it and look from outside, in order to get closer to a truly enlightened ideology. You must oppose it with resolve.
>
> Let me say it again: We need to revolutionize our religion.
>
> Honorable Imam [the Grand Shaykh of al-Azhar], you bear responsibility before Allah. The world in its entirety awaits your words, because the Islamic nation is being torn apart, destroyed, and is heading to perdition. We ourselves are bringing it to perdition through our silence."[60]

Unlike Mubarak, al-Sisi is profoundly pious.[61] Despite this more marked engagement, both with regard to Christians and to a reform of Islamic discourse, the president's position recalls that of the al-Wasat Party and the recommended measures that Mubarak adopted in vain. As described in Chapter 1 of this book, al-Wasat often called for conservative religious unity against atheism, materialism, and religious radicals; it defined communal moral values for Eastern Christians and Muslims. Mubarak had tried to mobilize al-Azhar to limit the expansion of radicalized discourse; this had been a failure.

The president's statements vary. If the denunciation of dominant religious discourse appears as a constant, he does not establish a specific policy to reform it. In general, he points to al-Azhar's essential role in reforming religious discourse and in integrating this righteous understanding of religion into all aspects of life. But the revolution pushed al-Azhar to seek autonomy vis-à-vis the state.[62] He calls on Egyptians and invites them to show the true meaning of Islam as tolerant: in his attempts to give lessons in Islam, would he garner more success than his predecessor, Mursi? The Islamization of Egyptian society since the 1980s has been characterized by the diversification and the individualization of religious practices. And the revolution revealed another prominent trait of new religious practices: their rejection of traditional Islamic authorities and of all religious authorities with hegemonic pretensions.[63]

Sometimes he seems to stall. After months of attacks in the Sinai, at a time when Egypt is enmeshed with several regional wars, the Egyptian journalist Sherif al-Shubashi called for women to demonstrate in Tahrir Square on May 1, 2015, and remove their veils—reminiscent of a famous gesture by the feminist Huda al-Sha'arawi at the beginning of the twentieth century. Al-Sisi, whose wife and daughter wear the veil, asked those dealing with the issue of religious reform "to be careful." "Do not pressure public opinion and scare people in their homes. People hold nothing more dear than their religion. This issue should be addressed delicately and responsibly." Ibrahim 'Issa, who hosts a popular television talk show and has long been critical of the Brotherhood, al-Azhar, and Salafist groups, said al-Sisi's statements could only be interpreted as pulling the carpet out from beneath the debate on religious reform that he had initiated. The conservative religious establishment, claimed 'Issa, had clearly convinced al-Sisi that an ongoing discussion on the role of religion in Egypt could harm his popularity.[64]

The presidential discourse represents a continuity of Egyptian governmental practices, both in what it takes for granted and in what it provokes. It tries to reconcile the "conservative" tendency of Egyptian society with the ethical desires expressed by the revolutionaries against the corruption that drove

Egyptians to indignation. But it only channels these desires toward consensual enemies, minorities with only vaguely defined outlines, minorities without institutions: atheists and homosexuals. During the first decade of the twenty-first century several taboos had been lifted one after the other: Article 2, the Coptic issue, any critique of the president, sexual harassment, and so on. After January 25, 2011, two more ramparts fell: the military budget and atheism. For the first time in Egypt, atheism became the object of debates in the press, and a few individuals openly declared their atheism. As with the case of conversion, it was the public declaration more than the fact itself that resonated. Arrests and trials for blasphemy or insults to religion multiplied between 2012 and 2014.[65]

After Mursi's rule and the violence by Brotherhood militants, in tandem with the widely broadcast exploits of the Islamic State, denouncing radical Islamism signified to Egyptians that the president was working for peace, despite appearances. This was without doubt the only point of agreement between Mubarak and the majority of Egyptians: he knew how to preserve the peace, and al-Sisi has only backpedaled on this with the war in Yemen. Through this denunciation al-Sisi gives Egypt the image its inhabitants wanted to see: that of a country in which Christians and Muslims live happily together. But an enemy is not an enemy unless it is external—though this implies to sometimes externalize the internal. The reactivation of the conspiracy rhetoric permits not only a demonizing of the designated enemy but a way of discrediting the revolution itself. Indeed, after having presented itself as a revolutionary power and the incarnation of the will of the people, the new government launched operations to neutralize the revolutionaries' prestige, without needing to attack again. Concerned with the legitimacy of the military coup after Mursi's overthrow, the Biblawi government[66] had decided in October 2013 to create a memorial in Tahrir Square for the martyrs of the two "revolutions"—those of January 25, 2011, and June 30, 2013. Representing the emergence of a plurality of political subjects affirming their inalienable rights, the martyrs were embroiled in the counterrevolutionary narrative that froze them as the mute embodiment of the nation. At the moment, the president goes even further and takes aim at the revolutionary event itself. Since January 2014 al-Sisi and other military officers have voluntarily used the expression "fourth generation war." Popularized after the January 25, 2011, revolution by public figures hostile to the uprising, the formula designates wars provoked in a nation by external forces.[67] Al-Sisi sometimes uses this in reference to the regional level—for example, to justify support for Saudi Arabia (which has been the main and most powerful counterrevolutionary force in the region since the

1960s): "Egypt faces a fourth-generation war, one of the most dangerous [kinds of] wars. . . . We all should be aware of the attempts to stir dispute between Egypt and Gulf nations; I will not let anybody assault any other sides. . . . No one, whatever his strength and cunning, could drive a wedge between us."[68] The principal target of al-Sisi's speech is Islamists, though it extends to the protestors from January 25. From Mubarak to As'ad, the incumbent governments have always tried to present any uprisings as the work of a foreign, enemy hand, and the argument of the "foreign hand" is often employed to explain so-called sectarian conflicts.

In so doing, the presidential address defines for agents of the state—judges, the police—which outbursts will be tolerated, or even encouraged, and which abuses will be accepted. In this way discovering, or even searching for, a direct line of causality between the multiple death sentences for Muslim Brothers, or for cases of blasphemy, is unnecessary. The presidential position has assumed existing values and practices. His speeches set the tone and legitimate many excesses.

CONCLUSION

One image haunts the January 25 revolution: the image of Christian-Muslim unity. One variant on this theme peppers the walls of the capital and punctuates demonstrations throughout the country: it shows the Copt Mina Danial, who died in the Maspero military massacre in Cairo in October 2011, and Shaykh 'Imad 'Iffat, a high member of Dar al-Ifta', who was killed by a bullet in December 2011 during a street battle between protesters and the police, the army, and the Muslim Brothers.[1]

Arising from a constellation of symbols and narratives, the allegory of Islamo-Christian unity embodies the very paradox of Egyptianness. This image unfolds with a nation- and state-building process that performed a double operation: it distinguished itself from the occupying powers and turned Islam into an identity marker, thereby subjugating Christians, in the judicial, political, and symbolic realms. Raised in the enthusiasm of the 1919 struggle for national emancipation, the image of Islamo-Christian unity asserts an undefined "Egyptianness" as the foundation of political authority and the national emancipation project. In the aftermath of a crisis that polarized Christians and Muslims,[2] it was born in circumstances nonetheless marked by civility between the "two elements of the nation" and in the cadre of a political action oriented by joint opposition to an enemy. But in exhibiting the union, it reveals the initial division and, by the same token, that this identity, devoid of intrinsic qualities, only takes shape through negation and stands on a split. National construction, thus, secured the people to the nation and *le politique* to identity.

Yet national sentiment, then nationalism, crystallized in the aftermath of Muhammad 'Ali's state modernization measures. Nation and state took shape with a delay. Nation and state-building—these two processes, overlapped, often bolstering, but sometimes undermining, one another. As it happens, was not Egyptian nationalism forged through acts of resistance to a repressive military-police apparatus, thus to state-building? Countering the argument that conscription would "play a notable role in the awakening of the Egyptian peasants from their long slumber, and would reveal their true nature, hidden until then," Khalid Fahmy highlights rural acts of resistance to conscription. He shows how this refusal does not express the peasantry's "umbilical attachment to the earth, but its aversion to Mehmed Ali's policies and the elitist practices of the officers."[3] The officers of this era were justly perceived as foreign, the highest posts of the military hierarchy being reserved for the Turkic-Circassian elites. From 'Urabi (1882) to Nasser, the progressive Egyptianization of the army and the state apparatus in general, its opening, albeit limited, to the lower-middle classes in the early 1930s, and then its determinant role on the international political scene during the struggle for emancipation, have woven the state, the nation, and nationalism into one another, surreptitiously robbing the "people" of a voice that would henceforth be uttered on their behalf, and in their absence.[4] Since the presidency of Gamal Abdel Nasser, the state apparatus has absorbed the nation-people allegory and the nationalist narrative, and exhibited its official representations, beginning with the image of Nasser and Cyril VI. Their political friendship symbolized the quest for national emancipation as, in Egypt as well as in many other countries under the colonial yoke, religious institutions had supported nationalist politics.[5] Under Mubarak's presidency narratives and representations both displayed fraternity between Copts and Muslims, from the public appearances of religious representatives from Christian and Muslim institutions—most often after an outburst of "interreligious" violence—to the publications promoted by Mubarak's government. Thus, a consensual representation par excellence, Christian-Muslim unity as an allegory for the nation was hoisted by all parties and groups to different ends.

"To achieve the goal [our predecessors in 1919] abandoned and left unfinished," wrote Samer Soliman, "we should begin to talk of the State and not of the Nation. To speak of the Nation is to evade the sectarian issue once more and to bequeath it to future generations who will be burned by its fire, as we ourselves have been burned."[6] The discourse on the nation and national unity—and Arabism—is not opposed to sectarian discourse. Elaborated at the same time, they nourish each other, and both rely on identitarian logic. And identitarian logic is a binary logic working through division and exclusion. It does not allow for equality, except for those who are the same. It excludes plurality.

Thus, identitarian, as well as authoritarian, dynamics put to work an affective tempo punctuated by fear of the different and desire for the similar: the fear and the desire often being intertwined. Sectarianism, continued Soliman, constitutes in one part an administrative, judicial, and political legacy of the Ottoman Empire. Also, the "coexistence between equal citizens only happens once the reform of state institutions leads to the installation of a national democratic state."[7] If the state is the principal agent enhancing the processes of minoritization, then only the state can initiate this transformation. Indeed, the Christians' fate in Egypt remains reliant on the establishment of state institutions independent of the regime, economic elites, and rulers. But the state is not given to act as a neutral entity. The constitutional, security, and legal *dispositifs*—which consist of the practices of institutional agents—have enshrined sectarianism. For the affective dynamic that governs identitarian practices not only feeds the national narratives; it permeates the very institutions that produce, and are products of, the "communitarian subject." Affect is encysted in the institutions.

The state consists of an array of coercive apparatuses, means of control, and techniques of power, which are carried out by individual practices. But this thousand-headed and thousand-armed Leviathan does not perpetuate itself automatically. The regime-ruling party orients, encourages, and legitimizes certain practices, and it obstructs, forbids, or punishes others. Although processes of minoritization operate in several distinct sites, and in spite of the proliferation of centers of power in an Egyptian state now far less centralized than that of Nasser's era, these diversified practices form a coherent whole, a signifying order, which implies specific regimes of veridiction and legitimization. Authoritarian and sectarian dynamics overdetermine each other, producing an identitarian order with an Islamic reference. Identity, thus, becomes the principle of intelligibility and legitimization of the security-state and of its random, arbitrary, and informal operating modes.

Yet the "Coptic issue" both legitimates this order and calls it into question. It exposes the aporia of the Egyptian state: in the name of identity-unity the nation-state constantly defines itself based on a foundational fracture—"the unity of the two elements of the nation"—and in the name of security it ceaselessly recreates an internal enemy. And the Coptic Church has long been one of its favorite enemies. An institution of the state, it is an integral part of the authoritarian coercive apparatus, all the while providing a space in which to produce countercultures. But the diversification and the individualization of religious, social, and cultural practices in the Coptic community have not yet called into question the sectarian order. Despite lively intracommunity tensions—whether between the lower and higher clergy, between Upper and Lower Egypt, between laity and clergy, between youth and clergy, etc.—and despite the Copts' social and political diversity, the church remains a reference point and a place of communion for most Copts.

The ruling party represented the principal operator of state governmentality. The controlled pluralization of political and media life was not meant to ensure power sharing. Certainly, the attempt at hereditary power transmission has failed. But the pluralization of the electoral and media scene before the revolution, characterized by growing rivalries between Islamist currents and the NDP, as well as by a renewal of political dissent, had triggered antagonisms, for better or worse: manifestations of hatred, as well as initiatives intended to address multiform sectarian violence. The power of hegemonic logics of sense relies on their capacity to integrate contrarian and critical leanings. It is precisely this power of neutralization that permits defining them as structuring. This does not mean, however, that the structure remains unchanged or that the subversive elements are absorbed without influencing it. The persistence of structural tendencies rests on their aptitude to be transformed, while remaining hegemonic, unless the transformation leads to a reversal.

Could they be reversed, or at least transformed, through a revolution? Yes, if, as was the case with the revolution begun on January 25 and put on "standby"[8] in July 2013, what is at stake is not simply the overthrow of a government under the pressure of street insurrection. Revolution, as a radical transformation, strikes the founding principles of the political order, signals that the power has lost its symbolic efficiency, and reveals, as much as it precipitates, the elaboration "of a new world experience, intellectual, moral, religious, or metaphysical."[9] As in one aforementioned example, the diversification and individualization of religious practices, unfolding in continuity with new perceptions of religious authorities and the outright rejection of traditional religious authority, attest to these social changes. The long-term effects of the revolutionary experience and ongoing social mutations remain unknown. It takes a long time for eventual subversive practices to radically transform the state apparatus, including bending and even reversing the structural tendencies. All the more so when counterrevolutionary forces keep a firm grip on coercive *dispositifs*, relying on the majority of a population usually prone to favor the status quo and rarely disposed to revolution.

How, then, to reassess the impact of advocacy activism? By partially integrating not only the mouthpieces of criticism but the very concepts of critique, did the Mubarak regime completely neutralize their efficiency? Social scientists have given differing interpretations of civil society activism in the Arab world. For some, civil society organizations "are a place of neutralization and domestication of political dissent, inasmuch as their leaders participate in the logic of co-optation by the established régime."[10] For others they play the role of uncomfortable antechambers of politics: "between denunciation and participation, civil society leaders are embedded in complex networks and less excluded from the game than searching for new forms of participation. Some have left and others have turned their backs on the register of violent confrontation, radical questioning, or revolution."[11] Several studies have shown that the emergence of civil society, defined by the development of advocacy groups and NGOs, does not constitute a determinant element in democratic transition. Joel Beinin states that not all the organizations "embrace democratic values" and that some of them transmit neoliberal orthodoxy by assuming "the responsibilities abandoned by shrinking states."[12] Maha Abdelrahman observes that some of them perpetuate the authoritarian pattern,[13] and Vicki Langhor shows how they nurture a class of professional activists distanced from political action and devoid of decision-making power but depend on the incumbent regimes.[14] Lacking a social basis, these organizations did little to contribute to the waves of social mobilization that played a pivotal role in the January 25 revolution.[15]

It is worth nuancing these results, however, by taking another starting point and, thereby, reframing the problem. What I am considering here is advocacy activism, dedicated to defending basic rights of the person—freedom of religion, belief, expression, etc.—several cases of which I have looked at in this book. To what extent is it relevant to gauge the effect of advocacy activism in the theoretical framework of democratic transition? Reassessing the efficiency and the political sense of advocacy activism in Egypt invites one to first identify its goals and fields of action. To this end I have identified specific actions and their immediate results: the examples analyzed herein permit the conclusion that, in certain cases, the results are positive in that they have achieved their intended objective. In the medium term the question arises of the relationships between the regime and advocacy activists, turned into a class of professional activists devoid of decision-making power. Indeed, these activists generally cut themselves off from political action narrowly defined by the competition for power, decision-making responsibility, membership in a political party, or political activism directly challenging political leaders, economic elites, or the regime. Moreover, activists often undertake tasks in cooperation with state and government agencies, while remaining subjugated. However, the professionalization of activists, and the sectoralization of their actions, allows them to work on specific techniques of power, that is to say on the exercise of domination in circumscribed areas, whose number increases as advocacy associations multiply. Thus, they initiate a transformation of institutional practices as they knead the dough of the institution itself, at the risk, certainly, of being wrapped into it. In the long term the efficiency of their actions remains to be understood not so much through the lens of their power to mobilize as with regard to the transformation of norms, practices, and representations.

These findings lead to two further series of questions:

First, the power imbalance seems to produce a vicious circle. Whereas civil society remains under control, the regime has effective means to conduct conducts (*conduire des conduites*), facilitate or block, incite or forbid, by the force of habit, suggestion, or coercion. Yet, shouldn't we discard the "democratic transition" framework and start with the observation that societies and politics are entering the era of "de-democratization"?[16] If, in other words, authoritarian logics are gaining ground even in democratic situations, then, would the actions of advocacy groups and other citizen initiatives remain the only means by which to "re-democratize" or "democratize" societies, or, at least, mitigate the extension of authoritarian logics?

Second, if the January 25 revolution did not consist simply of an uprising against the regime but constituted an index of social transformation, changes in representations of power and authority, we might assume that the actions of organizations dedicated to the defense of rights played a role in this. Transforming the state governmentality requires challenging its regimes of veridiction and legitimation, not only by scrutinizing its principles but by transforming the practices that confer on them existence and consistence. Advocacy groups such as MARED and EIPR have undeniably challenged the structuring principles of the sectarian order, notably by allowing an extension of the scope of law in some cases, at the expense of arbitrary rule. Yet other case studies have revealed the ambivalence of Coptic activism and transgressive actions, which could either shore up the established order or, on the contrary, contribute to undermining its foundations. By reiterating a particularistic discourse and symbols, while referring to international principles considered universal, some Coptic activists do not just double-bolt the ghetto door; they block the slow formation of concrete universal categories from Coptic singularities—as distinguished from particularities.

NOTES

INTRODUCTION

1. Not long after his ascension to the presidency of the republic, Sadat carried out a purge of the government apparatus, pushing aside ʿAli Sabri and his supporters, who thought they would easily manipulate Sadat. On May 15, 1971, ʿAli Sabri and scores of other important figures of the Nasserist era were arrested and accused of having plotted a coup d'état.

2. In 1980 Sadat had amended Article 2 of the 1971 Constitution, which stated: "Islam is the religion of the State, Arabic is its official language, and the principles of shariʿa are *a* principal source of legislation" (emphasis added). Sadat's changes stipulated that the shariʿa constituted *the* source, and no longer *a* source of legislation (see Chapter 3). The Coptic patriarch Shenuda III expressed his disapproval by announcing that the church would not celebrate the Easter holiday and would refuse to accept governmental delegates, who would customarily come to present their holiday greetings. Furthermore, activists in the diaspora community, equally opposed to the amendment, had greeted Sadat with protest demonstrations a few months earlier when the Egyptian president made a visit to the United States to hold diplomatic meetings that would lead to the signature of the Camp David Accords (see Chapter 3).

3. "Discours historique de Sadate," *al-Ahram*, May 15, 1980, 1.

4. To further clarify: *dhimma* signifies "protection," whereas *dhimmī* signifies "protected peoples." The *dhimmī* are non-Muslim populations who, in the *dār al-islām*, could be tolerated under certain conditions. The *ahl al-kitāb* (People of the Book) are, among non-Muslim religious groups, those who adhere to a holy book and transcription or testimony of divine revelation. These include Christians, Jews, Samaritans, and Sabians. The definition of *ahl al-dhimma* has varied historically and geographically, depending on several parameters (religious composition of the population, financial needs in governance, prevailing attitudes with regard to non-Muslims, etc.).

5. Samer Soliman, "The Radical Turn of Coptic Activism: Path to Democracy or to Sectarian Politics," *Cairo Papers in Social Science* 29 (Summer-Fall 2006): 135–55.

6. Alain Roussillon, "Visibilité nouvelle de la 'question copte': Entre refus de la sédition et revendication citoyenne," in *L'Égypte dans l'année 2005*, ed. Florian Kosthall

(Cairo: Centre d'Études et de Documentation Économiques, Juridiques et sociales [hereafter CEDEJ], 2006), 137–75.

7. Samer Soliman, "al-Ḥaraka al-dīmuqrāṭiyya fī muwājaha al-ṭā'ifiyya," *al-Bosla*, Oct. 2005.

8. By this I do not mean that religion, Islam, is reduced to a principle of intelligibility and legitimation by the security state, nor do I mean that the new Muslim religiosities and the diverse forms of Islamization of society in Egypt and elsewhere fall under a claim to identity. I am simply defining the field of investigation that does not include a study of the diversification and individualization of Muslim practices and their significance. Moreover, the use of *identitarian* allows me to distinguish between an understanding of "identity" whose claim does not necessarily lead to sectarianism, and which is not necessarily embedded in a matrix of war, and an "identity" turned into a hegemonic and exclusive principle, as is the case in the authoritarian-identitarian situation under study.

9. Vivienne Jabri, "La guerre et l'État libéral démocratique," *Cultures et conflits* 61 (Spring 2006): 46.

10. See, e.g., Bat Ye'or, *The Dhimmi: Jews and Christians Under Islam* (Madison, NJ: Fairleigh Dickinson University Press, 1985).

11. See Paul Sedra, "Class Cleavages and Ethnic Conflict: Coptic Christian Communities in Modern Egyptian Politics," *Islam and Christian-Muslim Relations* 10, no. 2 (1999): 219–35.

12. See, e.g., Magdi Sami, *Dhimmitude: L'oppression des coptes d'Égypte* (Paris: L'Harmattan, 2008).

13. See Tariq al-Bishri, *al-Muslimūn wa-l-aqbāṭ fī iṭār al-jamā'a al-waṭaniyya* (Beirut: Dār al-waḥda, 2004); Barbara Carter, *The Copts in Egyptian Politics* (London: Croom Helm, 1986); and Dina El-Khawaga, "Le renouveau copte: La communauté comme acteur politique" (PhD diss., Institut des études politiques, 1993).

14. See Muhammad Hasanayn Haykal, *L'automne de la colère* (Paris: Ramsay, 1983); Musa Sabri, *al-Sādāt, al-ḥaqīqa wa-l-usṭūra* (Cairo: al-maktaba al-maṣrī al-hadīth, 1985); and Ghali Shukri, *L'Égypte: Contre-révolution* (Paris: Le Sycomore, 1979).

15. Sedra, "Class Cleavages," 233.

16. See Alastair Hamilton, *The Copts and the West, 1439–1822: The European Discovery of the Egyptian Church* (Oxford: Oxford University Press, 2006); Paul Sedra, *From Mission to Modernity: Evangelicals, Reformers and Education in Nineteenth-Century Egypt* (I.B. Tauris, 2011); and Heather Sharkey, *American Evangelicals in Egypt* (Princeton, NJ: Princeton University Press, 2008).

17. See Febe Armanios, "The Coptic Charismatic Renewal in Egypt: Historical Roots and Recent Developments," paper presented at the International Association of Coptic Studies Quadrennial Congress, Rome, Italy, Sept. 15–22, 2012; Gaétan DuRoy, "Abuna Sam'an and the 'Evangelical Trend' Within the Coptic Church," in *Reconsidering Coptic Studies*, ed. Nelly Van Doorn-Hoarder (Winston-Salem, NC: Wake Forest

University, 2012); and Carolyn Ramzy, "To Die Is a Gain: Singing a Heavenly Citizenship Among Egypt's Coptic Christians," *Ethnos* 80, no. 5 (2015): 649–70.

18. See Kurt Werthmuller, *Coptic Identity and Ayyubid Politics in Egypt, 1218–1250* (Cairo: American University Press, 2010); and Armanios, "Coptic Charismatic Renewal."

19. See Séverine Gabry, "Processus et enjeux de la patrimonialisation de la musique copte," in *Pratiques du patrimoine en Égypte et au Soudan*, ed. Omnia Aboukorah and Jean-Gabriel Leturcq (Cairo: CEDEJ, 2009), 132–53; Carolyn Ramzy, "*Taratīl* as Popular Music and the Transformation of a Coptic Folk Genre," *Journal of the Canadian Society for Coptic Studies* 1 (2010): 121–32. On media see Elizabeth Iskander, *Sectarian Conflict in Egypt: Coptic Media, Identity, and Representation* (New York: Routledge, 2012).

20. See Maurits Berger, "Public Policy and Islamic Law: The Modern Dhimmī in Contemporary Family Law," *Islamic Law and Society* 8, no. 1 (2001): 88–136; Maurits Berger, "Conflicts Law and Public Policy in Egyptian Family Law: Islamic Law Through the Backdoor," *American Journal of Comparative Law* 50, no. 3 (2002): 555–94; Maurits Berger, "Apostasy and Public Policy in Contemporary Egypt: An Evaluation of Recent Cases from Egypt's Highest Courts," *Human Rights Quarterly* 25, no. 3 (2003): 720–40; and Nathalie Bernard-Maugiron, "L'amendement du règlement sur le statut personnel des coptes orthodoxes en Égypte: À quand une loi unifiée pour la famille?" *Revue internationale de droit comparé* (RIDC) 62, no. 1 (2010): 75–103.

21. See Laure Guirguis, "Contestations coptes contemporaines," in *Protestations sociales, révolutions civiles: Transformations du politique dans la Méditerranée arabe*, ed. Sarah Ben Néfissa and Blandine Destremeau (Paris: Armand Colin, 2011), 139–63; Iskander, *Sectarian Conflict in Egypt*; Roussillon, "Visibilité nouvelle"; Soliman, "The Radical Turn"; and Mariz Tadros, *Copts at the Crossroads* (Cairo: AUC Press, 2013).

22. Claude Lefort, "Penser la révolution dans la révolution française," *Annales, Économies, Sociétés, Civilisations* 35, no. 2 (1980): 336.

23. Claude Lefort, "Permanence du théologico-politique?" in *Essais sur le politique* (Paris: Seuil, 1986), 282.

24. Foucault introduced the notion of *governmentality* in a lecture at the Collège de France on February 1, 1978, in a reflection on the passage (as seen in some seventeenth-century texts but mostly carried out in eighteenth-century Europe) from the exercise of power as the reign on a political entity (city, empire) to political power as the government of men, as conducting conducts. Foucault traces the genealogy of political power as the government of men to the organization of pastoral power and the idea of a spiritual direction. (For an analysis of pastoral power see Michel Foucault, *Sécurité, territoire, population: Cours au Collège de France, 1977–1978* [Paris: Gallimard, 2004], 136–232.) This transformation of the role of the sovereign appears in conjunction with reconfiguration of power relations in Europe after the treaty of Westphalia and the socioeconomic mutations that had enhanced the emergence of population

as a problem. See Foucault, *Sécurité, territoire, population*, 293; and Henry Kissinger, *Diplomacy* (New York: Simon and Schuster, 1994).

25. Foucault, *Sécurité, territoire, population*, 366.

26. Michel Foucault, *Society Must Be Defended: Lectures at the Collège de France, 1975–1976*, trans. David Macey (New York: Picador, 2003), 27–28.

27. Anthony Giddens, *Central Problems in Social Theory: Action, Structure, and Contradiction in Social Analysis* (Berkeley: University of California Press, 1979), 66.

28. Michel Camau, introduction to *Démocraties et autoritarismes: Fragmentation et hybridation des régimes*, ed. Michel Camau and Gilles Massardier (Aix-en-Provence: Karthala, 2009), 8–9.

29. See Carl Schmitt, *La notion de politique: Théorie du partisan* (Paris: Calmann-Lévy, 1989).

30. See Sedra, "Class Cleavages."

31. See El-Khawaga, "Le renouveau copte"; Vivian Ibrahim, *The Copts of Egypt: Challenges of Modernisation and Identity* (London: I.B. Tauris, 2010); Laure Guirguis, "Égypte: l'autre succession—l'Église copte à l'approche d'un tournant," *Religioscope* (2010): http://religion.info/french/articles/article_501.shtml; Guirguis, "Contestations"; Paul Sedra, "Copts and the Millet Partnership: The Intra-communal Dynamics Behind Egyptian Sectarianism," *Journal of Law and Religion* 29, no. 3 (2014): 491–509; and Mariz Tadros, "Vicissitudes in the Entente Between the Coptic Orthodox Church and the State in Egypt (1952–2007)," *International Journal of Middle East Studies* 41, no. 2 (2009): 269–87.

32. Charles Suaud comes to the same conclusion when he shows how the Vendéen cultural counterdiscourse does not affect the state against which it is developed but rather fosters state culture; see Charles Suaud, "La force symbolique de l'État," *Actes de la recherche en sciences sociales* 116–17, no. 1 (1996): 3–23.

33. See Soliman, "The Radical Turn"; and Guirguis, "Contestations." On Coptic mobilization after 2008 and before the fall of Mubarak see Tadros, *Copts at the Crossroads*.

34. See Tadros, *Copts at the Crossroads*, chaps. 7, 11.

35. Camau, introduction, 8–9.

36. Tadros, *Copts at the Crossroads*.

37. Michel Camau and Gilles Massardier, eds., *Démocraties et autoritarismes: Fragmentation et hybridation des régimes* (Aix-en-Provence: Karthala, 2009); and Olivier Dabène, Vincent Geisser, and Gilles Massardier, eds., *Autoritarismes démocratiques et démocraties autoritaires* (Paris: La Découverte, 2008).

38. Camau, introduction, 8–9.

39. Ibid. Camau references Guy Hermet, "Un régime à pluralisme limité? À propos de la gouvernance démocratique," *Revue française de science politique* 54, no. 1 (2004): 159–78. On authoritarian dispositifs in Egypt and the Arab world see Dabène, Geisser, and Massardier, Autoritarismes démocratiques; Marsha Posusney, "Enduring Authori-

tarianism: Middle East Lessons for Comparative Theory," *Comparative Politics* 36, no. 2 (2004): 127–38.

40. See Judith Butler, *Ce qui fait une vie* (Paris: Zone, 2009).

41. Wendy Brown, "American Nightmare: Neoliberalism, Neoconservatism, and De-democratization," *Political Theory* 34, no. 6 (2006): 690–714.

CHAPTER 1

1. On the departure of Egypt's Jews see Joel Beinin, *The Dispersion of Egyptian Jewry: Culture, Politics, and the Formation of a Modern Diaspora* (Cairo: American University Press, 2005). On Egypt's Jews see Dario Miccoli, *Histories of the Jews of Egypt: An Imagined Bourgeoisie, 1880s–1950s* (London: Routledge, 2015).

2. *Al-Ahram*, June 22, 1981; reproduced in Center of Economic, Juridical, and Social Research and Documentation, *Revue de la presse égyptienne* (Cairo: CEDEJ, 1981).

3. Michel Foucault, *Society Must Be Defended: Lectures at the Collège de France, 1975–1976*, trans. David Macey (New York: Picador, 2003), 25.

4. On the Free Officer's movement see Tewfik Aclimandos, "Les activistes politiques au sein de l'armée égyptienne: 1936–1954" (PhD diss., Institut d'études politiques, 2004). On the Nasserite era see Anwar Abdel Malek, *Égypte, société militaire* (Paris: Seuil, 1962); and Kirk J. Beattie, *Egypt During the Nasser Years: Ideology, Politics, and Civil Society* (Boulder, CO: Westview Press, 1994).

5. Gamal al-ʻUtayfi then became president of the Constitutional and Legislative Affairs Committee and, in this capacity, one of the most important protagonists in the government strategies concerning the project of the application of *shariʻa* law. In 1972 the governmental committee formed after the Khanka events contained six members (three Copts and three Muslims). The report was published in the Egyptian press on November 29, 1972, and was reproduced in Ghali Shukri, *al-Aqbāṭ fī waṭan mutaghayīr* (Cairo: Dār al-shurūq, 1991), 210–37.

6. On the Assiut conference see al-Bishri, *al-Muslimūn wa al-aqbāṭ*, 72–105; Barbara Carter, *The Copts in Egyptian Politics* (London: Croom Helm, 1986), 58; Dina El-Khawaga, "Le renouveau copte: La communauté comme acteur politique" (PhD diss., Institut des études politiques, 1993), 91–95; Mustafa al-Feqi, *Les Coptes en politique égyptienne: Le rôle de Makram Ebeid dans le mouvement national* (Paris: L'Harmattan, 2007), 47–52; and Paul Sedra, "Copts and the Millet Partnership: The Intra-communal Dynamics Behind Egyptian Sectarianism," *Journal of Law and Religion* 29, no. 3 (2014): 491–509.

7. On the Tanzimat see Henry Laurens, *L'Orient arabe: Arabisme et islamisme de 1798 à 1945* (Paris: Armand Colin, 2004), 59–110; and Bernard Lewis, *The Emergence of Modern Turkey* (London: Oxford University Press, issued under the auspices of the Royal Institute of International Affairs, 1968).

8. On the ten conditions necessary to construct a church see Shukri, *al-Aqbāṭ*, 207–12.

9. Ibid., 87.

10. See also contemporary testimonials. For example, Mariz Tadros, "Vicissitudes in the Entente Between the Coptic Orthodox Church and the State in Egypt (1952–2007)," *International Journal of Middle East Studies* 41, no. 2 (2009): 269–87 also refers to those of Musa Sabri (Musa Sabri, *al-Sādāt, al-haqīqa wa al-usṭūra* [Cairo: al-maktaba al-maṣrī al-hadīth, 1985]); and Muhammad Hasanayn Haykal (Muhammad Hasanayn Haykal, *L'automne de la colère* [Paris: Ramsay, 1983]), concerning the obstacles that State Security agents pose to construction of churches, particularly under Minister of the Interior al-Nabawi Isma'il (1925–2009), who served as minister from 1985 to 1997.

11. Yusif Sidhum, *Watani*, August 13, 2006.

12. *Watani*, April 22, 2007: see the interview with al-Juwayli inquiring about the reasons that the draft had not yet been approved, or even examined, by the assembly.

13. Ibid.

14. Literally, "Islamic organizations," a term that in the plural signifies Islamic groups. Its singular form signifies one of them in particular: the *Jama'at al-Islamiyya*, a prominent radical Islamist group in Egypt that was formed on college campuses in the 1970s by members of the Muslim Brotherhood. The group borrows from the centralized and strictly hierarchized organization, unlike *al-Jihad* (a precursor to what would later become the Egyptian Islamic Jihad), which operated in a network of cells primarily united by ideological orientation. The *Jama'a* renounced violence in 1997 and attempted to integrate into the political scene. Among other groups, *Tafkir wa-l-Hijra* preached exile from a society of *jāhiliyya* (ignorance, referring to the post-Islamic period). On the activities of Islamist groups in the 1970s see Ali E. Hillal Dessouki, "The Resurgence of Islamic Organisations in Egypt," in *Islam and Power*, ed. Alexander S. Cudsi and Ali E. Hillal Dessouki (Baltimore: Johns Hopkins University Press, 1981), 107–18; the testimony of Muntasir al-Zayyat, the lawyer who was at the origin of the agreement between the *Jamā'a* and the Egyptian government, Muntasir al-Zayyat, *al-jamā'āt al-islāmiyya: ru'ya min al-dākhil* (Cairo: Dār miṣr al-maḥrūsa, 2005); Ygal Carmon, Yotam Feldner, and David Lav, "The al-Gama'a al-Islamiyya Cessation of Violence: An Ideological Reversal," Middle East Media Research Institute (MEMRI), Inquiry and Analysis Series 309 (2006). On their current positions see Sameh Fawzi, "al-Ḥarakāt al-islāmiyya wa qadāyā al-muwāṭan: Qirā'a fī al-mawqif min al-aqbāṭ," in 'Amr al-Shubaki, *Al-muwāṭana fī muwājaha al-ṭā'ifiyya* (Cairo: Al-Ahram Center for Political and Strategical Studies, 2009), 121–51.

15. On the Islamization of political rhetoric during the implementation of Nasser's socialist politics see Olivier Carré, *L'idéologie politico-religieuse nassérienne à la lumière des manuels scolaires* (Paris: CERI, 1972). On Sadat's politics see Kirk J. Beattie, *Egypt During the Sadat Years* (New York: Palgrave, 2000); Ghali Shukri, *L'Égypte: Contre-révolution* (Paris: Le Sycomore, 1979); Haykal, *L'automne*; and Sabri, *al-Sādāt*.

16. Usama Salama, *Maṣīr al-aqbāṭ fī Miṣr* (Cairo: Dār al-Khayyāl, 1998), 77.

17. On the methods used under the rule of the powerful minister of interior al-Nabawi Isma'il, sacked by Mubarak in 1982, and on the dealings and ties between the police and the violent henchmen in the provinces of Assiut and Minya, see 'Ali 'Abd al-Rahim, *al-Mukhātara fī safqa al-ḥukūma wa jamā'āt al-'unf* (Cairo: Mīrīt li-l-nashr wa-l-ma'lūmāt, 2000). On al-Nabawi Isma'il see Mahmud Fawzi, *Ḥiwār 'alā nār hādi'a: al-Nabawī Ismā'īl wa judhūr minaṣṣat al-Sadāt* (Cairo: Bait al-lughāt al-duwaliyya, 2008).

18. On the Mubarak years see Vincent Battisti and François Ireton, eds., *L'Égypte au présent, inventaire d'une société* (Paris: Sindbad, Actes Sud, 2011); and Robert Springborg, *Mubarak's Egypt: Fragmentation of the Political Order* (Boulder, CO: Westview Press, 1989).

19. Nathalie Bernard-Maugiron, "Les tribunaux militaires et juridictions d'exception en Égypte," in *Juridictions militaires et tribunaux d'exception en mutation: Perspectives comparées et internationales*, ed. Elisabeth Lambert Abdelgawad (Paris: Archives contemporaines, 2007), 191–233.

20. An analysis of the formation of the "Islamic Republic of Imbaba" and the repression carried out against the neighborhood must take into account the informal urbanization, as well as the networks of solidarity and power that are created in these types of neighborhoods. Although they remain loosely tied to central spaces of power, they lack any administration or supervision by public power (and services); see Éric Denis, "La mise en scène des 'ashwaiyyāt: Premier acte: Imbaba, décembre 1992," in "L'Égypte en débats," ed. Alain Roussillon, *Égypte/Monde arabe*, no. 20, 1st ser. (1994): 117–32; and Patrick Haenni, *L'ordre des caïds: Conjurer la dissidence urbaine au Caire* (Cairo: CEDEJ-Karthala, 2005).

21. On the attacks at al-Kushih see William Wissa's detailed survey: *al-Kushiḥ: al-Haqīqa al-ghā'iba* (Cairo: Logos Center, 2004). See also *al-Ahram Weekly*, no. 512 (Dec. 14–20, 2000); and no. 545 (August 2–8, 2001). On the hijacking of the debate following the violence at al-Kushih and on the construction of a consensus on national identity against the intervention of foreign organizations see Maha Abdelrahman, "The Politics of 'Uncivil' Society in Egypt," *Review of African Political Economy* 29, no. 91 (2002): 21–36; Nicola Pratt, "Identity, Culture and Democratization: The Case of Egypt," *New Political Science* 27, no. 1 (2005): 69–86; and Elizabeth Iskander, *Sectarian Conflict in Egypt: Coptic Media, Identity, and Representation* (New York: Routledge, 2012).

22. EIPR, *Two Years of Sectarian Violence: What Happened? Where Do We Begin?* (Cairo: EIPR, 2010) (available at eipr.org); and Tadros, "Vicissitudes."

23. See Marwan al-Ashaal, "Reports on Reconciliation Sessions in the Egyptian Legal System," *Arab West Report*, Feb. 23, 2010, www.arabwestreport.info/year-2010/week-2/5-report-reconciliation-egyptian-legal-system; Rochelle Curtis, "Reconciliation Sessions in the Egyptian Newspapers: Analysis and Observations," *Arab West Report*, Feb. 27, 2010, www.arabwestreport.info/year-2010/week-2/4-reconciliation-sessions-egyptian-newspapers-analysis-and-observations; and Jayson Caspers, "Social Reconciliation: Pre- and Post-Conflict in the Egyptian Setting," *Arab West Report*, Feb. 22,

2010, www.arabwestreport.info/year-2010/week-2/2-social-reconciliation-pre-and-post-conflict-egyptian-setting. A similar process of repetition of violence in the same locations occurred in India; see Paul Brass, *The Production of Hindu-Muslim Violence in Contemporary India* (Seattle: University of Washington Press, 2003).

24. "Egypt Executes Man for 2010 Coptic Shooting," Reuters, Oct. 10, 2011, www.reuters.com/article/2011/10/10/us-egypt-execution-idUSTRE7993FQ20111010.

25. The government did little more than follow the example of various associations and churches. Catholic and Protestant churches engaged in interfaith dialogues starting in the 1970s. Constrained by several laws, issued from 1930 to 1960, that restricted the domains in which they could exercise influence, they changed course and merely renounced frenetically proselytizing in the country. Besides interfaith dialogue, they also privileged cooperation in rural development and literacy projects. See also Heather Sharkey, *American Evangelicals in Egypt* (Princeton, NJ: Princeton University Press, 2008), 179. Egyptian Protestants were particularly active in this domain. Under the presidency of Samuel Habib the CEOSS (Coptic Evangelical Organization for Social Services) organized several meetings where the highest representatives from Egypt's Islamic religious institutions participated. The Coptic Orthodox clergy, although it lends itself to the game of publicly expressing "interfaith benevolence" at Muslim and Christian holidays and participated in the activities of the World Council of Churches, has been long reticent when it comes to Islamic-Christian dialogue. Many Coptic laypersons, however, like Samir Murqus, engage in regular discussions with Muslim intellectuals and publish the content of these exchanges, as well as reflections on their activities; see Samir Murqus, *al-Akhir, al-ḥiwār, al-muwāṭana* (Cairo: Maktaba al-shurūq al-duwaliyya, 2005).

26. On Shaykh Sha'rawi see Farag Fuda, Yunan Labib Rizk, and Khalil 'Abd al-Karim, *al-Ṭā'ifiyya . . . ilā ayn?* (Cairo: Dār wa maṭābi' al-mustaqbal, 1987), 32. Farag Fuda was assassinated in June 1992 by two members of the Jama'a al-Islamiyya.

27. See Malika Zeghal, *Gardiens de l'islam: Les oulémas d'al-Azhar dans l'Égypte contemporaine* (Paris: Presses de Sciences-Po, 1996), esp. chap. 5. For a contemporary study on the relationship between the Muslim Brotherhood and al-Azhar see Rachel Scott, "What Might the Muslim Brotherhood Do with al-Azhar? Religious Authority in Egypt," *Die Welt des Islam* 52, no. 2 (2012): 31–165.

28. Ministry of Awqaf, *Samāḥāt al-islām wa ḥuqūq ghayr al-muslimīn* (Cairo: Ministry of Awqaf, 1991), 39–43.

29. Ibid., 65.

30. Edwar Ghali al-Dahabi, *al-Namūzaj al-maṣrī li al-waḥda al-waṭaniyya* (Cairo: Maktaba al-'usra, 1998), 125.

31. Husayn Kafafi, *al-Masiḥiyya wa-l-islām fī miṣr* (Cairo: Maktaba al-'usra, 1998), 23.

32. Sigmund Freud, *Moses and Monotheism* (Letghworth, Hertfordshire: Hogarth, 1939). Freud's text was translated into Arabic. See also Jacques Derrida's analyses in

Jacques Derrida, "Mal d'archives" (Paris: Galilée, 1995); and Jan Assman, *Moïse l'égyptien: Un essai d'histoire de la mémoire* (Paris: Aubier, 2001).

33. Sherif Younes is a historian and professor at the University of Helwan, in Cairo. He is not Christian. Specializing in the Nasserist period and the history of ideas in Egypt, he is the author of *The Name of the People: A Critical History of Nasserist Ideology* (in Arabic), of a study on Sayyid Qutb, as well as a stimulating and original essay on the Israeli-Palestinian question. A long version of the text cited in the research presentation was published in the collection of papers presented at the second MARED conference: Sherif Younes, "al-Tārīkh al-maṣriyya: al-Tamyīz al-dīnī fī manāhij al-dirāsāt al-ijtimā'iyya," in *al-Ta'līm wa al-muwāṭana: al-Mu'tamar al-waṭanī al-thānī li munāhaḍa al-tamyīz al-dīnī*, arranged by Muhammad Munir Megahed (Cairo: MARED, 2010), 165–94. The given references refer to the abridged version, which I have translated into French: Sherif Younes, "L'histoire meurtrie: La discrimination religieuse dans les manuels d'histoire égyptiens," *Altermed* 4 (2011): 149–55.

34. *Egypt and the Civilizations of the Ancient World*, official textbook for social studies in 2008–9, read by students in their ninth year of education (237), quoted in Sherif Younes, "L'histoire meurtrie," 150.

35. Official textbook for social studies for the year 2008–9 read by students in elementary school, second section: 77, cited by Sherif Younes, "L'histoire meurtrie," 150.

36. Younes, "L'histoire meurtrie," 151.

37. On Brotherhood activity in the unions see Husam Tamam, *Taḥawwulāt al-ikhwān al-muslimūn* (Cairo: Maktaba madbūlī, 2006); and Carrie R. Wickham, *Mobilizing Islam: Religion, Activism, and Political Change in Egypt* (New York: Columbia University Press, 2002). On the al-Wasat Party's foundation see Meir Hatina, "The 'Other Islam': The Egyptian Wasat Party," *Critique: Critical Middle Eastern Studies* 14, no. 2 (2005): 171–84; and Tal'at Ramih, *al-Wasat wa-l-ikhwān: al-wathā'iq wa al-qissa al-kāmila li akhtar sira' siyāsī fī al-tis'īnāt* (Cairo: Markaz yāfā li-l-dirāsāt wa-l-abḥāth, 1997).

38. Rafiq Habib, interview by the author, Cairo, March 2010.

39. Mahdi 'Akif, Supreme Guide of the Muslim Brothers from 2004 to 2014, was born in 1928 in the Daqahliyya Province and would have joined the association as an adolescent. He led the camps of the Faculty of Law at 'Ain Shams in the guerrilla war until the 1952 revolution, when he became director of the student and "physical education" section at the Brotherhood headquarters. After several arrests he was referred to military court in 1996 as the head of the Brothers' international organization and condemned to three years in prison; he was freed in 1999. Married to the sister of Mahmud 'Izzat, who wears the *niqab*, and father of four children, he lived in Nasser City, had a Mercedes, and was known to have loved *Quo Vadis*, *Viva Zapata*, and *Gone with the Wind*, though he did not go to the cinema after 1974.

40. Rafiq Habib, son of Samuel Habib—late president of Protestant Churches and the founders of CEOSS—had a background in sociology and was the author of several

texts on the history of Egyptian churches and Christian political currents, inviting the patriarch's displeasure toward his father. After the 1990s he drifted toward the Muslim Brotherhood. The principal artisan of the al-Wasat Party and of a theory of "civilizational" Islam that includes Christians, he was part of the Freedom and Justice Party and recently published a text on the Muslim Brothers: *al-Ikhwān al-muslimūn: Ma'ārik al-siyāsa wa-l-iṣlāḥ* (Cairo: al-markaz al-ḥaḍārī li-l-dirāsāt al-mustaqbaliyya, 2010).

41. Salim al-'Awwa, *al-Aqbāṭ wa-l-islām, ḥiwār* (Cairo: CEDEJ, 1987), 41.

42. Salim al-'Awwa, *al-Dīn wa-l-waṭan* (Cairo: Nahḍa Maṣr li al-ṭabā'a wa-l-nashr wa al-tawzī', 2006).

43. Rafiq Habib, ed., *Awraq ḥizb al-Wasat* (Cairo: n.p., 1997). See also the more recent text: Abu al-'Ila Madi, *al-Mas'ala al-qibṭiyya . . . wa-l-shari'a wa-l-ṣaḥwa al-islāmiyya* (Cairo: Safīr al-duwaliyya li al-nashr, 2007).

44. For a postcolonial reading of the concept in reference to the Coptic case see Saba Mahmood, "Religious Freedom, the Minority Question, and Geopolitics in the Middle East," *Comparative Studies in Society and History* 54, no. 2 (2012): 418–46; and Saba Mahmood, *Religious Difference in a Secular Age: A Minority Report* (Princeton, NJ: Princeton University Press, 2015).

45. Habib interview.

46. Qur'an, "al-Baqara," 2.256.

47. *Al-Jumhuriyya*, August 8, 2007.

48. *Nahda Masr*, August 7, 2007.

49. *Al-Masri al-Yawm*, August 7, 2007.

50. *Nahda Masr*, August 9, 2007.

51. *Al-Masri al-Yawm*, August 6, 2007.

52. *Al-Fajr*, August 13, 2007.

53. *Al-Masri al-Yawm*, August 6, 2007.

54. *Al-Masri al-Yawm*, August 6, 2007. Yusif al-Badri is a member of the Academy of Islamic Research; he has brought forward hundreds of cases against Egyptian intellectuals accused of having defamed Islam. He was among those who brought ḥisba proceedings against Nasr Hamid Abu Zayd in 1996; see Baudouin Dupret and Jean-Noël Ferrié, "Participer au pouvoir, c'est imposer la norme: Sur l'affaire Abu Zayd (Égypte, 1992–1996)," *Revue française de science politique* 47, no. 6 (1997): 762–75.

55. *Al-Jumhuriyya*, August 12, 2007.

56. *Al-Usbu'*, August 18, 2007.

57. *Ruz al-Yusuf*, August 18, 2007.

58. *Nahda Masr*, August 19, 2007.

59. Haykal's article appeared in *al-Ahram* on April 22, 1994: "Egypt's Copts Are Not a Minority: Letter to the Editor-in-Chief of *al-Wafd*." (The editor-in-chief of *al-Wafd* was Gamal Badawi.) For a good survey of the debates see *Ruz al-Yusuf*, May 2, 9, 16, and 23, 1994; and Dina El-Khawaga's article on media strategies in Egyptian papers and

of several public personalities on the polemic around the conference: "Le débat sur les Coptes: Le dit et le non-dit," in "L'Égypte en débats," ed. Alain Roussillon, *Égypte/Monde arabe*, no. 20, 1st ser. (1994): 67–76.

60. The published work retraced the history of Copts in Egypt; the authors wanted to show that Copts had been the subject of uninterrupted repression in Egypt since the introduction of Islam into the country. The only newspaper to offer a summary of the text was *al-Badil*, August 14, 2007.

61. According to Article 48 of law 143/1994 that governs the civil state (*qānūn al-aḥwāl al-madaniyya*), every citizen is required to hold an identity card on which is listed his or her current religious affiliation. The obligation to hold an identity card at the age of sixteen exists according to law 181/1955 on personal identification cards. Failure to comply is subject to fine.

62. The Egyptian state does not recognize Bahaism as a heavenly religion. Since digitizing the procedures to obtain identity cards in 1995, Bahais no longer have the option of leaving the "religion" line blank. Some prefer not to complete the forms at all and live undocumented rather than deny their religious identity or declare themselves Muslims. Rather than eliminating the "religion" line, several alternatives were proposed in debates on the subject: adding an "other" box or one for "nonheavenly" religions. For a historical perspective on the relationship between Bahai and the Egyptian state see Johanna Pink, "The Concept of Freedom of Belief and Its Boundaries in Egypt: The Jehovah's Witnesses and the Bahai Faith: Between Established Religions and an Authoritarian State," *Culture and Religion* 6, no. 1 (2007): 135–60. On contemporary suits brought by Bahai see a report from the National Council on Human Rights (CNDH) dated August 8, 2006; and, especially, a very thorough report citing numerous examples, published by EIPR and Human Rights Watch, *Prohibited Identities: State Interference with Religious Freedom* (Cairo and New York: EIPR and Human Rights Watch, 2007).

63. The term *personal status* was used "seemingly for the first time in the official code of Qadri Pasha in 1875, following a belated distinction between real and personal rights," referring to the laws that set forth the "rights and duties attached to or arising from a particular personal status." See Bernard Botiveau, *Loi islamique et droit dans les sociétés arabes* (Paris: Karthala-IREMAM, 1993), 217.

64. On the reform of confessional courts and Coptic resistance to them see Nathan Brown, *The Rule of Law in the Arab World: Courts in Egypt and the Gulf* (Cambridge: Cambridge University Press, 1997).

65. Conversation with Muhammad 'Afifi, Cairo, 2009. I thank Husam Bahgat and Adel Ramadan, EIPR, for having provided me with a reproduction of circular no. 40 of 1969.

66. Numerous observers of the Coptic scene interpret the rumor about the authorities' decision to suppress these sessions to be a response to the patriarchal attitude during the Wafa' Qustantin affair. On this occasion the church had demanded that State

Security agents and the president of the republic hand over the wife of a priest, Wafa' Qustantin, who had converted to Islam. Angry demonstrators and the clerical hierarchy justified their demands by arguing that, as the consultation sessions had not taken place, Wafa' had not yet legally taken Islam as her religion. (In reality it seemed that the village priest had refused to organize the counseling sessions and guidance because of her special status as the wife of a priest.) Since this affair, the minister of the interior has ceased to inform the church of requests to convert to Islam, while also instructing al-Azhar not to accept all requests.

67. Circular no. 5, distributed June 10, 1971. See also EIPR and Human Rights Watch, *Prohibited Identities*, 65.

68. Maurits Berger, "Apostasy and Public Policy in Contemporary Egypt: An Evaluation of Recent Cases from Egypt's Highest Courts," *Human Rights Quarterly* 25, no. 3 (2003): 720–40.

69. Qur'an, "al-'Imrān," 3.104. The Cairo Appellate Court would validate the legality of *ḥisba* procedure in the case of Nasr Hamid Abu Zayd, whereas the Court of First Instance, Litigation Division of Personal Status, had ruled that the request of lawyers was inadmissible on the grounds that the applicant had no legal interest in bringing proceedings (they were requesting a judgment of apostasy, implying the invalidation of all contracts and, thereby, separation from his wife); see Dupret and Ferrié, "Participer au pouvoir."

70. Qur'an, "al-Tawba," 9.74.

71. Gamal al-Banna is the brother of Hassan al-Banna, the founder of the Society of Muslim Brothers. See Gamal al-Banna, *Kitāb ḥurriyya al-i'tiqād fī al-islām* (Beirut: al-maktab al-islāmī, 1981), 66–71. On the project of the apostasy law as treated in Egyptian media see *al-I'tisam*, Jan. 1977, 2; Feb. 1977, 18–21; March 1977, 31; April 1977, 22–27; May 1977, 18–20; and *al-Ahram*, July 15, 1977. (Notice that the State Council had submitted the draft to the Ministry of Justice for submission to the Cabinet and then the People's Assembly), *al-Ahram*, August 6, 1977. (Notice that the State Council had approved the draft law on apostasy and submitted it to the People's Assembly. This was the last notice on the subject.) On the reaction of Copts to the draft see *al-Kiraza*, August 26 and Sept. 2, 1977; and *Watani*, Sept. 4, 1977, 1.

72. Qur'an, "al-Kahf," 18.29.

73. Qur'an, "al-Baqara," 2.256.

74. Declarations made at the seminar organized by the Union of Journalists, together with islamonline.net, Sept. 2007.

75. See "Questions, Answers on Islam," *Washington Post*, July 21, 2007, http://newsweek.washingtonpost.com/onfaith/muslims_speak_out/2007/07/sheikh_ali_gomah.html.

76. *Nahda Masr*, May 15, 2007.

77. On 'Ali Jum'a's reasoning see Tewfik Aclimandos, "L'amour vache. Conversions: Quelques remarques sur les discours et les imaginaires," in *Conversions religieuses et*

mutations politiques: Tares et avatars du communautarisme égyptien, ed. Laure Guirguis (Paris: Non Lieu, 2008), 49–83.

78. Qur'an, "al-'Imrān," 71. See Taha Jabir al-'Alwani, *Lā ikrāh fī al-dīn: Ishkāliyyāt al-ridda wa-l-murtaddīn min ṣadr al-islām ilā al-yawm* (Cairo: al-ma'had al-'ālamī li-l-fikr al-islāmī, dār al-shurūq al-duwaliyya, 2006). Taha Jabir al-'Alwani received his doctorate in *Uṣūl al-fiqh* at al-Azhar University.

79. On the controversy provoked by the publication of the text see the classic work by Albert Hourani, *Arabic Thought in the Liberal Age, 1789–1939* (1962; Cambridge: Cambridge University Press, 2003). For a reflection on the reformist experience see Alain Roussillon, *Réforme sociale et identité: Essai sur l'émergence de l'intellectuel et du champ politique modernes en Égypte* (Casablanca: Le Fennec, 1999). On contemporary conceptions of the religious/political nexus in Islam see Nasr Hamid Abu Zayd, *Reformation of Islamic Thought: A Critical Historical Analysis* (Amsterdam: Amsterdam University Press, 2006); Talal Asad, *Formation of the Secular: Christianity, Islam, Modernity* (Stanford: Stanford University Press, 2003); Alain Roussillon, *La pensée islamique contemporaine: Acteurs et enjeux* (Paris: Téraèdre-IISMM, 2005); and Fouad Zakariya, *Laïcité ou islamisme: Les Arabes à l'heure du choix* (Paris: La Découverte, 1991).

80. The EIPR's reports give numerous examples of trial or detention for falsification of papers. See esp. EIPR and Human Rights Watch, *Prohibited Identities*, as well as reports available on the organization's website: eipr.org.

81. Sadat had created permanent Courts of State Security with law 105/1980, at the exact moment when the state of emergency, in place in 1967, had been lifted. They were removed, and law 105/1980 was repealed in June 2003 at the request of Gamal Mubarak, who was then secretary-general of the NDP's Political Committee. On special courts see Bernard-Maugiron, "Les tribunaux militaires."

82. Ibid.

83. The church refused to grant divorce except in cases of adultery. A number of Christians have converted to Islam or another Christian denomination to divorce without having to enter into a confrontation with the clerical authorities or having to admit having committed adultery themselves, the consequence of which is renouncing the right to remarry. In effect, if two spouses are not of the same confession (*ṭā'ifa*) or denomination (*milla*), personal status laws for Muslims apply. Because the conversion to Protestantism (or another denomination) for one of the spouses is taken into consideration only if it went into effect before filing for divorce, two people who want to end their marriage sometimes have no other solution than to convert to Islam, since in this case the date of conversion is not taken into account.

84. EIPR and Human Rights Watch, *Prohibited Identities*.

85. See, e.g., case no. 24673/58 (March 29, 2005) in EIPR and Human Rights Watch, *Prohibited Identities*.

86. Maurits Berger, "Conflicts Law and Public Policy in Egyptian Family Law: Islamic

Law Through the Backdoor," *American Journal of Comparative Law* 50, no. 3 (2002): 555–94.

87. On the 1923 Constitution see al-Bishri, *al-Muslimūn wa al-aqbāṭ*, 199–222; Nathalie Bernard-Maugiron, "Les constitutions égyptiennes (1923–2000): Ruptures et continuités," in "L'Égypte dans le siècle, 1901–2000," ed. Ghislaine Alleaume, *Égypte/Monde arabe*, no. 4/5, 2nd ser. (2001): 103–35; Elie Kedourie, "The Genesis of the Egyptian Constitution of 1923," in *Political and Social Change in Modern Egypt*, ed. Peter Malcolm Holt (Oxford: Oxford University Press, 1968), 347–61; and Samir Murqus, "al-aqbāṭ wa-l-shari'a bayn dustūr al-ḥaraka al-waṭaniyya (1923) wa dustūr walī al-amr (1971)," in *al-Muwāṭana fī muwājaha al-ṭā'ifiyya*, ed. 'Umru al-Shubaki (Cairo: al-Ahram Center for Political and Strategic Studies, 2009), 73–93.

On Article 2 of the Constitution refer to the text in which Nabîl 'Abd al-Fattah sheds light on the political implications of the problem of applying shari'a law between 1970 and 1980, showing how the reference to Islam determines a closure of political discourse and analyzing its impact on the tactics of political figures: 'Abd al-Fattah, "Le texte et la poudre: Shari'a islamique et droit positif dans le régime politique égyptien pendant les années 1970 et 1980, Politiques législatives. Égypte, Tunisie, Algérie, Maroc," *Dossiers du CEDEJ* (Cairo: CEDEJ, 1994).

88. Baudouin Dupret, "La shari'a comme référent législatif," in "Anthropologie de l'Égypte 2," ed. Jean-Noël Ferrié and Saadia Radi, *Égypte/Monde arabe*, no. 25, 1st ser. (1996): 121–75.

89. Botiveau, *Loi islamique et droit*, 286.

90. Thus the reasoning, for example, in cases 475, 478, 481/65 (August 5, 1996).

91. Nathalie Bernard-Maugiron, *Le politique à l'épreuve du judiciaire: La justice constitutionnelle en Égypte* (Bruxelles: Bruylant, 2003), 343.

92. For example, in case 24673/58 (April 26, 2005). All decisions of the Court of Administrative Justice in affairs of reconversion are based on similar reasoning.

93. Brown, *Rule of Law*.

CHAPTER 2

1. Hamit Bozarslan, "Sécularisme, religion et nation: Les cas turcs, pakistanais et israélien," *Esprit* 333 (March–April 2007): 235–41.

2. On the emergence of Egyptian nationalism see Tewfik Aclimandos, "Nationalismes machréquins et nassérisme," in *Nationalismes en perspective*, ed. Gil Delannoi and André Taguieff (Paris: Berg International, 2001); Ralph Coury, "Who Invented Egyptian Arab Nationalism?" *International Journal of Middle East Studies* 14, no. 3 (1982): 249–81, and no. 4 (1982): 459–79; Israel Gershoni and James Jankowski, *Egypt, Islam, and the Arab: The Search for Egyptian Nationhood* (New York: Oxford University Press, 1987); and Israel Gershoni and James Jankowski, *Rethinking the Egyptian Nation* (Cambridge: Cambridge University Press, 1995).

3. On theories of nationalism that present the formation of an intelligentsia as the main explicative factor see Ernst Gellner, *Nations and Nationalism* (Ithaca, NY: Cornell University Press, 1983).

4. Dina El-Khawaga, "Le renouveau copte: La communauté comme acteur politique" (PhD diss., Institut des études politiques, 1993).

5. Alastair Hamilton, *The Copts and the West, 1439–1822: The European Discovery of the Egyptian Church* (Oxford: Oxford University Press, 2006).

6. El-Khawaga, "Le renouveau copte," 42.

7. Henri Ayrout, *Mœurs et coutumes des fellahs d'Égypte* (Paris: Payot, 1938); Gabriel Baer, *Fellah and Townsman in the Middle East: Studies in Social History* (London: Cass, 1982); Gabriel Baer, *A History of Landownership in Modern Egypt, 1800–1950* (London: Oxford University Press, 1962); and Nessim Henry Henein, *Mârî Girgis: Village de Haute Égypte* (Cairo: IFPO, 1988).

8. See Catherine Mayeur-Jaouen, *Pèlerinages d'Égypte: Histoire de la piété copte et musulmane XVe–XXe siècles* (Paris: EHESS, 2005); and Brigitte Voile, *Les Coptes d'Égypte sous Nasser: Sainteté, miracles, apparitions* (Paris: CNRS, 2004).

9. Sévérine Gabry, "Processus et enjeux de la patrimonialisation de la musique copte," in *Pratiques du patrimoine en Égypte et au Soudan*, ed. Omnia Aboukorah and Jean-Gabriel Leturcq (Cairo: CEDEJ, 2009), 132–53.

10. Irénée-Henri Dalmais, *Les liturgies d'Orient* (Paris: Le Cerf, 1980).

11. On the development of a sectarian discourse involving the ethnicization of communitarian identity see Paul Sedra, "Class Cleavages and Ethnic Conflict: Coptic Christian Communities in Modern Egyptian Politics," *Islam and Christian-Muslim Relations* 10, no. 2 (1999): 219–35, esp. 222–24, 232. Sedra compares this discourse to the discourses of Coptic figures like Milad Hanna and Kilada, who bring national unity to the fore. Unlike Sedra I show how these two discourses form two sides of the same coin, inasmuch as they both rely on identity—national or community—and therefore do not challenge the principle of intelligibility of Egypt's authoritarian situation. Yet Sedra's argument, which integrates class cleavages into an analysis of sectarian conflicts and the evolution of intracommunitarian dynamics, is particularly relevant and well conducted.

12. Shawki Karas, *The Copts Since the Arab Invasion: Strangers in Their Land* (Jersey City, NJ: American Coptic Association, 1986). Shawki Karas, the "father" of Coptic diaspora activism, founded the first organization dedicated to defending the rights of Copts, the American Coptic Association. See also Chapter 6; and Sedra, "Class Cleavages," 222–24.

13. "Islam, Stranger in Its Own Country," *al-Liwa'*, June 17, 1908. Shaykh 'Abd al-'Aziz Jawish, of Tunisian origin, had succeeded Mustafa Kamil as the head of *al-Liwa'* in 1908. The controversy around the role of religion in the definition of the nation pitted the Coptic press (*Misr* and *al-Watan*) against the press involved with the reaction to the reformist project of Muhammad 'Abduh (*al-Mu'ayyid* and *al-Liwa'*). The paper *Misr*, founded

in 1895 by Tadros al-Mankabadi, benefited from the support of Butrus 'Ali Pasha, who had a poor relationship with 'Abd al-Sayyid, the founder of *al-Watan* in 1875. *Misr* acted as a mouthpiece for the more radical Coptic demands, marked by communitarianism. Its London correspondent at the time was Mikhail Kyriakos, "permanent representative of the Copts in the Britannic capital," to borrow the expression used by Mustafa al-Feqi, *Les Coptes en politique égyptienne: Le rôle de Makram Ebeid dans le mouvement national* (Paris: L'Harmattan, 2007). The two papers were rivals before joining causes after the Assiut conference in 1911. After 1917 *Misr* aligned with the party of Sa'ad Zaghlul. On the Coptic press see Ramy 'Ata Sadiq, *Ṣaḥāfat al-aqbāṭ wa qaḍāyā al-mujtama' al-maṣrī* (Cairo: Supreme Council of Culture, 2009); and Elizabeth Iskander, *Sectarian Conflict in Egypt: Coptic Media, Identity, and Representation* (New York: Routledge, 2012).

14. See Grégoire Delhaye, "La figure de 'la jeune fille convertie et mariée de force' dans le discours militant des coptes en diaspora," in *Conversions religieuses et mutations politiques: Tares et avatars du communautarisme égyptien*, ed. Laure Guirguis (Paris: Non Lieu, 2008), 133–51.

15. See Saba Mahmood, "Religious Freedom, the Minority Question, and Geopolitics in the Middle East," *Comparative Studies in Society and History* 54, no. 2 (2012): 418–46. On several cases of conversion and their political implications in the Ottoman Empire see Selim Deringil, "There Is No Compulsion in Religion: On Conversion and Apostasy in the Late Ottoman Empire, 1839–1856," *Comparative Studies in Society and History* 42, no. 3 (2000): 547–75; Tijana Krstic, *Contested Conversions to Islam: Narratives of Religious Change in the Early Modern Ottoman Empire* (Stanford: Stanford University Press, 2011); Turgut Subasi, "The Apostasy Question in the Context of Anglo-Ottoman Relations, 1843–44," *Middle Eastern Studies* 38, no. 2 (2002): 1–34; and Lucette Valensi, "Inter-communal Relations and Changes in Religious Affiliation in the Middle East (Seventeenth to Nineteenth Centuries)," *Comparative Studies in Society and History* 39, no. 2 (1997): 251–69.

16. Delhaye, "La figure."

17. Ibid.

18. Magdi Khalil, "L'islamisation forcée des jeunes filles coptes, " in *Conversions religieuses et mutations politiques: Tares et avatars du communautarisme égyptien*, ed. Laure Guirguis (Paris: Non Lieu, 2008): 151–63.

19. Ibid., 158.

20. Delhaye, "La figure."

21. William Wissa, interview by the author, Paris, summer 2008.

22. Adel Guindy, "Le droit de croyance en Égypte: Entre liberté et coercition," in *Conversions religieuses et mutations politiques: Tares et avatars du communautarisme égyptien*, ed. Laure Guirguis (Paris: Non Lieu, 2008), 173–97.

23. Janique Blattman, "Christian Solidarity International Claiming Forced Conversion of Coptic Girls to Islam," *Arab West Report*, Dec. 31, 2005.

24. Yara Sallam, interview by the author, Cairo, June 2009.

25. Febe Armanios, "The 'Virtuous Woman': Images of Gender in Modern Coptic Society," *Middle Eastern Studies* 38, no. 110 (2002): 110–30; Delhaye, "La figure."

26. Tewfik Aclimandos, "L'amour vache. Conversions: Quelques remarques sur les discours et les imaginaires," in *Conversions religieuses et mutations politiques: Tares et avatars du communautarisme égyptien*, ed. Laure Guirguis (Paris: Non Lieu, 2008), 49–83.

27. Armanios, "The 'Virtuous Woman,'" 117, cited in Aclimandos, "L'amour vache," 142.

28. Armanios, "The 'Virtuous Woman,'" 111.

29. See Paul Di Maggio, "Culture and Cognition," *Annual Review of Sociology* 23 (August 1997): 263–87.

30. Named prime minister and charged with forming a new government in June 1930, former Wafd member Isma'il Sidqi appeared as a strongman in the troubled Egyptian politics of this period. He managed to stay in place three years, which was rare during an era of ministerial waltzes. He formed a party, al-Sh'ab, suspended the constitution of 1923, coordinated the drafting of a new constitution that would reinforce royal power while reducing that of Parliament, censored the press, and repressed opposition, chiefly Wafd.

31. Barbara Carter, "On Spreading the Gospel to Egyptians Sitting in the Darkness: The Political Problem of Missionaries in Egypt in the 1930s," *Middle Eastern Studies* 20, no. 4 (1984): 18–36.

32. See Aclimandos, "L'amour vache," 49–83; and Richard P. Mitchell, *The Society of the Muslim Brothers* (New York: Oxford University Press, 1993).

33. Heather Sharkey, "Arabic Antimissionary Treatises: Muslim Responses to Christian Evangelism in the Modern Middle-East" and "Arabic Antimissionary Treatises: A Select Annotated Bibliography," *International Bulletin of Missionary Research* 28, no. 3 (2004): 98–106.

34. 'Abd al-Fattah Ghurab, "al-'Amal al-tanṣīrī fī al-'ālam al-'arabī" (master's thesis, Badr University in Cairo, 2007); and Aclimandos, "L'amour vache," 49–83.

35. Aclimandos, "L'amour vache," 51.

36. Thomas Brisson, "De l'islam au christianisme: Dire et mettre en scène la conversion," in *Conversions religieuses et mutations politiques: Tares et avatars du communautarisme égyptien*, ed. Laure Guirguis (Paris: Non Lieu, 2008), 222.

37. Ibid., 219–20.

38. "Coptic Girls Converting to Islam, Live in Fear," YouTube, uploaded on Oct. 18, 2008: www.youtube.com/watch?v=4WI_iXhzbXk.

39. "Egyptian Coptic Christian Woman Converted to Islam," YouTube, uploaded on March 16, 2009: www.youtube.com/watch?v=8K-uUE-ncq8&feature=related.

40. Iman Farag, "Invitation to Trouble and Confession," *al-Karama*, Oct. 25, 2005.

41. These remarks are rooted in my years of observations and discussion with various interlocutors, in addition to references cited herein.

42. Anwar Moghith, professor of philosophy at Helwan University, and Samir Zaki, lay leader of youth activity at Saint Teresa's Church in Shubra, interviews by the author, Cairo, March 2009.

43. See the anthropological study by Mary Douglas, *De la souillure* (Paris: La Découverte, 2001); and the political analysis by Wendy Brown, *Regulating Aversion: Tolerance in the Age of Identity and Empire* (Princeton, NJ: Princeton University Press, 2006).

44. Egyptian Initiative for Personal Rights (EIPR), *Two Years of Sectarian Violence: What Happened? Where Do We Begin?* (Cairo: EIPR, 2010).

45. Organ trafficking has become more pronounced and more organized in Egypt in the last decade. Upheavals in the media scene and increased competition have led to an eagerness for news items, scandals, and catastrophes of all kinds, particularly those that could denounce the corruption of leaders; Egyptian papers have revealed several cases of organ harvesting without a patient's knowledge or the kidnapping of children for their organs. The increasing number of testimonies circling by word of mouth on the subject of deliberate organ sale and the organization of these transactions indicate the existence of network infrastructure dedicated to this business.

46. *Al-Yawm al-al-Sabi'*, April 27, 28, 29, 30, and May 1, 3, and 5, 2009; *al-Jumhuriyya*, April 28 and May 3, 2009; *al-Masri al-Yawm*, April 29 and May 1, 3, and 4, 2009; *al-Musawwar*, April 29, 2009; *al-Dustur*, April 30 and May 1 and 5, 2009; *al-Ahrar*, May 1, 2009; *al-Ahram*, May 1 and 2, 2009; *al-'Arabi*, May 3, 2009; *Nahda Masr*, May 2, 2009; *al-Wafd*, May 3, 2009; *al-Shuruq*, May 3, 2009; *al-Mal*, May 3, 2009; *Ruz al-Yusuf*, May 3, 4, and 5, 2009; *al-Fajr*, May 4, 2009; *al-Watani al-Yawm*, May 5, 2009; *Daily News*, April 29 and May 1, 3, and 4, 2009; *New York Times*, April 30, 2009; and *L'Express*, April 30, 2009.

47. I thank Souad Ferrié for having communicated this information to me in the course of a conversation.

48. See, e.g., Baring Evelyn Cromer, *Modern Egypt* (London: Macmillan, 1908).

CHAPTER 3

1. On the Wafa' Qustantin affair see Muhammad al-Baz, *Ḍidd al-Bābā asrār wa azma al-kanīsa* (Cairo: Kunūz li-l-nashr wa-l-tawzi', 2006); Tariq al-Bishri, *al-Jamā'a al-waṭaniyya: al-'Uzla wa-l-indimāj* (Cairo: Dār al-hilāl, 2005); Rafiq Habib, *al-Jamā'a al-qibṭiyya: Bayn al-indimāj wa-l-in'zāl* (Cairo: Maktaba al-shurūq al-duwaliyya, 2006); 'Abd al-Latif al-Minawi, *al-aqbāṭ: al-kanīsa am al-waṭan?* (Cairo: Atlas li-l-nashr wa-l-intāj al-i'lāmī, 2005), 245; and Samer Soliman, "The Radical Turn of Coptic Activism: Path to Democracy or to Sectarian Politics," *Cairo Papers in Social Science* 29 (Summer-Fall 2006): 135–55.

2. The Majlis al-Milli, which translates very roughly to "Congregational Council," is a body of Coptic laymen with jurisdiction on Coptic secular affairs. For more on the history of the Majlis al-Milli see the subsequent section in this chapter.

3. *Al-Hayat*, Dec. 16, 2004.

4. See Stephen Davis, *The Early Coptic Papacy: The Egyptian Church and Its Leadership in Late Antiquity* (Cairo: American University Press, 2004); see also Christopher Haas, *Alexandria in Late Antiquity: Topography and Social Conflict* (Baltimore: Johns Hopkins University Press, 1997).

5. See Gawdat Gabra and Hany N. Takla, eds., *Christianity and Monasticism in Upper Egypt: Akhmim and Sohag* (Cairo: American University Press, 2008); Nelly Van Doorn-Harder and Kari Vogt, *Between Desert and City* (Oslo: Novus Forlag, 1997), 230–42. On Coptic monasticism see also Aziz Suryal Atiya, *The Coptic Encyclopedia* (New York: Macmillan, 1991); and, especially, the articles of Antoine Guillaumont and the works of Stephen Davis cited herein.

6. See Paul Veyne, *Quand notre monde est devenu chrétien (312–394)* (Paris: Le Livre de poche, 2007).

7. See Giuseppe Alberigo, ed., *Les Conciles œcuméniques: histoire et décrets*, 3 vols. (Paris: Cerf, 1994); Stephen Davis, *Coptic Christology in Practice: Incarnation and Divine Participation in Late Antique and Medieval Egypt* (New York: Oxford University Press, 2008).

8. On the history of Copts during this long period see the aforementioned works of Aziz Suryal Atiya, *A History of Eastern Christianity* (London: Methuen, 1968), as well as his articles in Aziz Suryal Atiya, editor in chief, *The Coptic Encyclopedia* (New York: Macmillan, 1991); Carl F. Petry, ed., *The Cambridge History of Egypt*, vol. 1, *Islamic Egypt, 640–1517* (Cambridge: Cambridge University Press, 1998); and Stephen Davis, *The Coptic Papacy in Islamic Egypt (641–1517)* (Cairo: American University Press, 2010).

9. For a nuanced appreciation see Jean-Michel Mouton, "L'islamisation de l'Égypte au Moyen Âge," in *Chrétiens du monde arabe: Un archipel en terre d'islam*, ed. Bernard Heyberger (Paris: Autrement, 2003), 110–26; Christian Décobert, "Sur l'arabisation et l'islamisation de l'Égypte médiévale," in *Itinéraires d'Égypte: Mélanges offerts au père Maurice Martin S. J.*, ed. Christian Décobert (Cairo: IFAO, 1992), 273–300.

10. This percentage, established in several official sources, is contested by the patriarch and some diaspora activists who believe the figure is much higher—even as high as 20 percent of the Egyptian population according to some of them. The most rigorous studies carried out by demographers, however, tend toward the side of the official statistics; see Youssef Courbage and Philippe Fargues, *Chrétiens et juifs dans l'islam arabe et turc* (Paris: Payot, 2005); and Éric Denis, "Cent ans de localisation de la population chrétienne égyptienne," *Astrolabe* 2 (1999): 25–40.

11. See Maurice Martin, "Note sur la communauté copte entre 1650 et 1850," *Annales islamologiques* 18 (1982): 193–215.

12. André Raymond, *Le Caire* (Paris: Fayard, 1993).

13. See Kurt J. Werthmuller, *Coptic Identity and Ayyubid Politics in Egypt: 1218–1250* (Cairo: American University Press, 2010); Febe Armanios, *Coptic Christianity in Ottoman Egypt* (New York: Oxford University Press, 2011); and Catherine Mayeur-Jaouen,

Pèlerinages d'Égypte: Histoire de la piété copte et musulmane XVe–XXe siècles (Paris: EHESS, 2005).

14. On the role of Patriarch Cyril IV (1854–61), the "father of reform," at the start of the Coptic Church's restructuring, in the context of the *Tanzimat* that upset the millet system, see Paul Sedra, "Copts and the Millet Partnership: The Intra-communal Dynamics Behind Egyptian Sectarianism," *Journal of Law and Religion* 29, no. 3 (2014): 491–509.

15. See Alastair Hamilton, *The Copts and the West, 1439–1822: The European Discovery of the Egyptian Church* (Oxford: Oxford University Press, 2006); Paul Sedra, "John Lieder and His Mission in Egypt: The Evangelical Ethos at Work Among the Nineteenth-Century Copts," *Journal of Religious History* 28 (Oct. 2004): 219–39; Paul Sedra, *From Mission to Modernity: Evangelicals, Reformers and Education in Nineteenth-Century Egypt* (I.B. Tauris, 2011); and Heather Sharkey, *American Evangelicals in Egypt* (Princeton, NJ: Princeton University Press, 2008).

16. Luc Barbulesco, "La communauté copte d'Égypte, 1881–1981: Attitudes collectives et orientations idéologiques" (PhD diss., Institut d'études politiques, 1990).

17. Nasim Sulaiman, "Habib Jirjis," in *The Coptic Encyclopedia*, vol. 4, ed. Aziz Suryal Atiya (New York: Macmillan, 1991), 1189; and Paul Sedra, "Class Cleavages and Ethnic Conflict: Coptic Christian Communities in Modern Egyptian Politics," *Islam and Christian-Muslim Relations* 10, no. 2 (1999): 219–35.

18. Brigitte Voile, *Les Coptes d'Égypte sous Nasser: Sainteté, miracles, apparitions* (Paris: CNRS, 2004), 155, citing A. al-Nur Sayfan, *Tārīkh al-qiddīs al-ʿaẓīm al-Anbā Shinūda* (Alexandria: n.p., 1959), 9.

19. On the relationship between the Egyptian and Ethiopian churches see Haggai Erlich, "Identity and Church, Egyptian-Ethiopian Dialogue, 1924–59," *International Journal of Middle East Studies* 32, no. 1 (2000): 23–46.

20. On the position of the Coptic Church with regard to Israel see documents in Ghali Shukri, *al-Aqbāṭ fī waṭan mutaghayīr* (Cairo: Dār al-shurūq, 1991), 63.

21. See Sedra, "Copts and the Millet Partnership."

22. On Cyril VI, and the relations between Nasser and Cyril IV, see Shukri, *al-Aqbāṭ*, 60; Mahmud Fawzi, *al-Bābā Kirillus wa ʿAbd al-Nāṣir* (Cairo: al-Waṭan li-l-Nashr, 1993); Usama Salama, *Maṣīr al-aqbāṭ fī Miṣr* (Cairo: Dār al-Khayyāl, 1998), 117; and Vivian Ibrahim, *The Copts of Egypt: Challenges of Modernisation and Identity* (London: I.B. Tauris, 2010).

23. "Adultery of the man or woman; one of the spouses' abandonment of the Christian religion; the uninterrupted absence of one of the spouses for five years with no sign of life; condemnation of one of the spouses to forced labor for at least five years; condemnation of one of the spouses to prison for at least five years; if one of the spouses is struck with dementia or an incurable disease for at least three years or impotent for at least three years; in the case of misconduct of one of the spouses; in the case of abuse or the violation of conjugal duties that result in a separation of more than three years; and

finally if one of the spouses joins religious orders," as referenced in Nathalie Bernard-Maugiron, "L'amendement du règlement sur le statut personnel des coptes orthodoxes en Égypte: À quand une loi unifiée pour la famille?" *Revue internationale de droit comparé (RIDC)* 62, no. 1 (2010): 75–103.

24. Based on the practice of the Majlis al-Milli before abolition in 1955, the 1938 regulations were effectively applied and had acquired customary (*'urfi*) value in the sense that Article 1 of the Civic Code of 1948, whereas that of 1955, was adopted after the withdrawal of the juridical powers of the Majlis al-Milli and had never been applied by them. It therefore had not acquired customary value. See ibid.

25. Ibid.

26. See James C. Scott, *Domination and the Arts of Resistance: Hidden Transcripts* (New Haven, CT: Yale University Press, 1990); and Charles Suaud, "La force symbolique de l'État," *Actes de la recherché en sciences sociales* 116–17, no. 1 (1996): 3–23.

27. See, e.g., H. H. Pope Shenouda III, *The Heresy of Jehovah's Witnesses*, www.orthodoxebooks.org/node/23; see also the articles written in October 2009 and published in the paper *Watani*.

28. Rafiq Habib, *al-Masīḥiyya al-siyāsiyya fī Miṣr: Madkhal ilā-l-tayārāt al-siyāsiyya lada al-aqbāṭ* (Cairo: Yāfā li-l-dirāsāt wa al-nashr, 1990).

29. Tewfik Aclimandos, "L'amour vache. Conversions: Quelques remarques sur les discours et les imaginaires," in *Conversions religieuses et mutations politiques: Tares et avatars du communautarisme égyptien*, ed. Laure Guirguis (Paris: Non Lieu, 2008), 49–83; and Muhammad al-Baz, *Zakaryā Buṭrus* (Cairo: Kunūz li-l-nashr wa-l-tawzi', 2010).

30. Dina El-Khawaga, "Le renouveau copte: La communauté comme acteur politique" (PhD diss., Institut des études politiques, 1993), 192–213.

31. Al-Baz, *Ḍidd al-Bābā*.

32. Jacques Masson, "La divinisation de l'homme: Les raisons de l'opposition de Chenouda III," *Proche-Orient Chrétien* 57, no. 3–4 (2007): 279–90.

33. On the "clericalization" and "Christianization" of the community see El-Khawaga, "Le renouveau copte," chaps. 5 and 6. On the attention given to those who had left the church see Febe Armanios, "The 'Virtuous Woman': Images of Gender in Modern Coptic Society," *Middle Eastern Studies* 38, no. 110 (2002): 110–30; and El-Khawaga, "Le renouveau copte," 238.

34. On Anba Musa see al-Baz, *Ḍidd al-Bābā*, 249.

35. This was not without hesitation, however: the clergy did not believe that the church was responsible for the well-being of the laity. After having changed position, Shenuda responded several times to questions about why he reversed course by saying that only communists could oppose the church's commitment to social services, since communists assumed that the state would provide all material goods to individuals. See Shukri, *al-Aqbāṭ*, 149.

36. Shenuda III, interview by Ghali Shukri, in Shukri, *al-Aqbāṭ*.

37. Wealth and income determine the selection of members of the electoral college; the suffrage is thus censitary based on the accepted definition by analogy with the procedure in place in the United States, where only individuals accountable to the census have the right to vote. In the contemporary era, where the majority of states have adopted universal suffrage, the idea of a "census" is still valid as a methodological tool necessary for analysis and reporting on economic and cultural inequality and modes of political participation. See Daniel Gaxie, *Le cens caché: Inégalités culturelles et ségrégation politique* (Paris: Seuil, 1978).

38. Adel Guindy, interview by the author, Paris, June 2010.

39. Myriam Revault D'Allonnes, *Le pouvoir des commencements* (Paris: Seuil, 2006). D'Allonnes adopts the notion from Jacques Derrida.

40. Max Weber, *Économie et société* (Paris: Plon, 2004), 285–355.

41. Claude Lefort, "Permanence du théologico-politique?" in *Essais sur le politique* (Paris: Seuil, 1986), 275–330.

42. Jean-Luc Nancy, *La communauté désœuvrée* (Paris: Christian Bourgois, 1990).

43. Abrar al-Ghannam, "Religious Censorship in Egypt: Attitudes Within the Coptic Orthodox Church of Egypt," *Arab West Report*, Dec. 10, 2008.

44. On the problem in the American context see Judith Butler, *Excitable Speech: A Politics of the Performative* (New York: Routledge, 2004).

45. Anba Bishuy endeavored to refute the historical errors and theological inaccuracies in the text. The controversy around the work lasted more than a year and revolved principally around errors or, conversely, the well-documented character of the text, depending on the stance of the author of the article toward the novel: accuser, defender, or impartial judge. More rarely, some, along with the author himself, would question the "right" of a novelist to take a historical period as the theme of its plot and to create a setting that could not reflect, as a historian might, all the aspects of the era. On *'Azāzil* in the press see (among others) *al-Hayat*, August 3, 2008; and the *Daily Star* (Cairo), Nov. 13, 2008.

46. Iman Farag, "Ya'qub revisité ou les enjeux des relectures nationales," in "L'expédition de Bonaparte vue d'Égypte," ed. Ghislaine Alleaume, *Égypte/Monde arabe*, no. 1, 2nd ser. (1999): 171–79.

47. See Shafiq Ghurbal, "Le général Ya'qûb, le chevalier Lascaris et le projet d'indépendance de l'Égypte en 1801," in "L'expédition de Bonaparte vue d'Égypte," ed. Ghislaine Alleaume, *Égypte/Monde arabe*, no. 1, 2nd ser. (1999): 179–203.

48. Ahmad Husayn al-Sawi, *Al-mu'allim Ya'qūb bayn al-usṭūra wa-l-ḥaqīqa* (Cairo: Dār al-fikr li-l-dirāsāt wa-l-nashr wa-l-tawzī', 1986), 13.

49. See Alain Roussillon, "Égyptianité, arabité, islamité: La recomposition des références identitaires," in "A propos de la nationalité: Questions sur l'identité nationale," ed. Iman Farag and Alain Roussillon, *Égypte/Monde arabe*, no. 11, 1st ser. (1992): 77–137; and *Réforme sociale et identité: Essai sur l'émergence de l'intellectuel et du champ politique modernes en Égypte* (Casablanca: Le Fennec, 1999).

50. On Ya'qub see the subtle analysis of Iman Farag, "Ya'qub revisité," included in the introduction to the translation of Shafiq Ghurbal's text (see note 47 above), as well as the study of Henry Laurens on the knight of Lascaris, an adventurer of modern times with whom Ya'qub embarked on the Pallas and at whose instigation he conceived of the project of Egypt's Liberation: Henry Laurens, *Orientales I: Autour de l'expédition d'Égypte* (Paris: CNRS, 2004). In the Egyptian press see *al-Yawm al-Sabi'*, May 28, 2009, and June 5, 2009; *al-Masri al-Yawm*, May 29, 2009; *al-Usbu'*, May 29, 2009; *Akhbar al-Adab*, May 31, 2009, and June 7, 2009; *Ruz al-Yusuf*, June 2, 4, and 6, 2009; *al-Musawwar*, June 3, 2009; *al-Karama*, June 8, 2009 (written by Ahmad al-Sawi); *al-Shuruq*, June 12 and 22, 2009; and *al-Ahram*, June 16, 2009. This debate created an occasion for diverse factions and actors to reaffirm their positions vis-à-vis the others: the church against the minister of culture, activists of the diaspora against Nabil Luqa Bibawi and Gamal As'ad, etc.: *Nahda Masr*, June 13, 2009; and *al-Wafd*, June 13, 2009. An article in which the author reframed the problem by taking a historical perspective appears in *al-Raya*, July 1, 2009. On Bonaparte's expeditions, outside the well-known references, see Sonallah Ibrahim's novel (read with pleasure): *Turbans et chapeaux*, trans. Richard Jacquemond (Arles: Actes Sud, 2011).

51. On *Bahibb al-Sīmā* see *al-Musawwar*, no. 4157, June 11, 2004; no. 4158, June 18, 2004 (particularly Murqus 'Aziz's point of view); and no. 4159, June 25, 2004 (Samir Farid's reaction to the priest); see also *al-Ahram Weekly*, no. 699, July 15–21, 2004; and no. 703, August 12–18, 2004.

52. *Al-Ahram Weekly*, no. 699, July 15–24, 2004.

53. Armanios, "The 'Virtuous Woman'"; and El-Khawaga, "Le renouveau copte," 238.

54. Mariz Tadros is particularly attentive to the diversity of Coptic actors; see Mariz Tadros, "Vicissitudes in the Entente Between the Coptic Orthodox Church and the State in Egypt (1952–2007)," *International Journal of Middle East Studies* 41, no. 2 (2009): 269–87; and Mariz Tadros, *Copts at the Crossroads* (Cairo: AUC Press, 2013).

55. On relations between Sadat and Shenuda III see the three authoritative testimonies of Egyptian journalists: Sabri, *al-sādāt*; Shukri, *L'Égypte* and *al-Aqbāṭ*; and Haykal, *L'automne*.

56. Dozens of stories circulate: Sadat, made to look ridiculous, is like the village idiot, which is why Nasser would have chosen him as vice president. In the same vein are numerous remarks about the last years of Mubarak's rule: Mubarak never nominated a vice president (before being forced to by the army in January 2011) because he could never find anyone more stupid than he was.

57. See Saba Mahmood, "Religious Freedom, the Minority Question, and Geopolitics in the Middle East," *Comparative Studies in Society and History* 54, no. 2 (2012): 418–46.

58. By amending Article 2, for example, Sadat intended primarily to ensure the

Islamist support for another constitutional amendment that would abrogate the limit for presidential mandates. In *al-Sharq al-Awsat* on April 13, 2011, an interview with former state prosecutor Muhammad Hamid al-Gamal provided several indications as to the backdoor negotiations on this article.

59. When he was interrogated on the matter, Shenuda responded at several points: "You reproach me for my involvement in politics at the same time as you demand it" (in intervening with emigrant activists).

60. The exchanges among Shenuda, leaders of American Coptic dissent, and the official regime intermediaries are reported accurately in Sabri, *al-Sādāt*; Shukri, *L'Égypte* and *al-Aqbāṭ*; and Haykal, *L'automne*. Salama, in *Maṣīr*, compares these three different narratives on Shenuda's role in the diaspora protests at the end of the 1970s.

61. Shenuda wrote several texts on this subject. He took the position not only from a political perspective but also a theological one as, at the World Council of Churches in New Delhi in 1961, the churches of the Third Synod had begun to discuss the problem of Jewish culpability in Christ's crucifixion and decided to absolve them in 1964.

62. For a detailed description and analysis of the Coptic mobilizations from 2000 to 2006 see Soliman, "The Radical Turn"; and Laure Guirguis, "Contestations coptes contemporaines," in *Protestations sociales, révolutions civiles: Transformations du politique dans la Méditerranée arabe*, ed. Sarah Ben Néfissa and Blandine Destremeau (Paris: Armand Colin, 2011), 139–63. On the CD issue see Alain Roussillon, "Visibilité nouvelle de la 'question copte': Entre refus de la sédition et revendication citoyenne," in *L'Égypte dans l'année 2005*, ed. Florian Kosthall (Cairo: CEDEJ, 2006).

63. See Voile, *Les Coptes*.

64. See al-Baz, *Ḍidd al-Bābā*.

65. Since 2004 Manqariyus has published the monthly *al-Katība al-tibiyya* (The Theban Legion) under the church's official supervision. The publication is named in reference to a legion of the Roman Army in Egypt, whose Christian soldiers claimed they were ready to fight for the emperor, but not to worship him, and were martyred for having refused to abandon their religion. The publication is spread in religious spaces only, as are most publications edited "by" and "for" Copts, except the weekly *Watani*, edited by Yusif Sidhum and distributed in kiosks.

66. Luc Barbulesco, "La communauté copte d'Égypte, 1881–1981: Attitudes collectives et orientations idéologiques" (PhD diss., Institut d'études politiques, 1990).

67. See Soliman, "The Radical Turn."

68. Max Michel made a much-noted entrance into the Egyptian media scene, after having failed in several attempts to endanger the unity of the mother church. In July 2006 Max Michel proclaimed himself the patriarch of the Coptic Church of Saint Athanasius in Muqattam (a hill east of Cairo, past the ancient necropolis). He adorned himself with patriarchal emblems, identical to those of Shenuda, and assumed the same title, under the name Maximos I. He advertised a more permissive reading of the biblical text on

matters of divorce to attract followers and showed himself willing to update the patristic Coptic heritage, momentarily attracting the curiosity of a few Coptic intellectuals. Steeped in rancor toward the true patriarch and the Coptic Church, whose clergy had disdained his theses, he was full of criticism toward Shenuda and accused him (without great originality) of being responsible for the resurgence of sectarian strife. For several decades Max Michel had searched for any means of a victorious return. He attempted to win over Samuel Habib (the previous head of the Egyptian Protestant Churches), among others, to issue him authorization to found a Protestant church (March 2009 interview with Rafiq Habib). When these efforts did not come to fruition, he finally secured the title of an American church, which none of the Orthodox churches recognize. According to several observers (mentioned in interviews with Hani Labib, who followed the matter in its minutiae, and with Nabil ʿAbd al-Fattah), he certainly would have needed assistance from State Security services to obtain identity documents declaring, incorrectly, that he held the title of "Anba," or, according to other observers, he would have at least required their total ignorance of clerical nomenclature.

69. On this episode see Tadros, "Vicissitudes," 269–87.

70. This formula usually expresses a critical stance with regard to patriarchal politics; see, e.g., al-Bishri, *al-Jamāʿa al-waṭaniyya*; and Habib, *al-Jamāʿa al-qibṭiyya*.

71. El-Khawaga, "Le renouveau copte," 219.

72. Among others, in the first centuries of Islamic conquest, for example, see Mounir Megally, "Bashmuric Revolts," in *The Coptic Encyclopedia*, vol. 2, ed. Aziz Suryal Atiya (New York: Macmillan, 1991), 349–51.

73. See Otto Meinardus, *Christians in Egypt: Orthodox, Catholic, and Protestant Communities Past and Present* (Cairo: American University Press, 2006), 19–32.

74. Pope Shenuda III, interview by Sanaʾ al-Saʿid, *al-Usbuʿ*, April 2, 2007.

75. Samir Murqus, "al-Aqbāṭ wa-l-shariʿa bayn dustūr al-ḥaraka al-waṭaniyya (1923) wa dustūr walī al-amr (1971)," in *al-Muwāṭana fī muwājaha al-ṭāʾifiyya*, ed. ʿAmr al-Shubaki (Cairo: al-Ahram Center for Political and Strategic Studies, 2009), 73–93. On the debates around the 2007 constitutional amendments see the collection of texts published by the Cairo Institute for Human Rights Studies (CIHRS), which launched a call to amend Article 2. In the press see al-Bishri's articles in *al-Ahram*, Feb. 28, 2007, and March 1, 2007; ʿAmr al-Shubaki, in *al-Masri al-Yawm*, March 8, 2007; and Fahmi Huwaydi, in *al-Ahram*, April 24, 2007, as well as the report from a panel discussion on the show *Atmosphere*, on the Orbit channel, which hosted Protestant priest Rifʿat al-Fikri, the journalist and author Hani Labib, and the Coptic political figure Gamal Asʿad—three personalities representing different positions on the constitutional article published in *Nahda Masr*, Feb. 8 and 9, 2007. For after the referendum see "The Church and the Referendum," *al-Masri al-Yawm*, March 26, 2007; and "The Christian Vote in the Referendum," *al-Masri al-Yawm*, March 28, 2007. On the 2009 exchanges between Adel Guindy and Fathy Surur on the subject see *al-Ahali*, June 10, 2009, July 8, 22, and 29, 2009, and August 5, 2009.

76. In Sana' al-Sa'id's interview, for example, Shenuda III declared, "A Coptic party is an experiment doomed to failure"; see *al-Usbu'*, Sept. 19, 2005.

77. *Al-Usbu'*, April 2, 2007. Refer also to 'Abd al-Fattah, "al-Mu'assasā al-dīniyya al-qibṭiyya al-urthuduksiyya wa qadāyā al-muwāṭana wa-l-waḥda al-waṭaniyya," in *al-Muwāṭana fī muwājaha al-ṭā'īfiyya*, ed. 'Amr al-Shubaki (Cairo: al-Ahram Center for Political and Strategical Studies, 2009), 93–121.

78. After his unremarkable and long-ignored beginnings as a drummer in a rock band, Ahmad 'Izz became enthusiastically involved in the cement industry, then in politics. He served as MP and spokesperson of the NDP at the People's Assembly. On Ahmad 'Izz see Tewfik Aclimandos, "'On ne prête qu'aux riches': Hommes d'affaire et politique," in *Chroniques égyptiennes 2008*, ed. Iman Farag (Cairo: CEDEJ, 2010), 196–241.

79. On growing corruption in the high clergy at the end of the 1990s see al-Baz, *Ḍidd al-Bābā*.

80. On Tharwat Basili see al-Baz, *Ḍidd al-Bābā*.

81. The patriarch reiterated in several interviews that "since the first Parliamentary elections after Sadat's accession to the presidency, they have asked that I choose a certain number of Copts to be nominated to the Assembly, but they have not taken a single one that I selected for them, so I have stopped selecting"; see, e.g., Salama, *Maṣīr*, 130. It is both true and false.

82. The majority of observers reacting to Shenuda's intervention evoked the distinction between the era of the plebiscite vote or referendum (*istiftā'*) and an election from among several candidates; see, e.g., *al-Masri al-Yawm*, August 12, 2005. Note that the Catholic Church also supported Hosni Mubarak's candidacy. On the patriarchal support for Mubarak in the elections and on the political activity of the church leadership see 'Abd al-Fattah, "al-Mu'assasā," 93–121; and in the press, e.g., *al-Ahram*, August 12, 2005; *Egypt Today*, Nov. 2005; *al-Fajr*, Nov. 28, 2005; and *al-Masri al-Yawm*, Dec. 13, 2005.

83. *Al-Ahram Weekly*, no. 756, August 18–24, 2005.

84. On Murqus 'Aziz see al-Baz, *Ḍidd al-Bābā*, 247.

85. *Nahda Masr*, Sept. 4, 2005.

86. *Al-Masri al-Yawm*, Sept. 5, 2005.

87. *Al-Akhbar*, August 6, 2005.

88. Ayman Nour had tried to court the Muslim Brotherhood vote while also benefiting from the support of Copts abroad, thanks to his party's affiliation with one of the most eminent Coptic activists, the late engineer 'Adli Abadir, based in Zurich: "Nur seeks the support of the Brothers in response to the Church's support for the National Party" (*al-Masri al-Yawm*, August 12, 2005). On Nour's attempts with Abadir and Filubatir's departure from al-Ghad after Nour promised to let the Brothers found a political party if he was elected, see *Nahda Masr*, Sept. 7, 2005. It is difficult to know how many Copts and how many Brothers were included in the 8 percent of votes that Nour received in the

election, particularly given that this figure itself is uncertain and may underestimate the actual number who voted for him.

89. A representative of the Giza diocese explained that Filubatir had been suspended from his duties for having criticized the Egyptian government, for his affiliation with an opposition party, and for shortcomings in fulfilling his clerical duties; see *Ruz al-Yusuf*, August 13, 2005. On the Filubatir affair see, e.g., *Sut al-Umma*, Nov. 28 and Dec. 12, 2005.

90. See Charles Taylor, *A Secular Age* (Cambridge: Belknap Press of Harvard University Press, 2007); and José Casanova, *Public Religions in the Modern World* (Chicago: University of Chicago Press, 1994).

91. On the Egyptian military and its role in the construction of the state and the nationalist narrative see Juan Cole, *Colonialism and Revolution in the Middle East: Social and Cultural Origins of Egypt's 'Urabi Movement* (Princeton, NJ: Princeton University Press, 1993); and Khaled Fahmy, "The Nation and Its Deserters: Conscription in Mehmed Ali's Egypt," *International Review of Social History* 43, no. 3 (1998): 421–36. On the military and State Security services see Zeinab Abu al-Magd, "The Army and the Economy in Egypt," *Jadaliyya*, Dec. 23, 2011; Yezid Sayigh, "Above the State: The Officers' Republic in Egypt," *Carnegie Papers* (Washington: Carnegie Middle East Center, 2012); Robert Springborg, "The President and the Field Marshall: Civil-Military Relations in Egypt Today," *Middle East Report and Information Project* 147 (July-August 1987): www.merip.org/mer/mer147/president-field-marshall; Ibrahim El-Houdaiby, "Changing Alliances and Continuous Oppression: The Rule of Egypt's Security Sector," *Arab Reform Initiative* (Jan. 2014); Hazem Qandil, *Soldiers, Spies and Statesmen: Egypt's Road to Revolt* (New York: Verso, 2012); Tewfik Aclimandos, "Nationalismes machréquins et nassérisme," in *Nationalismes en perspective*, ed. Gil Delannoi and André Taguieff (Paris: Berg International, 2001); and Tewfik Aclimandos, "Les activistes politiques au sein de l'armée égyptienne: 1936–1954" (PhD diss., Institut d'études politiques, 2004).

CHAPTER 4

1. See *al-Ahram*, July 26, 1954; and "Coptic Revolt Broken," *New York Times*, July 27, 1954.

2. Tewfik Aclimandos, conversation with the author, Cairo, Sept. 2009.

3. Al-Baz, conversation with the author, Cairo, Dec. 2009; and Kamal Zakhir, *al-'Ilmāniyūn wa-l-kanīsa: ṣirā'āt wa taḥālufāt* (Cairo: n.p., 2009), 170.

4. Muhammad 'Afifi, conversation with the author, Cairo, March 2010; and Zakhir, *al-'Ilmāniyūn*, 171.

5. Zakhir, *al-'Ilmāniyūn*, 168–69.

6. Yunan Labib Rizk, *al-Aḥzāb al-siyāsiyya min Miṣr, 1907–1984* (Cairo: Kitāb al-hilāl, 1984), 65.

7. Samira Bahr, *al-Aqbāṭ fī al-ḥayāt al-siyāsiyya al-miṣriyya* (Cairo: al-Anglo, 1979), 151–73.

8. Yusif Abu Sayf, *al-Aqbāṭ wa-l-qawmiyya al-ʿarabiyya* (Beirut: Markaz diraz, 1987); and Habib, *al-Masīḥiyya al-siyāsiyya.*

9. Ghali Shukri, *Egypt: Portrait of a President, 1971–1981. The Counter Revolution in Egypt; Sadat's Road to Jerusalem* (London: Zed, 1981), 281–82.

10. Anthony Gorman, *Historians, State and Politics in Twentieth Century Egypt: Contesting the Nation* (London: Routledge Curzon, 2003), 147–74.

11. Dina El-Khawaga, "Le renouveau copte: La communauté comme acteur politique" (PhD diss., Institut des études politiques, 1993), 102.

12. Muhammad ʿAfifi, conversation with the author, Cairo, March 2010.

13. On Ramsis Gabrawi's party see ʿAbd al-Fattah, "al-Muʾassasā al-dīniyya al-qibṭiyya al-urthuduksiyya wa qadāyā al-muwāṭana wa-l-waḥda al-waṭaniyya," in *al-Muwāṭana fī muwājaha al-ṭāʾifiyya*, ed. ʿAmr al-Shubaki (Cairo: al-Ahram Center for Political and Strategical Studies, 2009), 93–121; Vivian Ibrahim, *The Copts of Egypt: Challenges of Modernisation and Identity* (London: I.B. Tauris, 2010), 162–64; and Barbara Carter, *The Copts in Egyptian Politics* (London: Croom Helm, 1986), 280–81.

14. *Al-Masri al-Yawm*, May 6, 2010.

15. Zakhir, *al-ʿIlmāniyūn.*

16. For a comparative analysis on the social and professional backgrounds of lay reformers today and in the early twentieth century see Paul Sedra, "Class Cleavages and Ethnic Conflict: Coptic Christian Communities in Modern Egyptian Politics," *Islam and Christian-Muslim Relations* 10, no 2 (1999): 219–35, 228.

17. Kamal Zakhir, interview by the author, March 2007.

18. *Ruz al-Yusuf*, no. 4055, March 25–26, 2006.

19. Ibid.

20. On the role and status of clergymen and monks see *al-Fajr*, March 5 and April 16, 2007; *Ruz al-Yusuf*, March 9 and 16 and May 4, 2007; *al-Masri al-Yawm*, March 17, 2007; and Kamal Ghubriyal in *al-Qahira*, April 24, 2007. On Shenuda's arbitrary decisions concerning members of the clergy and abuses committed by Anba Bishuy see Muhammad al-Baz, *Ḍidd al-Bābā asrār wa azma al-kanīsa* (Cairo: Kunūz li-l-nashr wa-l-tawziʿ, 2006) (although information therein should be compared to others collected from Coptic actors).

21. For a critique of the current law and a proposal for a new one see Zakhir, *al-ʿIlmāniyūn.*

22. *Ruz al-Yusuf*, no. 4055, March 25–26, 2006.

23. Hani Labib, *al-Kanīsa al-miṣriyya: Tawāzunāt al-dīn wa-l-dawla* (Cairo: Dār Naḥda Miṣr, 2012).

24. Jacques Masson, "La divinisation de l'homme: Les raisons de l'opposition de Chenouda III," *Proche orient chrétien* 57, no 3–4 (2007): 279–90. For a postcolonial critique of orientalist and eulogistic works (those of Georges Antonius, Albert Hourani, and Elie Kedourie) on the influence of missionaries on reform see Paul Sedra, *From Mis-*

sion to Modernity: Evangelicals, Reformers and Education in Nineteenth-Century Egypt (London: I.B. Tauris, 2011); and Paul Sedra, "John Lieder and His Mission in Egypt: The Evangelical Ethos at Work Among the Nineteenth-Century Copts," *Journal of Religious History* 28 (Oct. 2004): 219–39; see also one of the texts to which he refers: Samir Seikaly, "Coptic Communal Reform: 1860–1914," *Middle Eastern Studies* 6, no. 3 (1970): 247–70.

25. *Ruz al-Yusuf*, no. 4195, Feb. 16–22, 2007.

26. *Al-Kiraza*, Feb. 23, 2007.

27. Masson, "La divinisation de l'homme," 282.

28. On Matta al-Maskin see, e.g., *al-Masri al-Yawm*, Nov. 5, 2006, and June 2007; *Ruz al-Yusuf*, Dec. 1 and 17, 2006; *Ruz al-Yusuf*, Feb. 16 and March 2, 2007; and *al-'Arabi*, Dec. 17, 2006.

29. Abūnā Matā al-Miskīn. Dīr al-Qadīs Anbā Maqār, *Morcos* 53 (special supplement) (2006) .

30. Kamal Zakhir, interview by the author, March 2012, Cairo.

31. Several usually reliable verbal sources attest that in 1971 all three papers carried the name of Nazir Gayid, who became Pope Shenuda. Some written testimonies also endorse this version of patriarchal election, notably that of Haykal; however, the accounts of this leading journalist often prove biased or incomplete. Others, typically just as reliable, insist that rigging was not possible, the kaimakam having displayed the two other papers straightaway. One testimony refers particularly to the memory of the child who pulled the name of the future patriarch. 'Atif Gendi, dean of the Faculty of Protestant Theology in Cairo, related this testimony, which the child recalled several years after the draw ('Atif Gendi, interview by the author, March 2012). The accuracy of the statement, however, is questionable given the age of the witness and the state in which, according to his own words, he found himself at the very moment of the draw.

32. On the constitution of the electoral college and the selection of candidate for the last two elections, Cyril (Kirillus) VI and Shenuda III, see Usama Salama, *Maṣīr al-aqbāṭ fī Miṣr* (Cairo: Dār al-Khayyāl, 1998).

33. See *al-Mal*, August 13, 2009.

34. For a more complete study in the early twenty-first century rivalries, in particular at the moment of succession, see al-Baz, *Ḍidd al-Bābā*; and Muhammad al-Baz, Zakaryā Buṭrus (Cairo: Kunūz li-l-nashr wa-l-tawzi', 2010); Laure Guirguis, "Égypte: l'autre succession—l'Église copte à l'approche d'un tournant," *Religioscope* (2010): http://religion.info/french/articles/article_501.shtml; and Mariz Tadros, *Copts at the Crossroads* (Cairo: AUC Press, 2013).

35. Celebration in honor of a saint's birthday.

36. See Catherine Mayeur-Jaouen, *Pèlerinages d'Égypte: Histoire de la piété copte et musulmane XVe–XXe siècles* (Paris: EHESS, 2005).

37. See Olivier Roy, "Le printemps arabe et le mythe de la nécessaire sécularisation," *Socio* 2 (2013): 25–36.

38. On the Jehovah's Witnesses in Egypt see Johanna Pink, "The Concept of Freedom of Belief and Its Boundaries in Egypt: The Jehovah's Witnesses and the Bahai Faith: Between Established Religions and an Authoritarian State," *Culture and Religion* 6, no. 1 (2007): 135–60. The Jehovah's Witnesses arrived in Egypt in 1935; the first convert was a Greek working in a café. Others followed, and an employee of the *Crédit Lyonnais*, Anis Fayyid, became their leader. They founded centers, and the movement grew. Despite a court decision in their favor, the government decided, by decree 155 of 1960, to forbid the group, close its centers, and confiscate its property. They have not gained legal recognition since then. To my knowledge no studies exist on current activities of the Jehovah's Witnesses in Egypt. In 1999 they submitted a request to the State Council to abrogate the negative decision taken in the Nasserist era and, therefore, to allow them to obtain organizational status. The State Council's Court of Administrative Justice finally ruled in 2009, after having required that they provide documents in which they explain their doctrine. In his reasoning the judge presiding over the court referred to supposed links between Jehovah's Witnesses and Zionists, as well as to their refusal to recognize any form of government. He argued that it was a political movement "working with Zionists and using sex to attract followers"; he then concluded that the doctrine and activities of such a group were harmful to public order and the morals of Egyptian society. See *al-Masri al-Yawm*, Dec. 31, 2009; and *al-Al-Yawm al-Sabi'*, Dec. 30, 2009.

Generally listed under recognized Protestant churches, adherents meet in private. Very discreet, they work primarily in the marginalized regions of Upper Egypt and the poor neighborhoods of Cairo. They prefer areas in which the local church has encountered difficulty and is not very active (according to residents' testimonies, they are present in al-Waraq, near Imbaba, Giza), as well as new neighborhoods where no church yet exists (like Tenth of Ramadan City on the northeastern outskirts of Cairo or the Ajami neighborhood in Alexandria). They mainly target poor families and offer assistance. They benefit from significant financial resources originating from the seat of the organization in Brooklyn, New York. They dangle emigration opportunities. Recently, they have entered into the most affluent suburbs and downtown Cairo: a Coptic family from a church in Heliopolis converted. Naturally, Jehovah's Witnesses cannot implement the same strategies in Egypt as in Europe or the United States, where they pass door-to-door and hand out leaflets in the street. They present themselves as Protestants and address people they know (for example, in the workplace), who are chosen for their infrequent church attendance despite being nominally Christian. It would seem, however, that they have paid home visits over the course of the past years; several individuals living in the center of Cairo had been solicited at home. Isolated, they do not work in conjunction with other Christian denominations, but their numbers grow. According to several estimates, the group may number around twenty-five thousand members across Egypt.

39. *Al-Masri al-Yawm*, March 1 and 2, 2008; see also the Sept. 16, 2007, and May 19,

2009, editions. See also H. H. Pope Shenouda III, *The Heresy of Jehovah's Witnesses*, www.orthodoxebooks.org/node/23.

40. The principal Protestant church is the Coptic Evangelical Church, with a Presbyterian leaning. This church numbers more than one hundred thousand members. The first representative of the Council of Protestant Churches was appointed by khedivial decree in 1878. The council was constituted of twenty members representing the fourteen recognized Protestant churches, divided into three groups: the most important, the Reformed churches (of which the Coptic Evangelical Church counted twelve members); the Church of the Brethren (Plymothian currents, Baptists, Methodists, etc.); and Pentecostal churches (these last two were represented by six members; the two other members of the Protestant council were women).

41. On Protestant missionary activity in the Middle East see Ussama Makdisi, *Artillery of Heaven: American Missionaries and the Failed Conversion of the Middle East* (Ithaca, NY: Cornell University Press, 2009); on Egypt see Alastair Hamilton, *The Copts and the West, 1439–1822: The European Discovery of the Egyptian Church* (Oxford: Oxford University Press, 2006); and Heather Sharkey, *American Evangelicals in Egypt* (Princeton, NJ: Princeton University Press, 2008).

42. Iris Habib el Masri, *The Story of the Copts: The True Story of Christianity in Egypt* (Merry Springs, CA: Middle East Council of Churches, 1978), www.orthodoxebooks.org/node/192.

43. This observation was noted in several interviews and conversations I held with Protestant figures in Egypt from 2005 to 2011 who wish to remain anonymous.

44. These are the most common criticisms that extended across my conversations with some forty individuals, as well as various third-party accounts.

45. See Tewfik Aclimandos, "L'amour vache. Conversions: quelques remarques sur les discours et les imaginaires," in *Conversions religieuses et mutations politiques: Tares et avatars du communautarisme égyptien*, ed. Laure Guirguis (Paris: Non Lieu, 2008), 49–83; al-Baz, *Zakaryā Buṭrus*; and Rafiq Habib, *al-Masīḥiyya al-siyāsiyya fī Miṣr: Madkhal ilā-l-tayārāt al siyāsiyya lada al-aqbāṭ* (Cairo: Yāfā lil dirāsāt wa al-nashr, 1990).

46. Gaétan Du Roy and Jamie Furniss, "Sœur Emmanuelle et les chiffonniers: Partage de vie et développement, 1971–1982," in *Mission et engagement politique après 1945*, ed. Caroline Sappia and Olivier Servais (Paris: Karthala, 2010).

47. Abuna Sam'an, interview in *Ruz al-Yusuf*, May 9, 2009. On the subject of Abuna Sam'an and of Muqattam, aside from the several investigations on the churches, conversations with Gaétan Du Roy and his writings on Muqattam were very informative. On Sam'an's biography see esp. Gaétan Du Roy, "Abuna Sam'an and the 'Evangelical Trend' Within the Coptic Church," in *Reconsidering Coptic Studies*, ed. Nelly Van Doorn-Harder (from the colloquium "The Future of Coptic Studies: Theories, Methods, Topics," Wake Forest University, Winston-Salem, NC, 2012).

48. *Ruz al-Yusuf*, May 9, 2009.

49. Du Roy, "Abuna Sam'an," 112.

50. Brigitte Voile, *Les Coptes d'Égypte sous Nasser: Sainteté, miracles, apparitions* (Paris: CNRS, 2004), 182.

CHAPTER 5

1. This is the principal critique that one could make of Rachel Scott's excellent work: to study ideology does not simply signify a textual analysis but all that makes sense and all that contributes to transforming a signifying order, which consists of an array of social, discursive, and symbolic practices, in a hegemonic system. The results of her investigations reveal another problem, that of sources. First, the Brothers generally do not offer researchers information on internal positions and rivalries. Second, the Society of Muslim Brothers most often assigns to a few selected Brothers the task of speaking with journalists and researchers.

2. Nathan J. Brown, "The Brotherhood Withdraws into Itself," in *Islam in a Changing Middle East: Rethinking Islamist Politics*, POMEPS Briefings (Feb. 2014): 18–23.

3. *Ruz al-Yusuf*, Nov. 20, 2005.

4. For a comparative reference point see Neera Chandhoke, *Beyond Secularism: The Right of Religious Minorities* (New Delhi: Oxford University Press, 1999), which relates the debates that unfold in the Indian context and addresses the issue of minority representation in the framework of the discussions between libertarians and communitarians; and Rajeev Bhargava, ed., *Secularism and Its Critics* (Delhi: Oxford University Press, 1998).

5. Tariq al-Bishri, *al-Muslimūn wa-l-aqbāṭ fī iṭār al-jamā'a al-waṭaniyya* (Beirut: Dār al-waḥda, 2004), 177.

6. The Wafd Party had boycotted the assembly to express its disagreement with the selection process of the assembly, whose members were nominated and not elected.

7. Mahmud 'Izmi, cited in Samer Soliman, "al-Ḥaraka al-dīmuqrāṭiyya fī muwājaha al-ṭā'ifiyya," *al-Bosla*, Oct. 2005.

8. Soliman, "al-Ḥaraka."

9. Mohamed Afifi, "Les requêtes adressées par les Coptes au Palais Royal-Égypte (1922–1952)," in *Droits et sociétés dans le monde arabe*, ed. Gilles Boëtsch, Baudouin Dupret, and Jean-Noël Ferrié (Aix-en-Provence: Presses universitaires d'Aix-Marseille, 1997), 51–59.

10. Barbara Carter, *The Copts in Egyptian Politics* (London: Croom Helm, 1986).

11. Samir Murqus, interview by the author, Cairo, Dec. 2009. In his youth Murqus was very committed to promoting church revival. Then he wrote extensively on the notion of citizenship and advocates for addressing Coptic problems on the basis of citizenship instead of referring to community, let alone communitarian, values.

12. *Al-Masri al-Yawm*, August 13, 2009; and *al-Yawm al-Sabi'*, August 9, 2009.

13. *Al-Dustur*, August 5, 2009.

14. Richard P. Mitchell, *The Society of the Muslim Brothers* (New York: Oxford University Press, 1993).

15. On Muslim reformism see Aziz al-Azmeh, *Islams and Modernities* (London: Verso, 1993); Albert Hourani, *Arabic Thought in the Liberal Age, 1789–1939* (1962; Cambridge: Cambridge University Press, 2003); and Alain Roussillon, *Réforme sociale et identité: Essai sur l'émergence de l'intellectuel et du champ politique modernes en Égypte* (Casablanca: Le Fennec, 1999).

16. Wael Eskandar, "Brothers and Officers: A History of Pacts," *Jadaliyya*, Jan. 25, 2013.

17. The only decision maker in the organization, al-Banna, had in all likelihood been preparing to take power since the beginning of the 1940s; see Tewfik Aclimandos, "Officiers et Frères musulmans: 1945–48," *Égypte/Monde arabe*, no. 4/5, 2nd ser. (2001): 255–306; see also the testimonies of other actors cited herein.

18. Aclimandos, "Officiers et Frères musulmans," 22 (reference is to the electronic edition page numbering).

19. Ibid., 27. On the reasons for 'Abd al-Ra'uf's joining the Society see 22–27. On Nasser's "conversion" see 27ff.

20. See Khalid Mohi al-Din, *Wa alān atakallam* (Cairo: al-Ahrām, 1997).

21. Aclimandos, "Officiers et Frères musulmans," 61.

22. Eskandar, "Brothers and Officers."

23. Gamal Essam El-Din, "How Gamal Brought the Whole Mubarak House Down," *Ahram Online*, April 16, 2011, http://english.ahram.org.eg/NewsContent/1/64/9988/Egypt/Politics-/How-Gamal-brought-the-whole-Mubarak-house-down.aspx.

24. On the Free Officer's Movement see Tewfik Aclimandos, "Les activistes politiques au sein de l'armée égyptienne: 1936–1954" (PhD diss., Institut d'études politiques, 2004). On the Nasserist era see Anwar Abdel Malek, *Égypte, société militaire* (Paris: Seuil, 1962); Said K. Aburish, *Nasser, the Last Arab* (New York: St. Martin's, 2004); and Kirk J. Beattie, *Egypt During the Nasser Years: Ideology, Politics, and Civil Society* (Boulder, CO: Westview Press, 1994).

25. Samer Soliman, "The Political Economy of Mubarak's Fall," in *Arab Spring in Egypt: Revolution and Beyond*, ed. Bahgat Korany and Rabab El-Mahdi (Cairo: AUC Press, 2012).

26. See Michel Camau and Vincent Geisser, *Le syndrome autoritaire: Politique en Tunisie de Bourguiba à Ben Ali* (Paris: Presses de Sciences Po, 2003).

27. Tewfik Aclimandos, "On ne prête qu'aux riches: Hommes d'affaire et politique," in *Chroniques égyptiennes, 2008*, ed. Iman Farag (Cairo: CEDEJ, 2010), 196–241.

28. On the organization and structure of the NDP see Amr Hisham Rabi, *al-Ḥizb al-Waṭanī al-Dīmuqrāṭī* (Cairo: al-Ahram Center for Strategic and Political Studies, 2004).

29. Chaymaa Hassabo, "Gamal Moubarak sous les projecteurs: Le lancement de sa campagne?" in *Chroniques égyptiennes, 2006*, ed. Chaymaa Hassabo and Enrique Klaus (Cairo: CEDEJ, 2007).

30. Military officer Zakariya 'Izmi, a confidant of Hosni Mubarak, led the Presidential Cabinet under Sadat, beginning in 1975, and then under Mubarak, after 1989. A member of the NDP Secretariat General since 1993, he was named financial affairs secretary in 2001 and then the party's deputy secretary general in 2006. Along with 'Izmi, Sawfar al-Sharif was a founding member of the NDP and became the secretary general of the political bureau in 2002. After more than fifteen years in the intelligence services, he rose through the ranks of the Information Ministry, becoming its head in 1982. Mufid Shihab, born in 1936, was in all likelihood co-opted for his juridical competence in light of the thirty-four constitutional articles that, in 2007, paved the way for succession. He was named minister of judicial affairs and legislative assemblies in 2005, a tailor-made post born of the fusion of the Ministry of Affairs of the People's Assembly and that of the Shura Council. After 2006 he held the position of deputy secretary general of judicial affairs in the NDP.

31. On economic development in Egypt, particularly during the last ten years of Mubarak's presidency, see Soliman, "The Political Economy."

32. On precarity in rural areas see François Ireton, "Économie politique de l'agriculture: De l'encadrement étatique à la déréglementation," in *L'Égypte au présent: Inventaire d'une société avant révolution*, ed. Vincent Battesti and François Ireton (Paris: Sindbad-Actes Sud, 2011).

33. On corruption see Ahmed El-Sayed El-Naggar, "Economic Policy: From State Control to Decay and Corruption," in *Egypt: The Moment of Change*, ed. Rabab El-Mahdi and Philip Marfleet (London: Zed, 2009).

34. Brigadier-General Husayn Hammouda, interview, *al-Shuruq*, April 8, 2011. Hammouda had worked in the State Security services.

35. Quoted in *al-Ahram Weekly*, March 16–22, 2006.

36. On the Egyptian military see Hazem Kandil, *Soldiers, Spies, and Statesmen: Egypt's Road to Revolt* (London: Verso, 2012).

37. For a comparative analysis of the role of Arab armies during the uprisings in winter 2010–11 see Philippe Droz-Vincent, "The Military Amidst Uprisings and Transitions in the Arab World," in *The New Middle East*, ed. Fawaz Gerges (Cambridge: Cambridge University Press, 2013).

38. For a study of electoral behavior see Sarah Ben Néfissa and Ala' al-din Arafat, *Vote et démocratie* (Paris: Karthala, 2005).

39. Although they had not legally formed a political party, the Muslim Brothers took part in elections through alliances with other parties by running independently or by supporting other candidates not affiliated with a party.

40. As'ad, however, did not sit in the Assembly then, because the electoral law in force at that time (114/1983, amending law 38/1972 on the People's Assembly) stipulated that only party lists "having achieved a minimum of eight percent of the national vote would be eligible to participate in the distribution of seats" (Article 17). The seats not

awarded after proportional repartition were returned to the majority party in the constituency (Article 17). See Nathalie Bernard-Maugiron, *Le politique à l'épreuve du judiciaire: La justice constitutionnelle en Égypte* (Bruxelles: Bruylant, 2003), 216.

41. According to law 188, amending once again the 1972 electoral law on the People's Assembly, this vote combined proportional party lists to elect 400 of 448 deputies and a two-round individual vote to elect the forty-eight other deputies, which could contain unaffiliated candidates. See Bernard-Maugiron, *Le politique à l'épreuve.*

42. *Al-Dustur*, Oct. 5, 2005.

43. *Al-Ahram Weekly*, no. 998, May 13–19, 2010.

44. See, e.g., *al-Fajr*, May 18, 2010.

45. Virginie Collombier, "Quand le PND se transforme en parti . . . Bilan d'étape," in *Chroniques égyptiennes, 2007*, ed. Hadjar Aouardji and Hélène Legeay (Cairo: CEDEJ, 2008), 41–62.

46. Virginie Collombier, "Le parti sera-t-il la solution? Le Parti National Démocratique égyptien, instrument de conquête du pouvoir dans un régime autoritaire en transition" (PhD diss., Institut d'études politiques, 2010), 196–97.

47. Mahmud 'Izzat, a professor at the Faculty of Medicine of Zagazig, joined the Brotherhood in 1962. He became a member of the Guidance Bureau in 1981. He was arrested twice, first in 1965, then again in 1995 during the Salsabil (name of a computer company) affair, which led to the discovery of several documents that described the stages of the Muslim Brothers' long march to gain control over the state apparatus. A dogmatic Qutbist (a follower of the doctrinal views of Sayyid Qutb), he gives great importance to educational issues and has long been head of the student section of the Brotherhood, as well as of the financial and administrative divisions. Along with 'Akif he is one of the last remaining members of the "secret apparatus." He used to instruct the MPs and the leaders of the regional sections of the Brotherhood.

48. Sawasiyya Center for Human Rights and Against Religious Discrimination, *Al-aqbāṭ wa-l-ṣu'ūd al-siyāsī li-l-ikhwān* (Cairo: Sawasiyya Center for Human Rights and Against Religious Discrimination, 2006).

49. Samih Fawzi, "al-Ikhwān al-muslimūn wa al-muwāṭana . . . Qirā' fī al-mawqif min al-aqbāṭ," in *Azma al-ikhwān al-muslimūn*, ed. 'Amr al-Shubaki (Cairo: al-Ahram Center for Political and Strategic Studies, 2009), 179–221.

50. Habib, *al-Aqbāṭ wa-l-ṣu'ūd*, 9.

51. Coptic scholars Samir Murqus and Samih Fawzi wrote a few articles on the Muslim Brothers' and other Egyptian Islamist trends' positions toward Copts; see Samih Fawzi, "al-Ḥaraka al-islāmiyya wa qaḍāya al-muwāṭana . . . qirā' fī-l-mawqif min al-aqbāṭ," in *al-Muwāṭana fī muwājaha al-ṭā'ifiyya*, ed. 'Amr al-Shubaki (Cairo: al-Ahram Center for Political and Strategical Studies, 2009), 121–51.

52. See Muhammad Salim al-'Awwa, *Fī al-niẓām al-siyāsī li-l-dawla al-islāmiyya* (Cairo: Dār al-shurūq, 1989), 237–60; and al-Bishri, *al-Muslimūn wa-l-aqbāṭ*.

53. Salim al-ʿAwwa, *al-Aqbāṭ wa-l-islām, ḥiwār* (Cairo: CEDEJ, 1987).

54. The writings of authors close to the Brotherhood dealing with the Coptic issue proliferated after 2005, and most of them attempted to provide a reassuring image of the Brotherhood; see, e.g., Muhammad Muru, *al-Muslimūn wa-l-aqbāṭ nāsij wāhid* (Cairo: Dār al-huda li-l-nashr wa-l-tawzīʿ, 2007); Mahmud Sultan, *al-Aqbāṭ wa-l-siyāsiyyā: taʾammulāt fī sanawāt al-ʿuzla* (Cairo: Dār al-ʿilm wa-lʾimān li-l-nashr wa-l-tawzīʿ, 2008); ʿAmr Shammah, *al-Ikhwān wa al-aqbāṭ man yaṭmʾunu man?* (Cairo: Maktaba waḥba, 2008).

55. Gamal Asʿad, Kawālīs al-kanīsa wa-l-aḥzab wa-l-ikhwān al-muslimīn (Cairo: Dār al-khayyāl, 2001).

56. On Zaghlul's mention of this sentence see al-Bishri, *al-Muslimūn wa-l-aqbāṭ*, 177.

57. Gamal Asʿad, *Kawālīs al-kanīsa wa al-aḥzāb wa al-ikhwān al-muslimūn* (Cairo: Dār al-khayyāl, 2001), 118; and *al-Shaʿb* (Cairo), Nov. 4, 1997.

58. *Al-daʿwa*, Dec. 1980.

59. Patrick Haenni, "La blogosphère en Égypte," *Études et analyses*, no. 17 (2008): www.religion.info/pdf/2008_09_blogegypte.pdf; and Marc Lynch, "Young Brothers in Cyberspace," *Middle East Report* 37 (Winter 2007): www.merip.org/mer/mer245/young-brothers-cyberspace&gt.

60. Husam Tammam, *Taḥawwulāt al-ikhwān al-muslimīn* (Cairo: Maktaba Madbūlī, 2006). See also Husam Tammam, ed., *ʿAbd al-Munʿim Abū al-Futūḥ, shahīd ʿalā tārīkh al-ḥaraka al-islāmiyya fī miṣr, 1970–1984* (Cairo: Dār al-Shurūq, 2010).

61. Khalil al-Anani, *al-Ikhwān al-muslimīn fī miṣr* (Cairo: Maktaba al-shurūq al-duwaliyya, 2007).

62. *Al-Karama*, Jan. 22, 2007.

63. Nathan J. Brown and Amr Hamzawi, "The Draft Party Platform of the Egyptian Muslim Brotherhood: Foray into Political Integration or Retreat into Old Position?" *Carnegie Papers, Middle East Series* 89 (Jan. 2008): http://carnegieendowment.org/files/cp89_muslim_brothers_final.pdf; and al-Anani, *al-Ikhwān*.

64. Tewfik Aclimandos, "Les Frères musulmans égyptiens: Pour une critique des vœux pieux," *Politique Africaine*, no. 108 (2007): 25–47; and al-Anani, *al-Ikhwān*.

65. Tammam, *Taḥawwulāt al-ikhwān al-muslimīn*, 54.

66. Husam Tammam, "Who's Afraid of the Salafists?" *al-Ahram online* (2011): http://english.ahram.org.eg/NewsContent/4/0/15601/Opinion/Whos-afraid-of-the-Salafists.aspx.

67. Alaa al-Din Arafat, "Le parti Nur dans les élections parlementaires de 2011–2012," in "Les élections de la révolution (2011–2012)," ed. Clément Steuer, *Égypte/Monde arabe*, no. 10, 3rd ser. (2013): https://ema.revues.org/3113.

68. Nabil ʿAbd al-Fattah, "al-Azhar dans un monde troublé: Crise et politiques d'adaptation," in "L'Égypte entame sa longue marche," ed. Tewfik Aclimandos and Laure Guirguis, special issue, *Les cahiers de l'Orient* 108 (2012): 67–80; and Rachel Scott, "What

Might the Muslim Brotherhood Do with al-Azhar? Religious Authority in Egypt," *Die Welt des Islams* 52, no. 2 (2012): 131–65.

69. During the March 2011 referendum, Egyptians had to agree on or reject the minimal constitutional amendments to allow modifying the electoral rules as specified in the Constitution and, thereby, allow the rapid organization of the upcoming elections. However, figures in the secular trends considered that, in the wave of the revolutionary enthusiasm, they should take the opportunity to demand the suppression of Article 2 (stipulating that "the principles of the shari'a are the main source of legislation and Islam is the religion of the state"). As the Constitution was supposed to be written later on, the committee set up to propose the constitutional changes did not want to raise the issue at this time, and Article 2 remained in place. For their part, the Muslim Brothers and the Salafis appropriated the "yes" position, arguing that voting "no" meant voting against Islam. After the referendum and the victory of the "yes" vote, the military extracted the amended articles related to electoral rules, and inserted them into a new basic and temporary constitutional text that was never submitted to referendum.

70. Tammam, "Who's Afraid of the Salafists?"

71. Irrespective of the Constitution's content, countrywide demonstrations challenged the autocratic gesture of President Mursi, who was then trying to impose the Constitution and the subsequent referendum on the people. Egyptians then made several jokes and humorous cartoons, one of them caricaturing the president of the Constituent Assembly as Colonel Sanders of KFC, carrying a fast-delivery constitution.

72. Nathalie Bernard-Maugiron, "Quelle Egypte dans la nouvelle Constitution," *Oasis*, Dec. 18, 2012. www.oasiscenter.eu/fr/articles/revolutions-arabes/2012/12/18/quelle-%C3%A9gypte-dans-la-nouvelle-constitution.

73. Ibid.

74. For a more detailed development see Laure Guirguis, *Égypte: Révolution et contre-révolution* (Montreal: Presses de l'université de Laval, 2014).

75. Born in 1941, Ahmad Shafiq had been a senior commander in the Egyptian Air Force. Though he was a survivor from the old regime and a close friend of Hosni Mubarak, he long remained a popular personality. He served as prime minister from January 31, 2011, to March 3, 2011, and then ran in the 2012 presidential elections.

76. See Ibrahim el-Houdaiby, "Changing Alliances and Continuous Oppression: The Rule of Egypt's Security Sector," *Arab Reform Initiative* (Jan. 2014).

77. See Hesham Sallam, "Morsi Past the Point of No Return," *Jadaliyya*, Dec. 8, 2012.

78. *Al-Fajr*, Dec. 4, 2012; and *al-Masri al-Yawm*, Dec. 6, 2012.

79. *Al-Masri al-Yawm*, April 9 and 10, 2013; and Issandr al-Amrani, "Attacks on Copts Are a Sign of Social Fragmentation," *National*, April 10, 2013, www.thenational.ae/thenationalconversation/comment/attacks-on-copts-are-a-sign-of-social-fragmentation.

80. Marc Lynch, introduction to "Islam in a Changing Middle East: Rethinking Islamist Politics," ed. Marc Lynch, *POMEPS Studies*, no. 6 (Feb. 2014): 4.

81. Husam Tammam and Patrick Haenni, "Les Frères musulmans égyptiennes face à la question sociale: Autopsie d'un malaise socio-théologique," *Études et Analyses*, no. 20 (2009): http://religion.info/french/articles/article_423.shtml.

82. Khalil al-Anani, "The Debacle of Orthodox Islamism," in "Islam in a Changing Middle East: Rethinking Islamist Politics," ed. Marc Lynch, *POMEPS Studies*, no. 6 (Feb. 2014): 8.

83. Caroline Barbary and Maria Adib Doss, "Tamarrod (Rébellion): Une autre lecture de l'action politique dans le processus révolutionnaire égyptien," *Confluences Méditerranée* 1, no. 88 (2014): 155–69; and Laure Guirguis, "Égypte: l'autre succession—l'Église copte à l'approche d'un tournant," *Religioscope* (2010): http://religion.info/french/articles/article_501.shtml.

CHAPTER 6

1. Jacques Rancière, *Le partage du sensible* (Paris: La Fabrique, 2000).

2. See the web pages of these organizations: www.amcoptic.com/; and www.copticnews.ca/.

3. On the organization and discourses of the first Coptic associations in the United States see Ziad Abdelnour, "Le rôle politique de la diaspora copte d'Amérique du Nord" (master's thesis, Institut d'études politiques, 1991).

4. See Grégoire Delhaye, "La réponse des États à la dissidence diasporique: Le cas de l'Égypte face au militantisme copte aux États-Unis," in *Loin des yeux, près du cœur: Les États et leurs expatriés*, ed. Stéphane Dufoix, Carine Guerassimoff-Pina, and Anne de Tinguy (Paris: Presses de Sciences Po, 2010), 323–41.

5. Ibid.; Margaret E. Keck and Kathryn Sikkink, *Activists Beyond Borders: Advocacy Networks in International Politics* (Ithaca, NY: Cornell University Press, 1998). See also Sidney Tarrow, "La contestation transnationale," *Cultures et conflits* 38–39 (Summer/Fall 2000): 187–223; and Sidney Tarrow, *The New Transnational Activism* (New York: Cambridge University Press, 2005).

6. Delhaye, "La réponse des États," 323–41.

7. Ibid., 327–28.

8. Hilmi Jirjis founded an association in the United Kingdom in 1995 and Ibrahim Habib in 1992, while Samir Ya'qub created one in France the same year. Violence happening in Egypt often triggers the formation of associations. For example, the murder of a young Christian in Dayrut prompted Samir Ya'qub to found the organization in France. For a presentation of the diverse Coptic associations abroad see Muhammad Zayan, *Aqbāṭ al-mahjar* (Cairo: Self-published, 2008).

9. Delhaye, "La réponse des États," 329–30.

10. Grégoire Delhaye, "Comprendre la mondialisation des normes: Les leçons de l'échec de la liberté religieuse universelle," in *Normer le monde*, ed. Yves Schemeil and Eberwein Wolf-Dieter (Paris: L'Harmattan, 2009).

11. On the ambivalent role of media in the engineering of a transnational Coptic identity see Elizabeth Iskander, *Sectarian Conflict in Egypt: Coptic Media, Identity, and Representation* (New York: Routledge, 2012), 48–69.

12. *Daily News* (Cairo), Sept. 30, 2007. On Murqus 'Aziz see Muhammad al-Baz, *Ḍidd al-Bābā asrār wa azma al-kanīsa* (Cairo: Kunūz li-l-nashr wa-l-tawzi', 2006), 247. Al-Baz speculates about the fact that the patriarch tolerated 'Aziz even though he departed from the political line dictated by the church.

13. See Dina El-Khawaga, "La génération seventies en Égypte: La société civile comme répertoire d'action alternatif," in *Résistances et protestations dans les sociétés musulmanes*, ed. Mounia Bennani-Chraïbi and Olivier Fillieule (Paris: Presses de Sciences Po, 2003), 3–13.

14. On late twentieth-century activism see Ahmed Abdallah, *The Student Movement and National Politics in Egypt* (London: al-Saqi, 1985); on more recent developments see Youssef el-Shazli and Chaymaa Hassabo, "Sociohistoire d'un processus révolutionnaire," in *Devenir révolutionnaires: Au cœur des révoltes arabes*, ed. Amin Allal and Thomas Pierret (Paris: Armand Colin, 2013).

15. Chaymaa Hassabo, "Du rassemblement à l'effritement des Jeunes pour le changement égyptiens: L'expérience de 'générations qui ont vécu et vivent toujours sous la loi d'urgence,'" *Revue internationale de politique comparée* 16, no. 2 (2009): 241–61.

16. Sarah Ben Néfissa, "Ça suffit! Le haut et le bas du politique en Égypte," *Politique africaine* 4, no. 108 (2007): 6; and Sarah Ben Néfissa, "Le déblocage du débat démocratique en Égypte, legs nassérien et poids du secteur privé," *Maghreb-Machrek* 182 (2005): 59–78.

17. On youth movements in Egypt before the January 25 revolution see Dina Shehata, "Youth Activism in Egypt," *Arab Reform Initiative*, Oct. 2008; and Nadine Abdalla, "Egypt's Revolutionary Youth: From Street Politics to Party Politics," *SWP Comments* 11 (March 2013): 1–8.

18. Nathalie Bernard-Maugiron, *Le politique à l'épreuve du judiciaire: La justice constitutionnelle en Égypte* (Bruxelles: Bruylant, 2003).

19. Nathalie Bernard-Maugiron, "Les juges et les élections dans l'Égypte post Moubarak: Acteurs ou victimes du politique?" *Confluences méditerranée* 3, no. 82 (2012): 117–32.

20. Nathalie Bernard-Maugiron, "Moderniser la Constitution ou renforcer l'autoritarisme de l'État? Les amendements constitutionnels de 2007," in *Chroniques égyptiennes 2007*, ed. Hadjar Aouardji and Hélène Legeay (Cairo: CEDEJ, 2008), 17–40, http://www.cedej-eg.org/IMG/pdf/01-Nathalie.pdf.

21. Benjamin Rey, "Entre nouvelles formes de mobilisations et gestion étatique: L'opposition égyptienne en 2004," in *L'Égypte dans l'année: Chronique politique 2004*, ed. Florian Kohstall (Cairo: CEDEJ, 2005), 25–46.

22. Marie Duboc, "La contestation sociale en Égypte depuis 2004: Précarisation et

mobilisation locale des ouvriers de l'industrie textile," in "Protestations sociales, révolutions civiles," ed. Sarah Ben Néfissa and Blandine Destremau, special edition, *Revue Tiers Monde*, no. 5 (2011): 95–115.

23. Marie Duboc, "Le 6 avril: Un jour de colère sans grèves," in *Chroniques égyptiennes 2008*, ed. Iman Farag (Cairo: CEDEJ, 2010).

24. See Joel Beinin, "Workers' Protest in Egypt: Neo-liberalism and Class Struggle in 21st Century," *Social Movement Studies* 8, no. 4 (2009): 449–54.

25. François Ireton, "La petite paysannerie dans la tourmente néolibérale," in *Chroniques égyptiennes 2006*, ed. Enrique Klaus and Chaymaa Hassabo (Cairo: CEDEJ, 2007), 29–58.

26. See Duboc, "La contestation sociale."

27. Kamal Abbas's remarks at the launch of Joel Beinin and Frédéric Vairel, eds., *The Struggle for Workers' Rights in Egypt*, held in Washington, DC, Feb. 16, 2010; cited by Joel Beinin in "Les ouvriers égyptiens et le 25 janvier," in "L'Égypte entame sa longue marche," ed. Tewfik Aclimandos and Laure Guirguis, special issue, *Les cahiers de l'Orient* 108 (2012): 97–114.

28. Liam Stack and Maram Mazen, "Striking Mahalla Workers Demand Government Fulfill Broken Promises," *Daily Star Egypt*, Sept. 27, 2007.

29. Jean Lachapelle, "Lessons from Egypt's Tax Collectors," *Middle East Report* 264 (Autumn 2012): www.merip.org/mer/mer264/lessons-egypts-tax-collectors-0; and Joel Beinin, "Workers, Trade Unions and Egypt's Political Future," *MERIP*, Jan. 18, 2013.

30. Beinin, "Workers, Trade Unions."

31. See Mariz Tadros, *Copts at the Crossroads* (Cairo: AUC Press, 2013); and Laure Guirguis, "Égypte: l'autre succession—l'Église copte à l'approche d'un tournant," *Religioscope* (2010): http://religion.info/french/articles/article_501.shtml.

32. See, e.g., Hani Fawzi's film *Bahibb al-sīmā* (2004).

33. Paul Sedra, "Martyrdom at Maspero: Searching for Meaning," *Egypt Independent*, Oct. 9, 2012; Sherif Younes, "The Maspero Massacre: The Military, the Media, and the 1952 Cairo Fire as Historical Blueprint," *Jadaliyya*, Oct. 19, 2011 (translated from the Arabic in *Akhbar al-adab*); Youssef Mervat, Araba Heba, and Anup Kumar, "Mediating Discourse of Democratic Uprising in Egypt: Militarized Language and the 'Battles' of Abbasiyya and Maspero," *International Journal of Communication* 8 (Jan. 2014): 871–89; and Tadros, *Copts at the Crossroads*.

34. For more details on the Maspero movement see Tadros, *Copts at the Crossroads*, chap. 9.

35. Muslimūn ḍidd al-tamyīz al-dīnī, "Bayān ṣādir 'an muslimīn ḍidd al-tamyīz: 30 April 2006," in *al-nashā' wa al-ahdāf wa al-mawāqif* (Cairo: Muslimūn ḍidd al-tamyīz al-dīnī, 2009), 19–22.

36. The papers from these colloquia were published under the titles *Egypt for All Egyptians: Papers from the First National Colloquium to Combat Religious Discrimination*

in Egypt (Cairo: April 11 and 12, 2008), under the coordination of Muhammad Munir Megahed, Markaz al-mahrūsa li-l-nashr wa-l-khadamāt al-saḥafiyya wa-l-maʿlūmāt (Cairo: Jan. 2009); and *Education and Citizenship: Papers from the Second National Colloquium to Combat Religious Discrimination in Egypt* (Cairo: April 24 and 25, 2009), ed. Muhammad Munir Megahed (the publisher's name is not available, Jan. 2010).

37. For example, the two children Mario and Andrew were registered by the administrative services with a Muslim identify after their father converted to Islam and then married a Muslim woman. Mario and Andrew later wanted to be officially registered as Christians, the religion of their birth and of their mother. Their mother, Camelia Lutfi, carried on an exhausting, years-long struggle to this end that brought her before several courts.

38. See Munir Migahid, "Pas de coercition en religion," in *Conversions religieuses et mutations politiques: Tares et avatars du communautarisme égyptien*, ed. Laure Guirguis (Paris: Non Lieu, 2008), 197–207.

39. See EIPR and Human Rights Watch, *Prohibited Identities: State Interference with Religious Freedom* (Cairo and New York: EIPR and Human Rights Watch, 2007).

40. Magdi Khalil appeared on the activist scene in the United States at the end of the 1990s. He wrote a number of texts on young women's abductions and forced conversion to Islam. See, e.g., www.meforum.org/2599/egypt-persecution-of-copts; www.islamist-watch.org/; www.danielpipes.org/; http://threatswatch.org/ (on pro-Israeli defense and national security); http://scotfella-directimpact.blogspot.com/2011/01/egyptian-american-writer-magdi-khalil.html (the website of a self-proclaimed Zionist tied to MEMRI); www.aina.org/news/20100917220629.htm (Assyrian International News Agency). After 2005 he became more active in Egypt.

41. On Gamal ʿAbd al-Rahim see http://gamalrahim.blogspot.com/. Without a true political affiliation, he was the author of a work on Ayman al-Zawahiri (formerly a member of the Muslim Brotherhood, al-Zawahiri joined the Islamic Jihad in 1979 and then worked alongside Usama Ben Laden). He grew up in a village in Suhag where an important Bahai community resides. One year after the illegal obstruction of the Journalists' Syndicate, he publicly called for the killing of his childhood neighbors precisely when the Bahais were being attacked in his home province.

42. *Baltagiyya*, sing. *baltagi*, literally "those who carry clubs." Often from the lower-class, marginalized zones of the capital, the *baltagiyya* are the official workforce of the regime and the police. Used to defend the Mubarak clan from peril during the revolution, they could be found at the sides of the revolutionaries. The issue of the *baltagiyya* emerged in the press and government discourse in the late 1990s.

43. See Andrei S. Markovitz and Mark Silverstein, *The Politics of Scandal: Power and Process in Liberal Democracies* (New York: Holmes and Meier, 1988).

44. Enrique Klaus, "Scandals as Sequentially-Organized Social Events. The 'Sexual Depravation Scandal in Upper Egypt'" (unpublished article sent by author, 2008).

45. Ibid.

46. Delhaye, "La réponse des États," 334–35.

47. Ibid., 337–338.

48. Husam Bahgat, interview by the author, Cairo, March 2010.

49. Samer Soliman, "La liberté de se convertir dans l'informel," in *Conversions religieuses et mutations politiques: Tares et avatars du communautarisme égyptien*, ed. Laure Guirguis (Paris: Non Lieu, 2008), 163–73.

50. See Giorgio Agamben, *State of Exception*, trans. Kevin Attell (Chicago: University of Chicago Press, 2005).

51. See Talal Asad, *Formation of the Secular: Christianity, Islam, Modernity* (Stanford, CA: Stanford University Press, 2003); and Nathan Brown, *The Rule of Law in the Arab World: Courts in Egypt and the Gulf* (Cambridge: Cambridge University Press, 1997).

52. On the three years after Mubarak's fall, as well as the dynamics leading to the uprising, see Laure Guirguis, *Égypte: Révolution et contre-révolution* (Montreal: Presses de l'université de Laval, 2014).

53. Alain Roussillon, "Égyptianité, arabité, islamité: La recomposition des références identitaires," in "A propos de la nationalité: Questions sur l'identité nationale," ed. Iman Farag and Alain Roussillon, *Égypte/Monde arabe*, no. 11, 1st ser. (1992): 77–137.

54. Quoted in Martin Malia, *Histoire des révolutions* (Paris: Tallandier, 2008), 409.

55. See Salwa Ismail, "The Egyptian Revolution Against the Police," *Social Research* 79, no. 2 (2012): 435–62; and Aida Seif al-Dawla, "Torture: A State Policy," in *Egypt: The Moment of Change*, ed. Rabab El-Mahdi and Philip Marfleet (London: Zed, 2009), 120–35.

56. See Chaymaa Hassabo, "Égypte, les illusions perdues des 'jeunes de la Révolution,'" *Orient XXI*, March 20, 2014.

57. Said Okasha, "La révolution du 25 janvier: Forces révolutionnaires, forces réactionnaires," in "L'Égypte entame sa longue marche," ed. Tewfik Aclimandos and Laure Guirguis, special issue, *Les cahiers de l'Orient* 108 (2012): 51–65.

58. On Mursi's reversal see Guirguis, *Égypte: Révolution*.

59. Summaries of al-Sisi's TV interviews on Dream Channel before May 2014 presidential election can be found on the website Mada Masr; see, e.g., www.madamasr.com/news/sisi-first-tv-interview-we-will-not-let-protests-destroy-country.

60. Al-Sisi's speech at al-Azhar, Dec. 28, 2014. A subtitled clip can be found at www.memritv.org/clip/en/4704.htm.

61. Khalil al-Anani, "Unpacking Sisi's Religiosity," *Mada Masr*, June 17, 2014, www.madamasr.com/opinion/unpacking-sisis-religiosity.

62. See Nabil 'Abd al-Fattah, "al-Azhar dans un monde troublé: Crise et politiques d'adaptation," in "L'Égypte entame sa longue marche," ed. Tewfik Aclimandos and Laure Guirguis, special issue, *Les cahiers de l'Orient* 108 (2012): 67–80.

63. Husam Tammam, "Who's Afraid of the Salafists?" *al-Ahram online* (2011): http://

english.ahram.org.eg/NewsContent/4/0/15601/Opinion/Whos-afraid-of-the-Salafists.aspx; and Olivier Roy, "Le printemps arabe et le mythe de la nécessaire sécularisation," *Socio* 2 (2013): 25–36.

64. Khaled Dawoud, "Drawing the Veil on Simmering Disputes," *Ahram Weekly*, no. 1243, April 23, 2015.

65. Ishak Ibrahim, "Tales of Blasphemy in Egypt," *Atlantic Council*, April 23, 2015; and Ishak Ibrahim, *Besieging Freedom of Thought: Defamation of Religion Cases in Two Years of the Revolution* (Cairo: EIPR, 2014).

66. The economist Hazem Biblawi, born in 1936, had pursued a career in international banks and institutions before he was named prime minister in July 2013. He tendered the resignation of his government in February 2014, paving the way for the official presidential candidacy of 'Abd al-Fattah al-Sisi in May 2014.

67. See Amr Adly, "Egypt's Conservative Nationalism: Discourse and Praxis of the New Régime," *Jadaliyya*, Oct. 14, 2014.

68. Ramadan Abdoh, "Egypt Faces 4th Generation War, Says Sisi," *al-Balad*, Feb. 22, 2015, www.el-balad.com/1403352.

CONCLUSION

1. Issandr al-Amrani, "Attacks on Copts Are a Sign of Social Fragmentation," *National*, April 10, 2013, www.thenational.ae/thenationalconversation/comment/attacks-on-copts-are-a-sign-of-social-fragmentation.

2. "Islam, Stranger in Its Own Country," by 'Abd al-'Aziz Jawish, published in *al-Liwa'* on June 17, 1908, marked the debut of hostilities between Christians and Muslims. The controversy over the role of religion in the definition of the nation, positioned the Coptic press (*Misr and al-Watan*) against the press involved in Muhammad 'Abduh's reform project (*al-Mu'ayyid* and *al-Liwa'*).

3. Khalid Fahmy, "The Nation and Its Deserters: Conscription in Mehmed Ali's Egypt," *International Review of Social History* 43, no. 3 (1998): 423.

4. See Younes Sherif, "Révolution égyptienne et crise de légitimité," in "L'Égypte entame sa longue marche," ed. Tewfik Aclimandos and Laure Guirguis, special issue, *Les cahiers de l'Orient* 108 (2012): 33–46.

5. On the position and role of religious institutions in the colonial situation see 'Abd al-Fattah, "al-Mu'assasā al-dīniyya al-qibṭiyya al-urthuduksiyya wa qadāyā al-muwāṭana wa-l-waḥda al-waṭaniyya," in *al-Muwāṭana fī muwājaha al-ṭā'ifiyya*, ed. 'Amr al-Shubaki (Cairo: al-Ahram Center for Political and Strategical Studies, 2009), 93–121.

6. Samer Soliman, "al-Ḥaraka al-dīmuqrāṭiyya fī muwājaha al-ṭā'ifiyya," *al-Bosla*, Oct. 2005.

7. Ibid.

8. Chaymaa Hassabo, "Égypte, les illusions perdues des 'jeunes de la Révolution,'" *Orient XXI*, March 20, 2014.

9. Claude Lefort, "Penser la révolution dans la révolution française," *Annales, Économies, Sociétés, Civilisations* 35, no. 2 (1980): 337.

10. Vincent Geisser, Karam Karam, and Frédéric Vairel, "Espaces du politique: Mobilisations et protestations," in *La politique dans le monde arabe*, ed. Elizabeth Picard (Paris: Armand Colin, 2006), 209–10.

11. Myriam Catusse, "Le charme discret de la société civile: Ressorts politiques de la formation d'un groupe dans le Maroc 'ajusté,'" *Revue internationale de politique comparée* 9, no. 2 (2002): 297–318.

12. Joel Beinin, "Civil Society, NGOs, and Egypt's 2011 Popular Uprising," *South Atlantic Quarterly* 113, no. 2 (2014): 398.

13. Maha Abdelrahman, *Civil Society Exposed: The Politics of NGOs in Egypt* (Cairo: American University in Cairo Press, 2004).

14. Vicki Langhor, "Too Much Civil Society, Too Little Politics: Egypt and Liberalizing Arab Regimes," *Comparative Politics* 36, no. 2 (2004): 181–204.

15. A counterexample is the case of Khaled Ali. He is one of the rare activists who, as a lawyer, not only has worked with the workers but has contributed to the "politicization" of their demands. After having worked in the Hisham Mubarak Center, created in 1999 with the lawyer Sayf al-Islam, Khaled Ali founded the Egyptian Center for Economic and Social Rights, which he helmed until he declared candidacy for the presidential elections in 2012. Representing a millworker in southern Cairo, he obtained a March 2010 verdict requiring the government to establish a minimum wage. Two months later, workers and activists demonstrated in front of Parliament to demand the application of this decision, taking it directly to the government and the head of state. On the role of civil society in the 2011 uprising see Beinin, "Civil Society."

16. See Wendy Brown, "American Nightmare: Neoliberalism, Neoconservatism, and De-democratization," *Political Theory* 34, no. 6 (2006): 690–714.

INDEX

Abadir, ʿAdli, 149–150, 164, 208–209n88
ʿAbd al-Fattah, Nabil, 111, 196n87
ʿAbd al-Nour, Mounir Fakhri, 130
ʿAbd al-Qadir, Faruq, 40
ʿAbd al-Quddus, Muhammad, 132
ʿAbd al Rahim, Gamal, 160, 223n41
ʿAbd al-Raʾuf, ʿAbd al-Monʾim, 124
Abdelrahman, Maha, 181
abduction. *See* disappearance of girls and women
Abu al-Futuh, Abd al-Monʾim, 27, 135, 136–137
Abu Sayf, Yusif, 102
Abu Zayd, Nasr Hamid, 192n54, 194n69
ACA (American Coptic Association), 147, 149–150, 197n12
Aclimandos, Tewfik, 52
al-ʿAdli, Habib, 127
adultery, 36, 64, 71, 195n83, 202–203n23
Adventists, 72, 112
advocacy activism, impacts of, 155–156, 161, 180–182
affirmative action, 92, 119–123
ʿAfifi, Muhammad, 100
Agamben, Giorgio, 167
ahl al-dhimma, 2, 183n2
ahl al-kitāb, 183n2
Ahmad, Makram Muhammad, 160–161
Akhenaton, religious unity and, 25
ʿAkif, Mahdi, 92, 135, 191n39
Ali, Khaled, 226n15
ʿAli Jumʿa, Grand Mufti, 37
al-ʿAlwani, Taha Jabir, 38
American Coptic Association (ACA), 147, 149–150, 197n12
American Coptic Union, 150
al-Anani, Khalil, 136
apostasy: death penalty for, 35; Higazi example, 29–32, 162–163; legality of, 32, 35; Muslim theologians on, 35–38; reconverts, 36, 39–40, 159, 223n37; shariʿa and, 35, 36, 40–41, 84. *See also* religious conversion
April 6 Youth Movement, 153
Arab Charter for Human Rights, 42
Arab Socialist Union, 17, 124–125
Armanios, Febe, 52–53, 81
Article 2 of the Constitution: apostasy and (1971), 40–41; discussion of omitting, 152, 175, 219n69; meaning of, 41, 140–141; Muslim Brotherhood and, 135; political implications of, 196n87; Sadat's amending of, 183n2, 205–206n58
Asʿad, Gamal, 129–130, 133–134, 148, 216–217n40
Assiut conference (1911), 17, 82, 119
atheism, 172, 174, 175
ʿAtiyya, Majid, 122
authoritarian logics, 6, 166, 182, 184n8
authority: charismatic, 77–79; of Egyptian regime, 89; Islamo-Christian unity and, 177; papal, 70, 75–79, 89, 96, 110; paternal, 53; revolutionary action and, 170, 182; of Samʿan, 114–115
ʿAwad, Louis, 80
ʿAwda, Jihad, 30

Stanford Studies in Middle Eastern and Islamic Societies and Cultures

---

Michael Farquhar, *Circuits of Faith: Migration, Education, and the Wahhabi Mission*
2016

Gilbert Achcar, *Morbid Symptoms: Relapse in the Arab Uprising*
2016

Jacob Mundy, *Imaginative Geographies of Algerian Violence: Conflict Science, Conflict Management, Antipolitics*
2015

Ilana Feldman, *Police Encounters: Security and Surveillance in Gaza under Egyptian Rule*
2015

Tamir Sorek, *Palestinian Commemoration in Israel: Calendars, Monuments, and Martyrs*
2015

Adi Kuntsman and Rebecca L. Stein, *Digital Militarism: Israel's Occupation in the Social Media Age*
2015

Laurie A. Brand, *Official Stories: Politics and National Narratives in Egypt and Algeria*
2014

Kabir Tambar, *The Reckonings of Pluralism: Citizenship and the Demands of History in Turkey*
2014

Diana Allan, *Refugees of the Revolution: Experiences of Palestinian Exile*
2013

Shira Robinson, *Citizen Strangers: Palestinians and the Birth of Israel's Liberal Settler State*
2013

Joel Beinin and Frédéric Vairel, *editors, Social Movements, Mobilization, and Contestation in the Middle East and North Africa*
2013 (Second Edition), 2011

Ariella Azoulay and Adi Ophir, *The One-State Condition: Occupation and Democracy in Israel/Palestine*
2012

Steven Heydemann and Reinoud Leenders, *editors, Middle East Authoritarianisms: Governance, Contestation, and Regime Resilience in Syria and Iran*
2012

Jonathan Marshall, *The Lebanese Connection: Corruption, Civil War, and the International Drug Traffic*
2012

Joshua Stacher, *Adaptable Autocrats: Regime Power in Egypt and Syria*
2012

Bassam Haddad, *Business Networks in Syria: The Political Economy of Authoritarian Resilience*
2011

Noah Coburn, *Bazaar Politics: Power and Pottery in an Afghan Market Town*
2011

Laura Bier, *Revolutionary Womanhood: Feminisms, Modernity, and the State in Nasser's Egypt*
2011

Samer Soliman, *The Autumn of Dictatorship: Fiscal Crisis and Political Change in Egypt under Mubarak*
2011